# Trauma: Explorations in Memory

# TRAUMA

## Explorations in Memory

Edited, with Introductions, by

**CATHY CARUTH**

The Johns Hopkins University Press

BALTIMORE AND LONDON

© 1995 The Johns Hopkins University Press
All rights reserved. Published 1995
Printed in the United States of America on acid-free paper
04 03 02 01 00 99 98 97 96          5 4 3 2

The Johns Hopkins University Press
2715 North Charles Street
Baltimore, Maryland 21218-4319
The Johns Hopkins Press Ltd., London

Library of Congress Cataloging-in-Publication Data will be found
at the end of this book.

A catalog record for this book is available from the British Library.

ISBN 0-8018-5009-6
ISBN 0-8018-5007-X (pbk.)

# CONTENTS

## II. Recapturing the Past

# PREFACE

*I do not want to take drugs for my nightmares, because I must
remain a memorial to my dead friends.*
—VIETNAM VET

Psychic trauma involves intense personal suffering, but it also involves
the recognition of realities that most of us have not begun to face. In the past
several years, public interest in the suffering entailed in trauma, as well as
professional research in the field, has grown considerably, and with the
events in Bosnia-Herzegovina and the increasing violence in our own country, many people have recognized the urgency of learning more about the
traumatic reaction to violent events and about the means of helping to
alleviate suffering. These methods have provided significant intervention in
both individual and group trauma. But the study and treatment of trauma
continue to face a crucial problem at the heart of this unique and difficult
phenomenon: the problem of how to help relieve suffering, and how to
understand the nature of the suffering, without eliminating the force and
truth of the reality that trauma survivors face and quite often try to transmit
to us. To cure oneself—whether by drugs or the telling of one's story or
both—seems to many survivors to imply the giving-up of an important
reality, or the dilution of a special truth into the reassuring terms of therapy.
Indeed, in Freud's own early writings on trauma, the possibility of integrat-
ing the lost event into a series of associative memories, as part of the cure,
was seen precisely as a way to permit the event to be forgotten. The difficulty
of listening and responding to traumatic stories in a way that does not lose
their impact, that does not reduce them to clichés or turn them all into
versions of the same story, is a problem that remains central to the task of
therapists, literary critics, neurobiologists, and filmmakers alike. The unique
and continuing contribution of the essays in this volume—which were originally published in earlier versions in two issues of *American Imago* that
appeared in 1991—is to ask how we can listen to trauma beyond its pathology

for the truth that it tells us, and how we might perhaps find a way of learning to express this truth beyond the painful repetitions of traumatic suffering.

This task of learning to listen anew calls for different ways of thinking about what it means to understand and what kinds of truth we are looking for, and in this respect the essays collected here have anticipated some of the central problems concerning memory and truth that have emerged in the last several years. There are two prominent examples of these growing concerns, one more central in the public eye and one more limited to professional circles. The first is the current debate surrounding so-called "false recovered memories." In response to the increasing focus on the recovery of traumatic memories, and the occasional lawsuits emerging from them, a group made up primarily of accused parents and relatives has attempted to put in question the veracity of many assertions of traumatic recall and of the methods used to uncover memories. It is, of course, important to learn to distinguish between wholly false, suggested memories and memories that are essentially true, especially when the outcome involves legal actions, and much work is being done in this area as a response to the concerns raised by the accused parents. But the concern with false memories also teaches us, I believe, another and equally important lesson: the difficulty that many people have in believing memories that seem to them to be false simply because they do not appear in easily recognizable forms, and the urgency of creating new ways of listening and recognizing the truth of memories that would, under traditional criteria, be considered to be false.

A different but related set of issues has been raised in the professional arena, at the same time, in the debate over the introduction into the American Psychiatric Association's *Diagnostic and Statistical Manual of Mental Disorders* of a category called DESNOS (Disorders of Extreme Stress Not Otherwise Specified), which would describe the more subtle and characterologically imprinted effects of long-term, chronic trauma, and would allow for the recognition of a distinct kind of traumatic experience in those for whom the experiences may not be available as flashbacks or simple memories but may be exhibited in more subtle kinds of behavior. The issues raised around the acceptance of DESNOS, like the debates concerning recovered memories, suggest that the problem of what it means to remember traumatic experience and what it means to know or recognize trauma in others remain complex issues tied to the fact that traumatic recall or reenactment is defined, in part, by the very way that it pushes memory away. As the noted child psychiatrist Lenore Terr suggests in her recent book *Unchained Memories: True Stories of Traumatic Memories Lost and Found*, there may not be one simple, generalizable set of rules that can determine in advance the truth of any particular case, and we may thus ultimately have to struggle with the particularity of each individual story in order to learn anew, each time, what it means for a memory to be true. The writers in this volume contribute, exemplarily, to this task by showing how the particularity of traumatic histories, and the complex relation between knowing and not knowing that defines them, can be approached through the different disciplines represented in this volume.

What these writers so forcefully suggest, and may continue to offer in the ongoing world of trauma research, is that there is no single approach to listening to the many different traumatic experiences and histories we encounter, and that the irreducible specificity of traumatic stories requires in its turn the varied responses—responses of knowing and of acting—of literature, film, psychiatry, neurobiology, sociology, and political and social activism. This volume is unique, I believe, in showing the richness of the many ways in which a variety of disciplines can contribute to the ongoing work on trauma, and indeed in demonstrating the necessity of this multifaceted approach. It may be only through this variety that we can learn, in effect, not only to ease suffering but to open, in the individual and the community, new possibilities for change, a change that would acknowledge the unthinkable realities to which traumatic experience bears witness.

## Acknowledgments

Versions of the essays in this volume were originally published in 1991 in two issues (1 and 4) of *American Imago* under the title "Psychoanalysis, Culture and Trauma." I would like to thank Donald Moss, M.D., for involving me with the journal. I am also grateful to Marjorie Allard for her excellent and prompt research and for other aspects of manuscript preparation.

# I

## Trauma and Experience

# INTRODUCTION

## CATHY CARUTH

In the years since Vietnam, the fields of psychiatry, psychoanalysis, and sociology have taken a renewed interest in the problem of trauma. In 1980, the American Psychiatric Association finally officially acknowledged the long-recognized but frequently ignored phenomenon under the title "Post-Traumatic Stress Disorder" (PTSD), which included the symptoms of what had previously been called shell shock, combat stress, delayed stress syndrome, and traumatic neurosis, and referred to responses to both human and natural catastrophes. On the one hand, this classification and its attendant official acknowledgment of a pathology has provided a category of diagnosis so powerful that it has seemed to engulf everything around it: suddenly responses not only to combat and to natural catastrophes but also to rape, child abuse, and a number of other violent occurrences have been understood in terms of PTSD, and diagnoses of some dissociative disorders have also been switched to that of trauma. On the other hand, this powerful new tool has provided anything but a solid explanation of disease: indeed, the impact of trauma as a concept and a category, if it has helped diagnosis, has done so only at the cost of a fundamental disruption in our received modes of understanding and of cure, and a challenge to our very comprehension of what constitutes pathology. This can be seen in the debates that surround "category A" of the American Psychiatric Association's definition of PTSD (a response to an event "outside the range of usual human experience"), concerning how closely PTSD must be tied to specific kinds of events;[1] or in the psychoanalytic problem of whether trauma is indeed pathological in the usual sense, in relation to distortions caused by desires, wishes, and repressions. Indeed, the more we satisfactorily locate and classify the symptoms of

PTSD, the more we seem to have dislocated the boundaries of our modes of understanding—so that psychoanalysis and medically oriented psychiatry, sociology, history, and even literature all seem to be called upon to explain, to cure, or to show why it is that we can no longer simply explain or simply cure. The phenomenon of trauma has seemed to become all-inclusive, but it has done so precisely because it brings us to the limits of our understanding: if psychoanalysis, psychiatry, sociology, and even literature are beginning to hear each other anew in the study of trauma, it is because they are listening through the radical disruption and gaps of traumatic experience.

In this volume I have asked leading thinkers in many different disciplines to respond to this disruption and to the insight it makes possible, to speak to each other through the new ignorance that trauma introduces among us. The aim of this volume, as I have thus formulated it, is to examine the impact of the experience, and the notion, of trauma on psychoanalytic practice and theory, as well as on other aspects of culture such as literature and pedagogy, the construction of history in writing and film, and social or political activism. I am interested not so much in further defining trauma, that is, than in attempting to understand its surprising impact: to examine how trauma unsettles and forces us to rethink our notions of experience, and of communication, in therapy, in the classroom, and in literature, as well as in psychoanalytic theory. In this introduction I will suggest briefly what I see as the challenges that trauma poses to psychoanalytic theory, as well as the possibilities it opens within psychoanalysis and more generally within contemporary thought.

While the precise definition of post-traumatic stress disorder is contested, most descriptions generally agree that there is a response, sometimes delayed, to an overwhelming event or events, which takes the form of repeated, intrusive hallucinations, dreams, thoughts or behaviors stemming from the event, along with numbing that may have begun during or after the experience, and possibly also increased arousal to (and avoidance of) stimuli recalling the event.[2] This simple definition belies a very peculiar fact: the pathology cannot be defined either by the event itself—which may or may not be catastrophic, and may not traumatize everyone equally—nor can it be defined in terms of a *distortion* of the event, achieving its haunting power as a result of distorting personal significances attached to it. The pathology consists, rather, solely in the *structure of its experience* or reception: the event is not assimilated or experienced fully at the time, but only belatedly, in its repeated *possession* of the one who experiences it. To be traumatized is precisely to be possessed by an image or event. And thus the traumatic symptom cannot be interpreted, simply, as a distortion of reality, nor as the lending of unconscious meaning to a reality it wishes to ignore, nor as the repression of what once was wished. Indeed, in 1920, faced with the onset of "war neuroses" from World War I, Freud was astonished at their resistance to the whole field of wish and unconscious meaning, comparing them to another long-resistant phenomenon he had dealt with, the accident neurosis:

> Dreams occurring in traumatic neuroses have the characteristic of repeatedly bringing the patient back into the situation of his accident, a situation from which he wakes up in another fright. This astonishes people far too little. . . . Anyone who accepts it as something self-evident that dreams should put them back at night into the situation that caused them to fall ill has misunderstood the nature of dreams. (*SE* 18:13)

The returning traumatic dream startles Freud because it cannot be understood in terms of any wish or unconscious meaning, but is, purely and inexplicably, the literal return of the event against the will of the one it inhabits. Indeed, modern analysts as well have remarked on the surprising *literality* and nonsymbolic nature of traumatic dreams and flashbacks, which resist cure to the extent that they remain, precisely, literal. It is this literality and its insistent return which thus constitutes trauma and points toward its enigmatic core: the delay or incompletion in knowing, or even in seeing, an overwhelming occurrence that then remains, in its insistent return, absolutely *true* to the event. It is indeed this truth of traumatic experience that forms the center of its pathology or symptoms; it is not a pathology, that is, of falsehood or displacement of meaning, but of history itself. If PTSD must be understood as a pathological symptom, then it is not so much a symptom of the unconscious, as it is a symptom of history. The traumatized, we might say, carry an impossible history within them, or they become themselves the symptom of a history that they cannot entirely possess.

Yet what can it mean that history occurs as a symptom? It is indeed this curious phenomenon that makes trauma, or PTSD, in its definition, and in the impact it has on the lives of those who live it, intimately bound up with a question of truth. The problem arises not only in regard to those who listen to the traumatized, not knowing how to establish the reality of their hallucinations and dreams; it occurs rather and most disturbingly often within the very knowledge and experience of the traumatized themselves. For on the one hand, the dreams, hallucinations and thoughts are absolutely literal, unassimilable to associative chains of meaning. It is this literality as we have said that possesses the receiver and resists psychoanalytic interpretation and cure.[3] Yet the fact that this scene or thought is not a possessed knowledge, but itself possesses, at will, the one it inhabits, often produces a deep uncertainty as to its very truth:

> A child survivor of the Holocaust who had been at Theresienstadt continually had flashbacks of trains, and didn't know where they came from; she thought she was going crazy. Until one day, in a group survivor meeting, a man says, "Yes, at Theresienstadt you could see the trains through the bars of the children's barracks." She was relieved to discover she was not mad. (Kinsler, 1990)

The survivors' uncertainty is not a simple amnesia; for the event returns, as Freud points out, insistently and against their will. Nor is it a matter of indirect access to an event, since the hallucinations are generally of events all too accessible in their horrible truth. It is not, that is, having too little or indirect access to an experience that places its truth in question, in this case, but paradoxically enough, its very overwhelming immediacy, that produces its belated uncertainty. Indeed, behind these local experiences of uncertainty, I would propose, is a larger question raised by the fact of trauma, what Shoshana Felman, in her essay in this volume, calls the "larger, more profound, less definable crisis of truth . . . proceeding from contemporary trauma." Such a crisis of truth extends beyond the question of individual cure and asks how we in this era can have access to our own historical experience, to a history that is in its immediacy a crisis to whose truth there is no simple access.

I would suggest that it is this crisis of truth, the historical enigma betrayed by trauma, that poses the greatest challenge to psychoanalysis, and is being felt more broadly at the center of trauma research today. For the attempt to understand trauma brings one repeatedly to this peculiar paradox: that in trauma the greatest confrontation with reality may also occur as an absolute numbing to it, that immediacy, paradoxically enough, may take the form of belatedness. Economic and psychological explanations never quite seem to match the full implications of this strange fact. Henry Krystal, calling on the work of Cohen and Kinston, refers in his essay for this volume to the impact of an event in which "no trace of a registration of any kind is left in the psyche, instead, a void, a hole is found." Similarly, Dori Laub has suggested that massive psychic trauma "precludes its registration"; it is "a record that has yet to be made" (Laub, 1991). The peculiarity of an event whose force is marked by its lack of registration is developed in Dr. Laub's piece for this volume, in which he suggests that the Holocaust involved a "collapse of witnessing":

> History was taking place with no witness: it was also the very circumstance of *being inside the event* that made unthinkable the very notion that a witness could exist. . . . The historical imperative to bear witness could essentially *not be met during the actual occurrence.*

While Dr. Laub's remarks define a specific quality of the Holocaust in particular which we would not wish too quickly to generalize, he touches on something nonetheless that seems oddly to inhabit all traumatic experience: the inability fully to witness the event as it occurs, or the ability to witness the *event* fully only at the cost of witnessing oneself. Central to the very immediacy of this experience, that is, is a gap that carries the force of the event and does so precisely at the expense of simple knowledge and memory. The force of this experience would appear to arise precisely, in other words, in the collapse of its understanding.

It is indeed the link between this inexplicable traumatic void and the nature of historical experience that is the focus of Freud's great study of Jewish history, *Moses and Monotheism*, in which he compares the history of the Jews with the structure of a trauma. What is striking, for Freud, is the return of the event after a period of delay:

> It may happen that someone gets away, apparently unharmed, from the spot where he has suffered a shocking accident, for instance a train collision. In the course of the following weeks, however, he develops a series of grave psychical and motor symptoms, which can be ascribed only to his shock or whatever else happened at the time of the accident. He has developed a "traumatic neurosis." This appears quite incomprehensible and is therefore a novel fact. The time that elapsed between the accident and the first appearance of the symptoms is called the "incubation period," a transparent allusion to the pathology of infectious disease. . . . It is the feature one might term *latency.* (Freud, 1939, 84)

In the term "latency," the period during which the effects of the experience are not apparent, Freud seems to describe the trauma as the successive movement from an event to its repression to its return. Yet what is truly striking about the accident victim's experience of the event and what in fact constitutes the central enigma of Freud's example, is not so much the period of forgetting that occurs after the accident, but rather the fact that the victim of the crash was never fully conscious during the accident itself: the person gets away, Freud says, "apparently unharmed." The experience of trauma, the fact of latency, would thus seem to consist, not in the forgetting of a reality that can hence never be fully known, but in an inherent latency within the experience itself. The historical power of the trauma is not just that the experience is repeated after its forgetting, but that it is only in and through its inherent forgetting that it is first experienced at all. And it is this inherent latency of the event that paradoxically explains the peculiar, temporal structure, the belatedness, of historical experience: since the traumatic event is not experienced as it occurs, it is fully evident only in connection with another place, and in another time. If repression, in trauma, is replaced by latency, this is significant in so far as its blankness—the space of unconsciousness—is paradoxically what precisely preserves the event in its literality. For history to be a history of trauma means that it is referential precisely to the extent that it is not fully perceived as it occurs; or to put it somewhat differently, that a history can be grasped only in the very inaccessibility of its occurrence.[4]

Freud's late insight into this inextricable and paradoxical relation between history and trauma can tell us something about the challenge it presently poses for psychoanalysis; for it suggests that what trauma has to tell us—the historical and personal truth it transmits—is intricately bound up with its refusal of historical boundaries; that its truth is bound up with its crisis of truth. This is why, I would suggest, psychoanalysis has been beset by problems surrounding, precisely, the historical truth it accords to trauma, or whether it locates its ultimate origin inside or outside the psyche. On the one hand, many have noted in the debate surrounding the historical reality of trauma for Freud, that he was, from the beginning, always concerned with the relation between the occurrence of real traumatic events and the experience of pathology; many have pointed to the early *Studies on Hysteria* and "Preliminary Communication," but one could perhaps already see the beginnings of this interest in his first published book, *On Aphasia*, exploring physical trauma to the brain. On the other hand, many have suggested that Freud's apparent "giving up" of the reality of childhood seduction served—for Freud's followers, if not entirely for Freud himself—to relocate the origins of trauma entirely inside the psyche, in the individual's fantasy life, and hence to disavow the historical reality of violence (see, for example, Masson, 1984). While the insistence on the reality of violence is a necessary and important task, particularly as a corrective to analytic therapies that would reduce trauma to fantasy life or adult trauma to the events of childhood, nonetheless the debate concerning the location of the origins of traumatic experience as inside or outside the psyche may also miss the central Freudian insight into trauma, that the impact of the traumatic event lies precisely in its belatedness, in its refusal to be simply located, in its insistent appearance outside the boundaries of any single place or time. From his early claims, in the *Project for a Scientific Psychology*, that a trauma consists of two scenes— the earlier (in childhood) having sexual content but no meaning, the later (after puberty) having no sexual content but sexual meaning[5]—to his later claims, in *Moses and Monotheism*, that the trauma occurs only after a latency period, Freud seems to have been concerned, as we have suggested, with the way in which trauma is not a simple or single experience of events but that events, insofar as they are traumatic, assume their force precisely in their temporal delay. The apparent split between external and internal trauma in psychoanalytic theory, and related problems in other psychiatric definitions of trauma—whether to define it in terms of events or of symptomatic responses to events, or the relative contribution of previous traumas to the present one—would all be a function, in Freud's definition, of the split within immediate experience that characterizes the traumatic occurrence itself. It is the fundamental dislocation implied by all traumatic experience that is both its testimony to the event and to the impossibility of its direct access. And it is the challenge of this paradoxical notion to any preconceived understanding of experience that permits what Laura Brown calls the "radical potential of psychoanalysis" to "retell the lost truths of pain among us."

This historical conception of trauma can also be understood as conveying the urgent centrality for psychoanalytic thinking of the relation between crisis and survival. Harold Bloom's essay for this volume, focusing on the drive's "nonlocation" and interpreting Freud's notion of the drive as a "borderland concept" in terms of "the contamination of drive and defense," raises this question by implicitly drawing on the central paradox of the theory of the death drive that arose in Freud's confrontation with the war traumas of World War I: the notion that in inanimate matter the drive originated as a defense, and specifically as a defense against the traumatic imposition of life; that life began as a struggle to return to death (Bloom, 1982). Understood as an attempt to explain the experience of war trauma, Freud's difficult thought provides a deeply disturbing insight into the enigmatic relation between trauma and survival: the fact that, for those who undergo trauma, it is not only the moment of the event, but of the passing out of it that is traumatic; that *survival itself,* in other words, *can be a crisis.*

With this insight psychoanalysis is no longer simply a statement about others, but is itself a complex act, and statement *of* survival. Robert Jay Lifton would seem to suggest this, indeed, when he implicitly characterizes late

Freudian trauma theory, and the theory of the death drive, as resulting from a struggle for survival with the traumas of World War I. Psychoanalytic theory, he would have us recognize, occasionally speaks its obscurist thoughts out of an intense and not fully assimilated confrontation with death. And Bloom's characterization of Freud also asks us to listen to him not as a mere theorist but as a witness who speaks, enigmatically, out of the crisis of his own survival: "Freud's peculiar strength was to say what could not be said, or at least to attempt to say it, thus refusing to be silent in the face of the unsayable." Psychoanalytic theory and trauma would indeed meet, in this perspective, on the grounds of this impossible saying.

If on the one hand the essays in this volume remind us of the inaccessibility of trauma, of its resistance to full theoretical analysis and understanding, they also open up a perspective on the ways in which trauma can make possible survival, and on the means of engaging this possibility through the different modes of therapeutic, literary, and pedagogical encounter. By turning away, as we have suggested, from a notion of traumatic experience as a neurotic distortion, the authors of these essays bring us back continually to the ever-surprising fact that trauma is not experienced as a mere repression or defense, but as a temporal delay that carries the individual beyond the shock of the first moment. The trauma is a repeated suffering of the event, but it is also a continual leaving of its site. The traumatic reexperiencing of the event thus *carries with it* what Dori Laub calls the "collapse of witnessing," the impossibility of knowing that first constituted it. And by carrying that impossibility of knowing out of the empirical event itself, trauma opens up and challenges us to a new kind of listening, the witnessing, precisely, *of impossibility.*

How does one listen to what is impossible? Certainly one challenge of this listening is that it may no longer be simply a choice: to be able to listen to the impossible, that is, is also to have been *chosen* by it, *before* the possibility of mastering it with knowledge. This is its danger—the danger, as some have put it, of the trauma's "contagion," of the traumatization of the ones who listen (Terr, 1988). But it is also its only possibility for transmission. "Sometimes it is better," Dori Laub suggests, speaking as a clinician, "not to know too much" (Laub, 1991). To listen to the crisis of a trauma, that is, is not only to listen for the event, but to hear in the testimony the survivor's departure from it; the challenge of the therapeutic listener, in other words, is *how to listen to departure.*

The final import of the psychoanalytic and historical analysis of trauma is to suggest that the inherent departure, within trauma, from the moment of its first occurrence, is also a means of passing out of the isolation imposed by the event: that the history of a trauma, in its inherent belatedness, can only take place through the listening of another. The meaning of the trauma's address beyond itself concerns, indeed, not only individual isolation but a wider historical isolation that, in our time, is communicated on the level of our cultures. Such an address can be located, for example, in Freud's insisting, from his exile in England, on having his final book on trauma—*Moses and Monotheism*—translated into English before he died; or in the survivors of Hiroshima first communicating their stories to the United States through the narrative written by John Hersey, or more generally in the survivors of the catastrophes of one culture addressing the survivors of another.[6] This speaking and this listening—a speaking and a listening *from the site of trauma*— does not rely, I would suggest, on what we simply know of each other, but on what we don't yet know of our own traumatic pasts. In a catastrophic age, that is, trauma itself may provide the very link between cultures: not as a simple understanding of the pasts of others but rather, within the traumas of contemporary history, as our ability to listen through the departures we have all taken from ourselves.

## Notes

1. This definition was used through DSM III-R. The phrase was eliminated from category A in the DSM IV definition, which appeared in 1994 (after the original publication of this introduction). The debate concerning what kinds of events may be considered potentially traumatizing nonetheless continues.

2. See for example the definition of PTSD in American Psychiatric Association (1987) and the discussion of PTSD in the introduction to van der Kolk (1984).

3. See Cohen, 1990a, 1990b.

4. See Caruth, 1991.

5. See Laplanche, 1970.

6. *Moses and Monotheism* tells not only about the ancient trauma of the Jews but about Freud's own unsettling departure from Vienna in 1938. On the circumstances of the book's translation, see Gay (1988), 637, 638, and 643. With regard to the Hiroshima survivors, the publication of Hersey's *Hiroshima* (1985), written in the third person but based on directly received first-person accounts, produced the first widespread reaction in the United States to the human effects of the bombing.

## References

American Psychiatric Association. 1987. *Diagnostic and Statistical Manual of Mental Disorders*. 3d ed., rev. Washington, D.C.: APA.

Bloom, Harold. 1982. *Towards a Theory of Revisionism*. New York: Oxford University Press.

Caruth, Cathy. 1991. "Unclaimed Experience: Trauma and the Possibility of History." *Yale French Studies* 79 (1991).

Cohen, Jonathan. 1990a. "The Role of Interpretation in the Psychoanalytic Therapy of Traumatized Patients." Paper prepared for the Sixth Annual Meeting of the International Society for Traumatic Stress Studies, New Orleans.

———. 1990b. "The Trauma Paradigm in Psychoanalysis." Paper prepared for the Sixth Annual Meeting of the International Society for Traumatic Stress Studies, New Orleans.

Freud, Sigmund. 1939. *Moses and Monotheism*. Trans. Katherine Jones. New York: Vintage.

———. 1920 (1955). *The Standard Edition of the Complete Psychological Works of Sigmund Freud*. Vol. 18. Translated under the editorship of James Strachey in collaboration with Anna Freud, assisted by Alex Strachey and Alan Tyson. 24 vols. (1953–74). London: Hogarth.

Gay, Peter. 1988. *Freud: A Life for Our Time*. New York: Norton.

Hersey, John. 1985. *Hiroshima*. New York: Bantam.

Kinsler, Florabel. 1990. "The Dynamics of Brief Group Therapy in Homogeneous Populations: Child Survivors of the Holocaust." Paper prepared for the Sixth Annual Meeting of the International Society for Traumatic Stress Studies, New Orleans.

Laplanche, Jean. 1970. *Life and Death in Psychoanalysis*. Trans. Jeffrey Mehlman. Baltimore: Johns Hopkins University Press.

Laub, Dori. 1991. "No One Bears Witness to the Witness." In *Testimony: Crises of Witnessing in Literature, Psychoanalysis, and History*. ed. Shoshana Felman and Dori Laub. New York: Routledge.

Masson, Jeffrey. 1984. *The Assault on Truth: Freud's Suppression of the Seduction Theory*. New York: Penguin.

Terr, Lenore. 1988. "Remembered Images and Trauma: A Psychology of the Supernatural." *The Psychoanalytic Study of the Child*. New Haven: Yale University Press.

van der Kolk, Bessel A., ed. 1984. *Post-Traumatic Stress Disorder: Psychological and Biological Sequelae*. Washington, D.C.: American Psychiatric Press.

# Education and Crisis, or the Vicissitudes of Teaching

SHOSHANA FELMAN

## I

### TRAUMA AND PEDAGOGY

Is there a relation between crisis and the very enterprise of education? To put the question even more audaciously and sharply: Is there a relation between trauma and pedagogy? In a post-traumatic century, a century that has survived unthinkable historical catastrophes, is there anything that we have learned or that we should learn about education, that we did not know before? Can trauma *instruct* pedagogy, and can pedagogy shed light on the mystery of trauma? Can the task of teaching be instructed by the clinical experience, and can the clinical experience be instructed, on the other hand, by the task of teaching?

Psychoanalysis, as well as other disciplines of human mental welfare, proceed by taking testimonies from their patients. Can educators be in turn edified by the practice of the testimony, while attempting to enrich it and rethink it through some striking literary lessons? What does literature tell us about testimony? What does psychoanalysis tell us about testimony? Can the implications of the psychoanalytic lesson and the literary lesson about testimony *interact* in the pedagogical experience? Can the process of the testimony—that of bearing witness to a crisis or a trauma—be made use of in the classroom situation? What, indeed, does testimony mean in general, and what in general does it attempt to do? In a post-traumatic century, what and how can testimony teach us, not merely in the areas of law, of medicine, of history, which routinely use it in their daily practice, but in the larger areas of the *interactions between the clinical and the historical, between the literary and the pedagogical*?

### THE ALIGNMENT BETWEEN WITNESSES

In his book entitled *Kafka's Other Trial*, writer, critic, and Nobel prize laureate for literature Elias Canetti narrates the effect that Kafka's correspondence has had on him:

> I found those letters more gripping and absorbing than any literary work I have read for years past. They belong among those singular memoirs, autobiographies, collection of letters from which Kafka himself drew sustenance. He himself . . . [read] over and over again, the letters of Kleist, of Flaubert, and of Hebbel. . . .
>
> To call these letters documents would be saying too little, unless one were to apply the same title to the *life-testimonies* of Pascal, Kierkegaard, and Dostoevsky. For my part, I can only say that these letters have *penetrated me like an actual life*. (Canetti, 1974, 4; emphasis mine)

A "life-testimony" is not simply a testimony to a private life, but a point of conflation between text and life, a textual testimony which can *penetrate us like an actual life*. As such, Kafka's correspondence is testimony not merely to the life of Kafka, but to something larger than the life of Kafka, and which Canetti's title designates, suggestively and enigmatically, as *Kafka's Other Trial*. Both through Kafka's life and through his work, something crucial takes place which is of the order of a *trial*. Canetti's very reading of Kafka's correspondence, in line with Kafka's reading of the letters of Kleist, Hebbel, and Flaubert, thus adds its testimony—adds as yet another witness—to Kafka's *Trial*. Canetti writes:

> In the face of life's horror—luckily most people notice it only on occasion, but a few whom inner forces *appoint* to *bear witness* are always conscious of it—there is only one comfort: *its alignment with the horror experienced by previous witnesses*. (ibid.; emphasis mine)

How is the act of *writing* tied up with the act of *bearing witness*—and with the experience of the trial? Is the act of *reading* literary texts itself inherently related to the act of *facing horror*? If literature is the *alignment between witnesses*, what would this alignment mean? And by virtue of what sort of agency is one *appointed* to bear witness?

### THE APPOINTMENT

It is a strange appointment, from which the witness-appointee cannot relieve himself by any delegation, substitution, or representation. "If someone else could have written my stories," says Elie Wiesel, "I would not have written them. I have written them in order to testify. And this is the origin of the loneliness that can be glimpsed in each of my sentences, in each of my silences" (1984; my translation). Since the testimony cannot be simply relayed, repeated, or reported by another without thereby losing its function as a testimony, the burden of the witness—in spite of his or her alignment with other witnesses—is a radically unique, noninterchangeable, and solitary burden. "No one bears witness for the witness," writes the poet Paul Celan (Aschenglorie ["Ashes-Glory"]: "Niemand zeugt für den zeugen") (Celan, 1980a). To bear witness is to *bear the solitude* of a responsibility, and to *bear the responsibility*, precisely, of that solitude.

And yet, the *appointment* to bear witness is, paradoxically enough, an appointment to transgress the confines of that isolated stance, to speak *for* others and *to* others. The French philosopher Emmanuel Levinas can thus suggest that the witness' speech is one that, by its very definition, transcends the witness who is but its medium, the medium of realization of the testimony. "The witness," writes Levinas, "testifies to what has been said *through* him. Because the witness has said 'here I am' before the other" (Levinas, 1982, 115, my translation; emphasis mine). By virtue of the fact that the testimony is *addressed* to others, the witness, from within the solitude of his own stance, is the vehicle of an occurrence, a reality, a stance or a dimension *beyond himself.*

Is the appointment to the testimony voluntary or involuntary, given *to* or *against* the witness' will? The contemporary writer often dramatizes the predicament (whether chosen or imposed, whether conscious or unconscious) of a voluntary or of an unwitting, inadvertent, and sometimes *involuntary witness*: witness to a trauma, to a crime, or to an outrage; witness to a horror or an illness whose effects explode any capacity for explanation or rationalization.

### THE SCANDAL OF AN ILLNESS

In Albert Camus' *The Plague*, for instance, the narrator, a physician by profession, feels historically appointed—by the magnitude of the catastrophe he has survived and by the very nature of his vocation as a healer—to narrate the story and bear witness to the history of the deadly epidemic that has struck his town:

> This chronicle is drawing to an end, and this seems to be the moment for Dr. Bernard Rieux to confess that he is the narrator. . . . His profession put him in touch with a great many of our townspeople while plague was raging, and he had opportunities of hearing their various opinions. Thus he was well placed for giving a true account of all he saw and heard. . . .

Summoned to give evidence [*appelé à témoigner*] regarding what was a sort of crime, he has exercized the restraint that behooves a conscientious witness. All the same, following the dictates of his heart, he had deliberately taken the victims' side and tried to share with his fellow citizens the only certitudes they had in common—love, exile, and suffering. . . . Thus, decidedly, it was up to him to speak for all. . . . Dr. Rieux resolved to compile this chronicle, so that he should not be one of those who hold their peace but should bear witness in favour of those plague-stricken people; so that some memorial of the injustice done them might endure. (1972, 270, 287)

Camus' choice of the physician as the privileged narrator and the designated witness might suggest that the capacity to witness and the act of bearing witness in themselves embody some remedial quality and belong already, in obscure ways, to the healing process. But the presence of the doctor as key witness also tells us, on the other hand, that what there is to witness urgently in the human world, what alerts and mobilizes the attention of the witness and what necessitates the testimony is always fundamentally, in one way or another, the scandal of an illness, of a metaphorical or literal disease; and that the imperative of bearing witness, which here proceeds from the contagion of the Plague—from the eruption of an evil that is radically incurable—is itself somehow a philosophical and ethical correlative of a situation *with no cure*, and of a radical human condition of exposure and vulnerability.

## IN AN ERA OF TESTIMONY

Oftentimes, contemporary works of art use testimony both as the subject of their drama and as the medium of their literal transmission. Films like *Shoah* by Claude Lanzmann, *The Sorrow and the Pity* by Marcel Ophuls, or *Hiroshima mon amour* by Marguerite Duras and Alain Resnais, instruct us in the ways in which testimony has become a crucial mode of our relation to events of our times—our relation to the traumas of contemporary history: the Second World War, the Holocaust, the Nuclear bomb, and other war atrocities. As a relation to events, testimony seems to be composed of bits and pieces of a memory that has been overwhelmed by occurrences that have not settled into understanding or remembrance, acts that cannot be construed as knowledge nor assimilated into full cognition, events in excess of our frames of reference.

What the testimony does not offer is, however, a completed statement, a totalizable account of those events. In the testimony, language is in process and in trial, it does not possess itself as a conclusion, as the constatation of a verdict or the self-transparency of knowledge. Testimony is, in other words, a discursive *practice*, as opposed to a pure *theory*. To *testify*—to *vow to tell*, to *promise* and *produce* one's own speech as material evidence for truth—is to accomplish a *speech act*, rather than to simply formulate a statement. As a performative speech act, testimony in effect addresses what in history is *action* that exceeds any substantialized significance, and what in happenings is *impact* that dynamically explodes any conceptual reifications and any constative delimitations.

### CRISIS OF TRUTH

It has been suggested that testimony is the literary—or discursive—mode par excellence of our times, and that our era can precisely be defined as the age of testimony. "If the Greeks invented tragedy, the Romans the epistle, and the Renaissance the sonnet," writes Elie Wiesel, "our generation invented a new literature, that of testimony" (1977, 9). What is the significance of this growing predominance of testimony as a privileged contemporary mode of transmission and communication? *Why has testimony in effect become at once so central and so omnipresent in our recent cultural accounts of ourselves?*

In its most traditional, routine use in the legal context—in the court-room situation—testimony is provided, and is called for, when the facts upon which justice must pronounce its verdict are not clear, when historical accuracy is in doubt, and when both the truth and its supporting elements of evidence are called into question. The legal model of the trial dramatizes, in this way, a contained, and culturally channeled, institutionalized, *crisis of truth*. The trial both derives from and proceeds by, a crisis of evidence, which the verdict must resolve.

What, however, are the stakes of the larger, more profound, less defin-able crisis of truth which, in proceeding from contemporary trauma, has brought the discourse of the testimony to the fore of the contemporary cultural narrative, way beyond the implications of its limited, restricted usage in the legal context?

## II

### THE STORY OF A CLASS

As a way of investigating the significance of such a question, as well as of the questions raised in the beginning of this chapter concerning the inter-action between the clinical and the historical and the instructional relations among trauma, testimony, and the enterprise of education, I devised some years ago a course entitled, "Literature and Testimony." To extend the implications of the notion of the testimony and to indicate the cross-disciplinary relevance of the question in my tentative conception, I subtitled it: "(Literature, Psychoanalysis, and History)." I announced it as a graduate seminar at Yale. The title drew some thirty graduate students, mainly from the literary disciplines, but also from psychology, philosophy, sociology, history, medicine, and law.

I did not know then that I would myself, one day, have to articulate my testimony to that class, whose lesson—and whose unforeseeable eventness—turned out to be quite unforgettable both to the students and to their teacher, but not in ways either of us could have predicted. I had never given—and have never given since—any other class like it, and have never been as stupefied by the inadvertent lessons and the unforeseeable effects of teaching as I was by the experience of this course. I would like to recount that uncanny pedagogical experience as my own "life-testimony," to shake now the peculiar story of that real class whose narrative, in spite of its unique particularity, I will propose as a generic (testimonial) story (in a sense to which I will return, and from which I will later draw the implications): the story of how I, in fact, myself became a witness to the shock communicated by the subject-matter; the narrative of how the subject-matter was unwittingly *enacted*, set in motion in the class, and how testimony turned out to be at once more critically surprising and more critically important than anyone could have foreseen.

I have now repeated this course several times, but never with the same series of texts, never again in the same way and with the same framework of evidence. This was the first time that I taught that subject. It was in the fall of 1984.

I organized my choice of texts around literary, psychoanalytic, and historical accounts, which dramatize in different ways, through different genres and around different topics, the accounts of—or testimonies to—a crisis. The textual framework of the course included texts (or testimonies) by Camus, Dostoevsky, Freud, Mallarmé, Paul Celan, as well as autobiographical/historical life accounts borrowed from the Video Archive for Holocaust Testimonies at Yale. By thus conceiving of the course at once as a focused avenue of inquiry and as a varied constellation of texts, a diversity of works and genres in which testimony was inscribed in many ways and with a whole variety of implications, I had two tentative pedagogical objectives in mind: (1) to make the class feel, and progressively discover, how testimony is indeed *pervasive*, how it is implicated—sometimes unexpectedly—in almost every kind of writing; (2) to make the class feel, on the other hand, and—there again—progressively discover, how the testimony cannot be subsumed by its familiar notion, how the texts that testify do not simply *report facts* but, in different ways, encounter—and make us encounter—*strangeness*, how the concept of the testimony, speaking from a stance of superimposition of literature, psychoanalysis, and history, is in fact quite unfamiliar and *estranging*, and how—the more we look closely at texts, the more they show us that, unwittingly, we do not even know what testimony is, and that, in any case, it is not simply what we thought we knew it was.

How, indeed, has the significance of testimony itself been set in motion by the course, and how has it emerged, each time, at once in a new light and yet always still estranged, still a challenge for the task of understanding?

## III

### NARRATIVE AND TESTIMONY: ALBERT CAMUS

It is the most familiar notion of the testimony, the one which we encounter daily through its usage by the media and are thus most prepared for, because most acquainted with, with which we began the process of the exploration of the class. Taking as a starting point Camus' *The Plague*, we came first to believe—through the novel's underscored and most explicit indications—that the essence of the testimony is historical, and that its function is to record events and to report the facts of a historical occurrence. "To some," says the narrator of the novel, "these events [the outbreak of the Plague] will seem quite unnatural; to others, all but incredible":

> But, obviously, a narrator cannot take account of these differences of outlook. His business is only to say: "This is what happened", when he knows that it actually did happen, that it closely affected the life of a whole populace, and that there are thousands of eyewitnesses who can appraise in their hearts the truth of what he writes. (Camus, 1972, 6)

Thus, the narrator-doctor-witness feels both obligated and compelled to "chronicle" the "grave events" of the catastrophe he has survived and to "play the part of a historian" (ibid., 6), to "bear witness," as he puts it, "in favor of those plague-stricken people, so that some memorial of the injustice done them might endure" (ibid., 287). Since *The Plague* is a transparent allegory for the massive death inflicted by the Second World War and for the trauma of a Europe "quarantined" by German occupation and desperately struggling against the overwhelming deadliness of Nazism; since, indeed, a fragment of the novel was published literally as an *underground testimony*, as a French Resistance publication in Occupied France (in 1942), the witness borne by the doctor underscores, and at the same time tries to grasp and comprehend, the historical dimension of the testimony.

So did we, in class, focus, at the start, on this historical dimension. Surprisingly, however, the historical event *fails* to exhaustively account for the nature of the testimony, since the bearer of the testimony is not simply a "historian" but, primarily, a *doctor*, and since history appears, and is recorded, in the striking metaphor of a disease, a plague. Since the testimony dwells on historicity as a relationship to death, and since the act of writing—the act of making the artistic statement of the novel—is itself presented as an act of bearing witness to the trauma of survival, the *event* to which the testimony points and which it attempts to comprehend and grasp is enigmatically, at once historical and clinical. Is the testimony, therefore, a simple medium of historical transmission, or is it, in obscure ways, the unsuspected medium of a healing? If history has clinical dimensions, how can testimony *intervene*, pragmatically and efficaciously, at once historically (politically) *and* clinically?

## CONFESSION AND TESTIMONY: FYODOR DOSTOEVSKY

If the testimony is, however, always an agent in a process that, in some ways, bears upon the clinical, how should we understand this clinical dimension when the testimony, in the course of its own utterance, quite explicitly rejects the very goal of healing and precludes any therapeutic project? This, as the class was to discover, is the case of Dostoevsky's hero or narrator, writing his *Notes from the Underground*:

> I'm a sick man . . . a mean man. I think there's something wrong with my liver. . . . But, actually, I don't understand a damn thing about my sickness; I'm not even too sure what it is that's ailing me. I'm not under treatment and never have been, although I have great respect for medicine and doctors. Moreover, I'm morbidly superstitious, enough, at least, to respect medicine. With my education, I shouldn't be superstitious, but I am just the same. No, I'd say I refuse medical help just out of contrariness. I don't expect *you* to understand that, but it's so. Of course, I can't explain who I am trying to fool this way. I'm fully aware that I can't spite the doctors by refusing their help. I know very well that I'm harming

myself and no one else. But still, it's out of spite that I refuse to ask for the doctor's help. So my liver hurts? Good, let it hurt even more. (Dostoevsky, 1961, 90–91)

In thus presenting us with the "confession" of an illness that spites healing and does not seek cure, Dostoevsky's testimony, unlike Camus', seems to find its predilection in the clinical in a manner that subverts its very raison d'être and with such an exclusivity as to entirely preclude any larger perspective, any political or historical preoccupation. And yet, the clinical description, although crucial, is also crucially deceptive, and does not truly exhaust the testimonial stakes of Dostoevsky's text, whose complexity encompasses unwittingly a latent historical dimension: even though its very title, *Notes from the Underground* is written as a latent echo to a work Dostoevsky published two years earlier, *Notes from the House of the Dead*, in which the writer testifies to his historical and autobiographical experience as a political prisoner in a penitentiary in Siberia. Dostoevsky's early writings had placed him politically as a Russian liberal. Having joined a liberal circle of enthusiastic young men who met to discuss socialism, Dostoevsky was arrested, accused of complicity in a conspiracy (to set up a printing press), and condemned to death. The death sentence was commuted to a sentence of imprisonment, but, in a calculatedly cold-blooded farce devised by the tsarist authorities for the edification of subversives, the announcement of the pardon was made only in the middle of the ceremony of the execution, in the very face of the firing-squad. Some prisoners fainted. Two went permanently insane. Dostoevsky's epileptic fits, to which he had been subject since his childhood, were immeasurably aggravated.

In the guise of a confession that seeks above all to demystify and deconstruct itself, *Notes from the Underground* can indeed be read as a belated *testimony to a trauma*, a trauma that endows Dostoevsky with the sickness of the one who "knows"—with the underground vision of the one who has been made into a *witness* of his own firing-squad. The testimony to the sickness encompasses, in fact, at once the history that lurks behind the clinical manifestations and the political oppression that signals mutely from behind the clinical "confession."

Unpredictably, the notion of the testimony thus turns out to be tied up, precisely, with the notion of the underground. In much the same way as Camus published *The Plague* as a literal member of the so-called "underground"—of the French Resistance during Nazi occupation—Dostoevsky's testimony from the underground equally, though unpredictably, encompasses not just the subterranean drift of the apparent clinical event, but the political dimension of oppression and the ethical dimension of resistance that proceed from, and inscribe within the testimony, the historical occurrence.

## IV

### PSYCHOANALYSIS AND TESTIMONY: SIGMUND FREUD

It was at this point that psychoanalysis was introduced into the course, and that the import of its lesson brought about a turning point in the insight of the class. We studied in particular chapter 2 of *The Interpretation of Dreams*, with Freud's detailed account and interpretation of his "Irma dream" (Freud, 1900). In our tentative awakening into the latent *clinical* dimension of the literary testimonies we had been examining, it was significant to note that Freud's narrated dream at once derives from (in reality), and enacts (in phantasy), the problematization of a setting that, this time explicitly, is clinical: the dream is triggered by the doctor's concern with his only partially successful treatment of his patient Irma: "the patient was relieved of her hysterical anxiety but did not lose all her somatic symptoms" (ibid., 106). In the dream, the patient Irma is in fact complaining to the doctor, Freud, about her suffering and her continued pain. When Freud, while thinking of his dream, resorts to writing down for the first time ever all his free associations, he unexpectedly discovers, all at once, the dream's specific latent *meaning*, an unprecedented *method* of dream interpretation, and a *theory* of dreams as psychical fulfillments of unconscious wishes:

> The dream acquitted me of the responsibility for Irma's condition by showing that it was due to other factors—it produced a whole series of reasons. The dream represented a particular state of affairs as I should have wished it to be. *Thus its content was the fulfilment of a wish and its motive was a wish.* (ibid., 118–19)

Like Dostoevsky's *Notes* (although with an intention altogether different), Freud's *Dreams* in turn offer us, surprisingly enough, at once an autobiographical and a clinical *confession*. "I have other difficulties to overcome, which lie within myself," writes Freud: "There is some natural hesitation about revealing so many intimate facts about one's mental life; nor can there be any guarantee against misinterpretation by strangers":

> [But] it is safe to assume that my readers . . . will very soon find their initial interest in the indiscretions which I am bound to make replaced by

an absorbing immersion in the psychological problems upon which they throw light. (ibid., 105)

Once again, then, in Freud's writing of his dreams, as in Dostoevsky's writing of his *Notes*, the *testimony* differentiates itself from the content of the *manifest confession* which it uses as its vehicle, the confession is *displaced*, precisely, at the very moment that we think we grasp it, and it is in this surprise, in this displacement, that our sense of testimony will be shifted once again.

Considered as a testimony, Freud's discourse as a whole has an unprecedented status in the history of culture, in three respects: (1) the radical displacement that it operates in our understanding of the clinical dimension; (2) the validity and scientific recognition that it for the first time gives to unconscious testimony; (3) its unprecedented status as both a narrative and a theoretical event, as a narrative, in fact, of the advent of theory.

Freud's innovations as clinician stem, indeed, from his concern with how not to dismiss the patient's testimony—as medical doctors were accustomed to do in hysterics' cases—even when the physician does not understand this testimony. "So far," says Freud in the first of his *Five Lectures on Psychoanalysis*, "it has been an advantage to us to accompany the doctors; but the moment of parting is at hand. For you must not suppose that a patient's prospects of medical assistance are improved in essentials by the fact that a diagnosis of hysteria has been substituted for one of severe organic disease of the brain":

> Thus the recognition of the illness as hysteria makes little difference to the patient; but to the doctor quite the reverse. It is noticeable that his attitude towards hysterical patients is quite other than towards sufferers from organic diseases. He does not have the same sympathy for the former as for the latter. Through his studies the doctor has learned many things that remain a sealed book to the layman. . . . But all his knowledge—his training in anatomy, in physiology, and in pathology—leaves him in the lurch when he is confronted by the details of hysterical phenomena. He cannot understand hysteria, and in the face of it he is himself a layman. This is not a pleasant situation for anyone who as a rule sets so much store by his knowledge. So it comes about that hysterical patients forfeit his sympathy. He regards them as people who are transgressing the laws of his science—like heretics in the eyes of the orthodox. He attributes every kind of wickedness to them, accuses them of exaggeration, of deliberate deceit, of malingering. And he punishes them by withdrawing his interest from them. (*SE* 11:11–12)

In contrast, it is by stepping in his turn into the position of the patient, and by acknowledging an interchangeability between doctor and patient (a fact which the Irma dream dramatizes by Freud's own arthritic shoulder pain, echoing the pain of his patient Irma), that Freud creates the revolutionized clinical dimension of the *psychoanalytic dialogue*, an unprecedented kind of dialogue in which the doctor's testimony does not substitute itself for the patient's testimony, but *resonates with it*, because, as Freud discovers, *it takes two to witness the unconscious.*

In presenting his own testimony of the Irma dream as a correlative both to the dreams and to the symptoms of his patients, Freud makes a scientific statement of his discovery that there *is* in effect such a thing as an *unconscious testimony*, and that this unconscious, unintended, unintentional testimony has, as such, an incomparable heuristic and investigative value. Psychoanalysis, in this way, profoundly rethinks and radically renews the very concept of the testimony, by submitting, and by recognizing for the first time in the history of culture, that one does not have to *possess*, or *own* the truth, in order to effectively *bear witness* to it; that speech as such is unwittingly testimonial; and that the speaking subject constantly bears witness to a truth that nonetheless continues to escape him, a truth that is, essentially, *not available* to its own speaker.

In the underground of language, Freud encounters Dostoevsky. Psychoanalysis and literature have come both to contaminate and to enrich each other. Both, henceforth, will be considered as primarily *events of speech*; and their testimony, in both cases, will be understood as a mode of *truth's realization* beyond what is available as statement, beyond what is available, that is, as a truth transparent to itself and entirely known, given, in advance, prior to the very process of its utterance. The testimony will thereby be understood, in other words, not as a mode of *statement of*, but rather as a mode of *access to*, that truth. In literature as well as in psychoanalysis, and conceivably in history as well, the witness might be—as the term suggests and as Freud knew only too well (as is evidenced by his insistence on "der Zeuge"), the one who (in fact) *witnesses*—but also, the one who *begets*—the truth, through the speech process of the testimony. This begetting of the truth is also what Freud does, precisely, through his witness and his testimony to the Irma dream, out of which he will *give birth* to the entire theory of dreams, and to its undreamt-of implications.

Freud's whole attempt, henceforth, will be to bring the *evidence materialized* by the unconscious testimony into the realm of cognition. Through the material process of the act of *writing down* (which itself in some ways implicates the relevance, and the participation, in the psychoanalytic testimonial process, of the *literary act*): through a detailed recording and deciphering of the dream's associations, the Irma dream *bears witness* to the *unconscious* testimony of the dream in such a way as to transform it into the most reflective and most pointed *conscious* testimony, a conscious testimony that itself can only be grasped in the movement of its own production, and that increasingly embraces not just what is *witnessed*, but what is *begotten* by the unconscious testimony of the dream. The stupendous conscious testimony that the dream gives birth to will consist, therefore, not merely in the actual interpretation and elucidation of the dream, but in the transformation of this one particular event and of this one particular interpretation into a paradigmatic model not just of interpretation but of the very principle of psychoanalytic discovery, a model, that is, of the very birth of knowledge through the testimonial process. The unconscious testimony of one dream—through its conflation with the testimonies of other dreams—is transmuted into the pathbreaking conscious testimony of a universal *theory of dreams*, which itself, in turn, founds the entire *theory of psychoanalysis*. Psychoanalytic theory, however, is nothing other than a finally available *statement* (or approximation) of a truth that, at the outset, was unknown but that was gradually *accessed* through the practice and the process of the testimony. In this sense, the whole *Interpretation of Dreams* can be viewed, indeed, as Freud's most revolutionary testimonial work: a universal testimonial work that at the same time dramatizes—to return once again to Canetti's terms with respect to Kafka's correspondence— a particular *life-testimony*, which, in this case, happens to be Freud's. In the Preface to the Second Edition of *The Interpretation of Dreams*, written ten years after the original publication, Freud thus writes:

> The essence of what I have written about dreams and their interpreta-
> tion, as well as about the psychological theorems to be deduced from
> them—all this remains unaltered: subjectively at all events, it has stood
> the test of time. Anyone who is acquainted with my other writings . . .
> will know that I have never put forward inconclusive opinions as though
> they were established facts, and that I have always sought to modify my
> statements so that they may keep in step with my advancing knowledge.
> In the sphere of my dream-life I have been able to leave my original
> assertions unchanged. During the long years in which I have been work-
> ing at the problems of the neuroses I have often been in doubt and
> sometimes been shaken in my convictions. At such times it has always
> been *The Interpretation of Dreams* that has given me back my certainty.
> (*SE* 5 xxv–xxvi)

Much like Kafka's novel or Kafka's correspondence, much like Dostoevsky's *Underground* or Camus's *Plague*, Freud's dream narrative is equally,

indeed, *the story of a trial*: a trial symbolized by the dramatic, anecdotal way in which Freud sees himself, within the dream, both tried and judged by his colleagues; an oneiric trial which, however, is itself the emblem of a larger, more decisive trial, encompassing the ways in which the revolutionary theory of psychoanalysis is being put to trial by the contemporary world. In this way, the very idiosyncrasy of Freud's autobiographical and clinical confession, the very triviality of the oneiric story of the trial, unwittingly emerges into the dimension of the truth of a ground breaking *theoretical event*. As the first dream Freud submitted not just to his own endeavor of detailed interpretation, not just to the further work of his own conscious understanding, but to the conscious witnessing of the whole world, the story of the Irma dream unsettlingly becomes, thus, a *generic* testimonial story.

The curious thing about this stunning theoretical event is the way in which its very generality hinges, paradoxically, on its accidental nature: on the contingency of a particular, idiosyncratic, symptomatic dream. In the symptomatic and yet theoretical illumination of this radically new kind of intelligibility, psychoanalysis can be viewed as a momentously felicitous, and a momentously creative, *testimony to an accident*.

# V

## POETRY AND TESTIMONY: STÉPHANE MALLARMÉ, OR AN ACCIDENT OF VERSE

Curiously enough, it is also in such unexpected terms—those precisely of the testimony to an accident—that Mallarmé, the Nineteenth-Century French Symbolist and perhaps the greatest poet France has given to the world, speaks about contemporary poetry.

Having been invited to give a talk at Oxford University on new trends in French poetry—on the poetic revolution taking place around him in France—Mallarmé announces to his English audience:

> In effect, I am bringing news, and the most surprising. Such a case has never been seen.
> They have done violence to verse. . . .
> It is appropriate to relieve myself of that news right away—to talk about it now already—much like an invited traveler who, without delay, in breathless gasps, discharges himself of the testimony of an accident known, and pursuing him. (Mallarmé, 1945, 634–44; trans. by Felman [all subsequent translations are by Felman])[1]

The conjunction of the testimony and the accident that seemed at once to redefine the testimony in the psychoanalytic perspective and to pinpoint the newness of psychoanalysis, thus also describes, surprisingly enough, the altogether different realm of poetry in Mallarmé's perspective. Coincidentally, Mallarmé's and Freud's conceptual discoveries occur in the same year: Mallarmé's lecture in England is published in 1895, the very year in which Freud comes across the theory of dreams through the pivotal analysis of his Irma dream. I would suggest, indeed, that this remote conceptual and chronological encounter between Freud's and Mallarmé's juxtapositions of the testimony and the accident is not due purely to coincidence but that, in fact, in spite of the all too-apparent differences between the two endeavors, something crucial in the depth of their conceptions and in the innovative thrust of their perceptions indeed resonates. What makes Mallarmé, therefore, at once perceive and in his turn convey the very newness in French poetry as *testimony to an accident*? What is the nature of the accident referred to here by Mallarmé?

What the poetic revolution basically consists of is the introduction of "free verse" into French poetry, a change of form or a loosening of the poetic rules which entails a destitution or disintegration of the classical Alexandrine, the official French verse whose traditional twelve syllables and whose symmetric rhymes and rhythms had imposed themselves for centuries as the only possible mould—and as the only formal stamp—of French poetic writing.

If poetry can be essentially defined as an art of rhythm, Mallarmé redefines rhythm and thus radically rethinks the event of poetry as such through the rhythmical unpredictability of free verse which, in unsettling the predictability—the formal structure of anticipation—of the Alexandrine, reaches out for what precisely *cannot be anticipated*: "they have done violence to verse." In opposition to the forms of traditional verse, poetry with Mallarmé becomes an *art of accident* in that it is an art of rhythmical surprises, an art, precisely, of unsettling rhythmical, syntactic and semantic expectations.

What is crucially important is, however, Mallarmé's acute and singular perception of the celebration of free verse as the violent experience of linguistic rupture, as the historical advent of a linguistic fragmentation in which the verse is violently and deliberately "broken," in what Mallarmé describes as a "fundamental crisis"—what he calls, precisely, in a text so-titled, *Crise de vers*, "Crisis of Verse" (ibid., 360). As the testimony to an accident which is materially embodied in an *accidenting of the verse*, poetry henceforth speaks with the very power—with the very unanticipated impact—of its own explosion of its medium.

Apparently, the poetic revolution is purely esthetic, purely formal. And yet, in Mallarmé's perception the *formal* change is crucially, implicitly endowed with a *political* dimension:

> In effect, I am bringing news, and the most surprising.
> Such a case has never been seen. They have done violence to verse.
> Governments change: but always prosody remains intact: either, in the revolutions, it passes unnoticed, or the violent attempt upon it does not impose itself because of the opinion that this ultimate dogma can never vary.[2]

Mallarmé implicitly compares the effects of the poetic revolution to the ground-shaking processes unleashed by the French Revolution. Paradoxically enough, the political upheaval and the civil shaking of foundations brought about by the fall of governments and the collapse of institutions may not be, in fact, as profound and as radical a change as the one accomplished by a linguistic or a poetic transformation. Insofar as the accidenting of the verse narrates the drama of the accidenting—the disruption and the shattering—of "this ultimate dogma," insofar as the resistance of tradition is now finally and formally dissolved and the traditional hierarchical divisions between poetry and prose—between *classes* in language—are now disposed of and inherently unsettled, the breaking of the verse becomes itself a symptom and an emblem of the historical breaking of political and cultural grounds, and the freeing, or the *liberation*, of the verse—through its decanonization—implicates the process of a vaster desacralization, of a vaster liberation taking place in social consciousness and in culture at large.[3] "In effect, I am bringing news, and the most surprising." What is profoundly surprising, Mallarmé implies, is not simply that the verse is broken, but that the breaking of the verse picks up on something that the political dimensions of the French Revolution have inaugurated, in their accidenting both of classes and of dogmas, but failed to consummate, failed to achieve completely. The revolution in poetic form testifies, in other words, to political and cultural changes whose historical manifestation, and its revolutionary aspect, is now noticed accidentally—accidentally breaks into awareness—through an *accident of verse*. The poetic revolution is thus both a replica, and a sequence, an effect of, the French Revolution. What free verse by accident picks up on, therefore, is not merely former poetry which it now modifies, but the formerly unseen, ill-understood relationship that the accident reveals between culture and language, *between poetry and politics.*

The seeming triviality of the formal *location* of the accident in free verse—in a literal transgression of the rules of prosody and in a rupture of the Alexandrine—is thus fundamentally misleading. In much the same way as in Freud, the trivial story of the trial—in testifying to an *accident of dream—* amounts to a groundbreaking revolution in perception and in human understanding. Mallarmé's accident of verse in effect bears witness to far-reaching transformations in the rhythm of life and to momentous cultural, political, and historical processes of change.

Mallarmé's subject—his poetic testimony or the news he brings about the accident—is therefore by no means trivial, nor is it, in fact, what it appears to be: the scope of the accident is vaster, more profound and more difficult to grasp than the sheer formality of the concerns that convey it and that are its vehicle. Halfway through his Oxford lecture, Mallarmé acknowledges this *otherness* of his own subject, which he himself does not entirely possess:

> In effect I am bringing news, and the most surprising. . . .
> They have done violence to verse. . . .
>
> It is appropriate to relieve myself of that news right away—to talk about it now already—much like an invited traveler who, without delay, in breathless gasps, discharges himself of the testimony of an accident known and pursuing him. . . .
>
> Should I stop here, and where do I get the feeling that *I have come relatively to a subject vaster and to myself unknown*—vaster than this or that innovation of rites or rhymes; in order to *attempt to reach* this subject, if not to treat it. . . .
>
> Consciousness in us is lacking of what, above, explodes or splits. (643–47)[2]

In a way, Mallarmé suggests that he speaks too soon, before he is quite ready, before he quite knows what his subject is about. And yet, since he has been a witness to "an accident known," since he does *know* that an accident has taken place, and since the accident "pursues him," he has got to speak "*already,*" almost compulsively, even though he has not had as yet the time to catch his breath. He thus speaks in advance of the control of consciousness; his testimony is delivered "in breathless gasps": in essence it is a *precocious testimony.*

Such precocious testimony in effect becomes, with Mallarmé, the very principle of poetic insight and the very core of the event of poetry, which makes precisely language—through its breathless gasps—speak ahead of knowledge and awareness and break through the limits of its own conscious understanding. By its very innovative definition, poetry will henceforth speak *beyond its means*, to testify—precociously—to the ill-understood effects and to the impact of an accident whose origin cannot precisely be located but whose repercussions, in their very uncontrollable and unanticipated nature, still continue to evolve even in the very process of the testimony.

The accident is therefore "known," paradoxically enough, at once precociously but only through its aftermath, through its effects.[5] The accident is known, in other words, both to the extent that *it "pursues"* the witness and that *the witness is, in turn, in pursuit of it.* Indeed, the syntax of the French expression "ainsi qu'un invité voyageur se décharge du témoignage d'un accident su et le poursuivant" is radically ambiguous. As Barbara Johnson has pointed out, Mallarmé's unique poetic style—in its play on this syntactic ambiguity—leaves in suspension the question of who is pursuing whom, whether it is the accident that pursues the witness-traveler or whether it is the traveler, the witness, who pursues the accident:

> Is it the accident [—writes Johnson—] which pursues the traveller, or rather, the traveller who . . . pursues the accident? Where is the accident situated? . . . Is the witness the one who *sees*, the one who *undergoes*, or the one who *propagates*, the accident to which he bears witness? (Johnson, 1979, 169–70; my translation)

What difference does this ambiguity make in our understanding of the accident and of the testimony?

If it is the accident that *pursues the witness*, it is the compulsive character of the testimony that is brought into relief: the witness is "pursued," that is, at once compelled and bound by what, in the unexpected impact of the accident, is both incomprehensible and unforgettable. The accident does not let go: it is an accident from which the witness can no longer free himself.

But if, in a still less expected manner, it is the witness who *pursues the accident*, it is perhaps because the witness, on the contrary, has understood that from the accident a *liberation* can proceed and that *the accidenting*, unexpectedly, is also in some ways *a freeing*.

Mallarmé thus pursues the accident of *free verse* in the same way Freud pursues, after an accident of dream, the path of *free association*. Both *free verse* and *free association* undergo the process of a fragmentation—a breaking down, a disruption and a dislocation—of the dream, the verse, of language, of the apparent but misleading unities of syntax and of meaning. The passage through this fragmentation is a passage through a radical obscurity. "One does not write," Mallarmé says, "luminously, on an obscure field . . ; man pursues black on white":[6]

> To write—
> The inkwell, crystal as a consciousness, with its drop of darkness at the bottom, . . . casts the lamp aside. (Mallarmé, 1945, 370)[7]

"Hitherto," says Freud, ". . . all the paths along which we have traveled have led us toward the light—toward elucidation and fuller understanding":

> But as soon as we endeavor to penetrate more deeply into the mental process involved in dreaming, *every path will end in darkness.* There is no possibility of explaining dreams since to explain a thing means to trace it back to something already known. (*SE* 5, 509–11)

In Mallarmé's as well as in Freud's case, what constitutes the specificity of the innovative figure of the witness is, indeed, not the mere telling, not the mere fact of *reporting* of the accident, but the witness' readiness to become himself a *medium of the testimony*—and a *medium of the accident*—in his unshakeable conviction that the accident, formal or clinical, carries historical significance which goes beyond the individual and is thus, in effect, in spite of its idiosyncracy, *not trivial.* What makes the newness and the radicality of the poetic—and the psychoanalytical—performance of a testimony that is both "surprising" and momentous is, in other words, not just the inescapability of the vocation of the witness insofar as the accident pursues him, but the witness's readiness, precisely, to *pursue the accident,* to actively pursue its path and its direction through obscurity, through darkness, and through fragmentation, without quite grasping the full scope and meaning of its implications, without entirely foreseeing where the journey leads and what is the precise nature of its final destination.

### POETRY AND TESTIMONY: PAUL CELAN, OR
### THE ACCIDENTING OF ESTHETICS

Half a century after Mallarmé, another poet will proceed to write in Paris (though this time in German) poetry that dramatizes yet another, more acute and more severe crisis of verse which, in its turn, sets out to *pursue* an "accidenting," to explore another kind of historic cataclysm and bear witness to another "fundamental crisis"—a fundamental shift in thinking and in being—proceeding this time not from the renewal triggered by a revolution, but from the destruction and the devastation which the Second World War and in particular, the Holocaust, have set in motion. In exploding, once again—in the footsteps of the lesson taught by Mallarmé—its own poetic medium, in dislocating its own language and in breaking down its own verse, the poetry of Paul Celan gives testimony, in effect, no longer simply to what Mallarmé refers to as an undefined, generic "accident," but to a more specific, more particularly crushing and more recent, cultural and historical breakdown, to the individual and the communal, massive trauma of a catastrophic loss and a disastrous fate in which nothing any more can be construed as *accident* except, perhaps, for *the poet's own survival.* Mallarmé's crisis of verse has come now to express, concretely and specifically, Celan's particular historical reality and his literally shattering experience as a Holocaust survivor. *The breakage of the verse enacts the breakage of the world.*

Like Mallarmé, the witness to the accident, Celan, the witness to catastrophe, is in turn a traveler, a witness-traveler whose poetry precisely is researching, through its testimony, the obscure direction and the unknown destination of his journey. "I have written poems," says Celan, "so as to speak, to orient myself, to explore where I was and was meant to go, to sketch out reality for myself" (see Felstiner, 1982, 23). Unlike Mallarmé, however, who brings "surprising news" to England as an "invited traveler" ("an invited traveller who, without delay, in breathless gasps, discharges himself of the testimony of an accident known, and pursuing him"), Celan's witness is not that of an "invited," but rather that of an evicted, traveler, one whose journey has originated in the constraint of deportation, in the throes of an *ejection* from his native country.

Paul Ancel, who will after the war rename himself—anagrammatically—Celan, was born to German-Jewish parents in 1920 in Czernowitz, Bukovina, a northern province of Romania. In July 1941 an S.S. *Einsatzgruppe,* aided by Romanian troops, began destroying Czernowitz's Jewish community. In 1942, Celan's parents were deported to a concentration camp. Paul Celan managed to escape, but was sent to a forced labor camp, in which he hauled debris and shoveled rocks for eighteen months. The only letter Paul received from his mother informed him that his father, totally spent, had been killed by the S.S. A few months later, Paul learned from an escaped cousin that his mother was in turn murdered, shot through the back of the neck. A story published in a German newspaper in the late seventies suggests that Celan (uncannily not unlike Dostoevsky) escaped execution in the camp by crossing over a dividing line—by switching places *in extremis* from a formation marked for death to one designated for the fate of slave labor.

In 1944, Celan returns to Czernowitz, which has been liberated by Soviet troops. After the war, he moves to Bucharest, then to Vienna, and finally settles in Paris in 1948. His poetic translations from French, English and Russian into German, accompany the publication of his own poetic works, which win him both prestigious literary prizes and immediate critical acclaim in the German-speaking world.

In April 1970, at the age of forty nine, Paul Celan commits suicide by drowning himself in the Seine.

In spite of his mastery of many languages and of his fluency in many literatures, in spite of his own choice to live in Paris and to be conversant with French culture, Celan could not give up writing in German. "I do not believe in bilingualness in poetry," he said, in reply to a question about his linguistic choices. "Poetry—that is the fateful uniqueness of language" (see Felstiner, 1986, 122). To his biographer Israel Chalfen, Celan explained his loyalty to German: "Only in one's mother tongue can one express one's own truth. In a foreign language the poet lies" (see Washburn, 1986, vii). Yet, this bonding to the mother tongue, this intimate connection to the spoken legacy of his lost mother as the only language to which truth—his own unique truth—can be *native*, is also, quite unbearably, an indissoluble connection to the language of the murderers of his own parents, a subjugation to the very language from which death, humiliation, torture and destruction issued, in a verdict of his own annihilation. Celan's poetic writing therefore struggles with the German to annihilate his own annihilation in it, to reappropriate the language that has marked his own exclusion: the poems dislocate the language so as to remold it, to radically shift its semantic and grammatical assumptions and remake—creatively and critically—a new poetic language entirely Celan's own. Mallarmé's crisis of language here becomes the vital effort—and the critical endeavor—to reclaim and repossess the very language in which *testimony* must—and cannot simply and uncritically—be given. This radical, exacting working through of language and of memory at once, takes place through a desperate poetic and linguistic struggle to, precisely, reappropriate the very language of one's own expropriation, to reclaim the German from its Nazi past and to retrieve the mother tongue—the sole possession of the dispossessed—from the Holocaust it has inflicted. "These," says Celan, "are the efforts of someone . . . shelterless in a sense undreamt of till now . . . who goes with his very being to language, stricken by and seeking reality":

> Within reach, close and not lost, there remained, in the midst of the losses, this one thing: language.

This, the language, was not lost but remained, yes, in spite of everything. But it had to pass through its own answerlessness, pass through a frightful falling mute, pass through the thousand darknesses of death-bringing speech. It passed through and yielded no words for what was happening—but it went through those happenings. Went through and could come into the light of day again, "enriched" by all that.

In this language I have sought, then and in the years since then, to write poems—so as to speak, to orient myself, to explore where I was and was meant to go, to sketch out reality for myself.

This, you see, was event, movement, a being under way, an attempt to gain direction. And if I ask about its meaning, I think I must say that this question also involves the clockhand's meaning.

. . . These are the efforts of someone coursed over by the stars of human handiwork, someone also shelterless in a sense undreamt-of till now and thus most uncannily out in the open, who goes with his very being to language, stricken by and seeking reality [ *wirklichkeitswund und Wirklichkeit suchend* ]. (see Felstiner, 1982, 23)

To *seek* reality is both to set out to explore the injury inflicted by it—to turn back on, and to try to penetrate, the state of being *stricken, wounded* by reality [ *wirklichkeitswund* ]—and to attempt, at the same time, to re-emerge from the paralysis of this state, to engage reality [ *Wirklichkeit suchend* ] as an advent, a movement, and as a vital, critical necessity of *moving on*. It is beyond the shock of being stricken, but nonetheless within the wound and from within the woundedness that the event, incomprehensible though it may be, becomes accessible. The wound gives access to the darkness that the language had to go through and traverse in the very process of its "frightful falling-mute." To seek reality through language "with one's very being," to seek in language what the language had precisely to *pass through*, is thus to make of one's own "shelterlessness"—of the openness and the accessibility of one's own wounds—an unexpected and unprecedented means of *accessing reality*, the radical condition for a wrenching exploration of the testimonial function, and the testimonial power, of the language: it is to give reality one's own vulnerability, as a conditional of exceptional availability and of exceptionally sensitized, tuned-in attention to the *relation between language and events*.

One such poem that attempts to probe precisely this relation between language and events is *Todesfuge* ("Death Fugue"), Celan's first published poem, written toward the end of 1944, immediately upon the poet's own emergence from his devastating war experience. The poem dramatizes and evokes a concentration camp experience, not directly and explicitly, however, not through linear narrative, through personal confession or through testimonial reportage, but elliptically and circularly, through the polyphonic but ironically disjointed art of counterpoint, and through the obsessional, compulsive repetitions and the vertiginous explosion of a mad song whose lament—half-blasphemy, half-prayer—bursts at once into a speechless, voiceless crying and into the dancing tumult of drunken celebration. Amazingly enough, the poem that depicts the most unthinkable complexities of horror and the most outrageously degrading depths of suffering is not a poem about killing, but, primarily, a poem about *drinking*, and about the relation (and the non-relation) between "drinking" and "writing."

> Black milk of daybreak we drink it at sundown
> we drink it at noon in the morning we drink it at
>     night
> we drink and we drink it
> we dig a grave in the breezes there one lies
>     unconfined
> A man lives in the house he plays with the serpents
>     he writes
> he writes when dusk falls to Germany your golden
>     hair Margarete
> he writes it and steps out of doors and the stars are
>     flashing he whistles his pack out
> he whistles his Jews out in earth has them dig for a
>     grave
> he commands us strike up for the dance
>
> . . . . . . . . . . .
>
> he writes when dusk falls to Germany your golden
>     hair Margarete
> your ashen hair Shulamith we dig a grave in the
>     breezes there one lies unconfined.          (Celan, 1980a, 51)

The performance of the act of drinking, traditionally a poetic metaphor for yearning, for romantic thirst and for desire, is here transformed into the surprisingly abusive figure of an endless torture and a limitless exposure, a figure for the impotent predicament and the unbearable ordeal of having to endure, absorb, continue to *take in* with no end and no limit. This image of the drunkenness of torture ironically perverts, and ironically demystifies, on the one hand, the Hellenic-mythic connotation of libidinal, euphoric Dionysiac drinking of both wine and poetry, and on the other hand, the Christian connotation of ritual religious consecration and of Eucharistic, sacred drinking of Christ's blood—and of Christ's virtue. The prominent underlying Eucharistic image suggests, however, that the enigmatic drinking that the poem repetitiously invokes is, indeed, essentially drinking of blood.

The perversion of the metaphor of drinking is further aggravated by the enigmatic image of the "black milk," which, in its obsessive repetitions, suggests the further underlying—though unspeakable and inarticulated—image of a child striving to drink from the mother's breast. But the denatured "black milk," tainted possibly by blackened, burnt ashes, springs not from the mother's breast but from the darkness of murder and death, from the blackness of the night and of the "dusk" that "falls to Germany" when death uncannily becomes a "master." Ingesting through the liquefied black milk at once dark blood and burnt ashes, the drinking takes place not at the maternal source but at the deadly source, precisely, of the wound, at the bleeding site of reality as stigma.

The Christian figure of the wound, traditionally viewed as the mythic vehicle and as the metaphoric means for a *historical transcendence*—for the erasure of Christ's death in the advent of Resurrection—is reinvested by the poem with the literal concreteness of the death camp blood and ashes, and is made thus to include, within the wound, not resurrection and historical transcendence, but the specificity of history—of the concrete historical reality of massacre and race annihilation—as unerasable and untranscendable. What Celan does, in this way, is to force the language of the Christian metaphorics to *witness* in effect the Holocaust, and be in turn witnessed by it.

The entire poem is, indeed, not simply about violence but about the relation between violence and language, about the passage of the language through the violence and the passage of the violence through language. The violence enacted by the poem is in the *speech acts* of the German master, the commandant who directs the orchestra of the camp inmates to musically accompany their own grave-digging and to celebrate, in an ecstatic death fugue, at once the wounding of the earth and their own destruction and annihilation. But it is already in the very practice of his language that the commandant in effect annihilates the Jews, by actively denying them as *subjects*, by reducing their subjective individuality to a mass of indistinct, debased, inhuman *objects*, playthings of his whims, marionettes of his own pleasure of destruction and musical instruments of his own sadistic passion.

> he whistles his Jews out in earth has them dig for a
> grave
> he commands us strike up for the dance
>
> . . . . . . . . . .
>
> He calls out jab deeper into the earth you lot you
> others sing now and play
>
> . . . . . . . . .
>
> jab deeper you lot with your spades you others play
> on for the dance
>
> He calls out more sweetly play death death is a
> master from Germany
> he calls out more darkly now stroke your strings
> then as smoke you will rise into air
> then a grave you will have in the clouds there one
> lies unconfined

The violence is all the more obscene by being thus *estheticized* and by estheticizing its own dehumanization, by transforming its own murderous perversity into the cultural sophistication and the cultivated trances of a hedonistic art performance. But the poem works specifically and contrapuntally to dislocate this masquerade of cruelty as art, and to exhibit the obscenity of this estheticization, by opposing the melodious ecstasy of the esthetic pleasure to the dissonance of the commandant's speech acts and to the violence of his verbal abuse, and by reintroducing into the amnesia of the "fugue"—into the obliviousness of the *artistic drunkenness*—the drinking of black milk as *the impossibility of forgetting* and of getting a reprieve from suffering and memory, and as the sinister, insistent, *unforgettable return of what the esthetic pleasure has forgotten.*

> we drink and we drink you
> A man lives in the house he plays with the serpents
> he writes
> he writes when dusk falls to Germany your golden
> hair Margarete
> your ashen hair Shulamith we dig a grave in the
> breeze there one lies unconfined
>
> Black milk of daybreak we drink you at night
> we drink you at noon   . . .
>           . . .   we drink and we drink you
>
> death is a master from Germany his eyes are blue
> he strikes you with leaden bullets his aim is true

a man lives in the house your golden hair Margarete
he sets his pack on to us he grants us a grave in the
    air
he plays with the serpents and daydreams death is a
    master from Germany

Your golden hair Margarete
your ashen hair Shulamith

The entire poem is contingent upon various forms of apostrophe and of address. The dehumanizing and annihilating interjections of the murderous address—"you lot, you others"—the address that institutes the other not as *subject* but as *target* ("He strikes you with leaden bullets his aim is true"), meets and clashes with the dreamy yearnings of the desiring address, the address that institutes the other as a *subject of desire* and, as such, a *subject of response*, of a called-for *answer.*

your golden hair Margarete
your ashen hair Shulamith

Marguerite, Faust's object of desire and Goethe's incarnation of romantic love, evokes at once the general tradition of German literary yearning and the actual longing—possibly of the commandant—for his German beloved. Shulamith, a female emblem of both beauty and desire celebrated and admired in *The Song of Songs*, evokes the Jewish biblical and literary yearning and the longing for the Jewish beloved. The invocation of the cherished name is traversed by the same depth of joy and sadness, charged with the same energy of human longing and desire. The yearnings, as such, resonate with one another. And yet, a bitter difference and a shocking irony resound from within this echoing resemblance. In contrast to the golden hair of Marguerite, the ashen hair of Shulamith connotes not just a mark of racial difference between the fair haired maiden of the Aryan ideal and the ashen pallor of the Semitic beauty, but the hair reduced to ashes, the burnt hair of one race as opposed to the esthetic idealization and self-idealization of the other race. Like the light of "daybreak" turned into night and into darkness, the dissonance of golden and of ashen thus produces, once again, only "black milk" as an answer to one's thirst, one's longing, one's desire. The call to Shulamith—beauty reduced to smoke—is bound to remain unanswered.

Black milk of daybreak we drink you at night

. . . . . . . . . . . . . . . . . .

we drink and we drink you

> A man lives in the house he plays with the serpents
> he writes
> he writes when dusk falls to Germany your golden
> hair Margarete
> your ashen hair Shulamith we dig a grave in the
> breeze there one lies unconfined

The wound within the culture opens up in the discrepancy, the muteness, the abrupt disjunction, not only between "Marguerite" and "Shulamith," but, primarily, between "*we drink*," "*we dig*" and "*he writes*." The open wound is marked within the language by the incapacity of "*we*" to *address*, precisely, in this poem of apostrophe and of address, the "*he*." It is in this radical disruption of address between the "*we*" (who "drink" and "dig") and the "*he*" (who "writes" and who "commands"), that Celan locates the very essence of the violence, and the very essence of the Holocaust.

If "death is a master from Germany," it is a "master" not just in the sense that it brings death and that it totally controls its slaves, nor even merely, in addition, in the sense that it plays the *maestro*, the musician or the meistersinger, *master of arts* who strives, ironically enough, to produce death as artistic *masterpiece*, but in the sense that Germany, unwittingly, has instituted death as Meister, as a *master-teacher*. Death has taught a lesson that can henceforth never be forgotten. If art is to survive the Holocaust—to survive death as a master—it will have to break, in art, this mastery, which insidiously pervades the whole of culture and the whole of the esthetic project.

The necessity for art to *de-estheticize* itself and to justify henceforth its own existence, has been forcefully articulated by the German critic Theodor Adorno, in a famous dictum that defines, indeed, Celan's predicament but which has become itself (perhaps too readily) a critical cliché, too hastily consumed and too hastily reduced to a summary dismissal of Celan's troubling poetic efficacity in poems like "Death Fugue"; "After Auschwitz, it is no longer possible to write poems" (Adorno, 1973, 362): "The esthetic principle of stylization," writes Adorno, "... make[s] an unthinkable fate appear to have had some meaning; it is transfigured, something of its horror is removed. This alone does an injustice to the victims. ... [Some] works ... are even willingly absorbed as contributions to clearing up the past" (Adorno, 1982, 313). In Adorno's radical conception, it is, however, not just these specific works, nor simply lyric poetry as genre, but all of thinking, all of writing that has now to think, to write *against itself*:

If thinking is to be true—if it is to be true today, in any case—it must be thinking against itself. If thought is not measured by the extremity that eludes the concept, it is from the outset in the nature of the musical accompaniment with which the SS liked to drown out the screams of its victims. (Adorno, 1973, 365)

Adorno himself, however, will return to his statement about poetry and Auschwitz in a later essay, to redefine its emphasis, to underscore the aporetic, and not simply negative, intention of his radical pronouncement, and to emphasize the fact (less known and more complex) that, paradoxically enough, it is only art that can henceforth be equal to its own historical impossibility, that art alone can live up to the task of contemporary thinking and of meeting the incredible demands of suffering, of politics and of contemporary consciousness, and yet escape the subtly omnipresent and the almost unavoidable cultural betrayal both of history and of the victims.

I have no wish to soften the saying that to write lyric poetry after Auschwitz is barbaric. . . . But Enzensberger's retort also remains true, that *literature must resist this verdict*. . . . It is now virtually in art alone that suffering can still find its own voice, consolation, without immediately being betrayed by it.

Today, every phenomenon of culture, even if a model of integrity, is liable to be suffocated in the cultivation of kitch. Yet paradoxically in the same epoch it is to works of art that has fallen the burden of wordlessly asserting what is barred to politics. (Adorno, 1982, 312, 318)

The whole endeavor of Celan's poetic work can be defined precisely, in Adorno's terms, as poetry's creative and self-critical *resistance to the verdict* that it is barbaric, henceforth, to write lyrically, poetically; a verdict that the poetry receives, however, not from the outside but from inside itself, a verdict that "Death Fugue" encompasses already, and in fact enacts and sets in motion through the master's usurpation of the singing of the inmates.

Something of that usurpation has, however, inadvertently reproduced itself even in the very destiny of "Todesfuge," whose immense success and frequent anthologization in the German-speaking world has soon turned Celan into something like another celebrated "master." Celan himself, in later years, thus turned against his early poem, refused to allow its reprinting in further anthologies, and changed his writing style into a less explicit, less melodious, more disrupted and disruptively elliptical verse:

NO MORE SAND ART, no sand book, no masters.

Nothing won by dicing. How many
dumb ones?
Seventeen.

Your question—your answer.
Your song, what does it know?

Deepinsnow,
　　　　Eepinnow,
　　　　　　　Ee—i—o.

To prevent the possibility of an esthetic, drunken infatuation with its own verse, the later poetry rejects, within the language, not its music and its singing—which continue to define the essence of poetic language for Celan— but a certain predetermined kind of recognizably *melodious* musicality. In Celan's own words, the verse henceforth "distrusts the beautiful, . . . insists on having its 'musicality' placed in a region where it no longer has anything in common with that 'melodious sound' which more or less undisturbed sounded side by side with the greatest horror. The concern of this language is, in all the unalterable multivalence of the expression, *precision*. It doesn't transfigure, doesn't 'poeticize,' it names and places" (Celan, 1980b, 23; emphasis mine).

Deep in Time's crevasse
by the alveolate
waits, a crystal of breath,
your irreversible
witness.　　　　　　　　　　　　(Celan, 1980a, 189)

The quest for musical precision—which shuns melody and which refrains, above all, from "poeticizing"—is, however, coupled with a tendency toward silence. "Tendency toward silence," notes Celan, "—this, too, can't be said just so. We mustn't create new fetishes. Even the anti-fetish can become a fetish" (1980b, 45).

NO MORE SAND ART, no sand book, no masters.

"One of the truths hardest to demonstrate," writes Pierre Boulez in an analysis of contemporary music that could apply as well to Celan's revised poetic musicality, "one of the truths hardest to demonstrate is that music is not just the 'Art of sound'—that it must be defined rather as a counterpoint of sound and silence. [Contemporary music's] rhythmic innovation is this conception whereby sound and silence are linked in a precise organization directed toward the exhaustive exploitation of our powers of hearing" (see Washburn, 1986, xxv).

By introducing silence as a rhythmic *breakdown* and as a displacing *counterpoint* to sound not just *in between* his stanzas and his verses, but even *in the very midst* of the phonetic flow and the poetic diction of his *words* ("You my words being crippled / together with me . . . / with the hu, with the man, with the human being" (Celan, 1980a, 151)), Celan strives to defetishize his language and to dislocate his own esthetic mastery, by breaking down any self-possessed control of sense and by disrupting any unity, integrity, or continuity of conscious meaning. Through their very breakdown, the sounds testify, henceforth, precisely to a knowledge they do not possess, by unleashing, and by drifting into, their own buried depths of silence.

> Your question—your answer.
> Your song, what does it know?
>
> Deepinsnow,
>       Eepinnow,
>           Ee—i—o.

But this breakdown of the word, this drift of music and of sound of the song that resists recuperation and that does not know, and cannot own, its meaning, nonetheless reaches a *you*, attains the hearing—and perhaps the question, or the answer, of an Other: "*Your* question—*your* answer / *Your* song." The poem strives toward the *Du*, the *you*, the listener, over the historical abyss from which the singing has originated and across the violence and the unending, shattered resonances of the breakage of the word. "A poem," writes Celan, "as a manifest form of language and thus inherently dialogue, can be a message in a bottle, sent out in the (not always greatly hopeful) belief that it may somewhere and sometime wash up on land, on heartland perhaps":

> Poems in this sense are always under way, they are making toward something.
>     Toward what? Toward something standing open, occupiable, perhaps toward a "thou" that can be *addressed*, an *addressable* reality. (see Felstiner, 1982; emphasis mine)

As an event directed toward the recreation of a "thou," poetry becomes, precisely, the event of *creating an address* for the specificity of a historical experience that annihilated any possibility of address. If the lesson of death ( *Todes-fuge's executioner, commandant,* and *maestro*)—the lesson of the master—was precisely that a master is the one who *cannot be addressed,* the one to whom one cannot say "*you,*" Celan's poetry now strives not simply, as is often said, to seek out the responsive *you,* to recreate the listener, the hearer, but to subvert, to dislocate and to displace the very essence of esthetics as a *project of artistic mastery* by transforming poetry—as breakage of the word and as drifting testimony—into an inherent and unprecedented, testimonial *project of address.*

> As one speaks to stone, like
> you,
> from the chasm, from
> a home become a sister to me, hurled
> toward me, you,
> you that long ago
> you in the nothingness of a night,
> you in the multi-night en-
> countered, you
> multi-you—.                    (Celan, 1980a, 153)

> and at times when
> only the void stood between us we got
> all the way to each other.              (ibid., 135)

### CROSSING THE VOID, OR POETRY AS SETTING FREE

Along with the above-sketched journey of the various writers, theorists and poets, the class traveled its own path. Opened up to the diversity and touched by the concrete peculiarities of literary, clinical, historical, and poetic testimonies; captivated and surprised by the unexpected ways in which the very different texts nonetheless unwittingly evolved into each other, came to engage each other's depth and put each other in an increasingly complex perspective, the students reemerged from each textual encounter somewhat changed. The formal and historical vicissitudes of Celan's poetry found them ready: ready to receive the silent counterpoints of the breakage of the words and of the poem's broken sounds; ready to be solicited by the namelessness of Celan's experience; ready, in other words, to assume the position of the "thou," to become the "you" that "in the nothingness of the night" the poetry was seeking. Through its responsive yet subdued, contained vibrations (vibrations evident both in the students' writing and in the keenness of attention in the classroom discussions), the class became, in fact, this responsive "you," this deeply attentive addressee, prepared to accompany the poet into the very place—the very night, the very silence—from which his poems had originated.

As Celan's drifting musicality became, indeed, the rhythm of the class, the class seemed to experience also, curiously enough, something like a liberation, the process of a freeing up. "Whoever has art before his eyes and on his mind," Celan said in his famous speech entitled "The Meridian," "Whoever has art before his eyes and on his mind . . . has forgotten himself. Art produces a distance from the I":

> Perhaps—I'm just asking—perhaps literature, in the company of the I which has forgotten itself, travels the same path as art, toward that which is mysterious and alien. And once again—but where? but in what place? but how? but as what?—it *sets itself free*. . . .
>
> Can we now, perhaps, find the place where strangeness was present, the place where a person succeeded in setting himself free, as an—estranged—I? Can we find such a place, such a step? . . .
>
> *Is perhaps at this point, along with the I—with the estranged I, set free . . .—is perhaps at this point an Other set free?* (Celan, 1978, 33–35; emphasis mine)[8]

Through Celan's poetry the class, in fact, felt strangely and obscurely freed up—freed from form, from rhythm, from melodiousness, from words, freed in sum from the "esthetic project" and thus ready to become the addressee to the "message in the bottle" thrust into the sea "in the (not always greatly hopeful) believe that it may somewhere and sometime wash up on land, on heartland perhaps." The class became the inadvertent, unexpected heartland, on which Celan's poetic bottle did indeed—by chance—wash up. Opened to the risks incorporated by the chance—and the necessity—of the encounter with the drifting testimony, ready to receive, and resonate to, the obscurity, the suffering, the uncertainty—and yet the absoluteness—of the message in the bottle, the class was now prepared for the next step.

# VI

### LIFE TESTIMONIES

The next and final stage of the course itinerary was the screening of two testimonial videotapes borrowed from the Fortunoff Video Archive for

Holocaust Testimonies at Yale, an archival collection of filmed testimonies—of autobiographical life accounts given by Holocaust survivors to volunteer, professionally trained interviewers, most of whom are psychoanalysts or psychotherapists. Within the context of these dialogic interviews, many of these Holocaust survivors in fact narrate their story *in its entirety* for the first time in their lives, awakened to their memories and to their past both by the public purpose of the enterprise (the collection and the preservation of first-hand, live testimonial evidence about the Holocaust), and, more concretely, by the presence and involvement of the interviewers, who enable them for the first time to believe that it is possible, indeed, against all odds and against their past experience, to tell the story and *be heard*, to in fact *address* the significance of their biography—to *address*, that is, the suffering, the truth, and the necessity of this impossible narration—to a hearing "you," and to a listening community. In the spirit of Celan's poetical endeavor, though on an altogether different level, the Fortunoff Video Archive for Holocaust Testimonies at Yale is thus, in turn, the endeavor of *creating* (recreating) *an address*, specifically, for a historical experience which annihilated the very possibility of address.

## THE ENCOUNTER WITH THE REAL: A CONVERGENCE OF HISTORICAL, POETICAL AND CLINICAL DIMENSIONS

In the context of the course we have previously explored in sequence, one after the other, the historical (Camus/Dostoevsky), the clinical (Camus/Dostoevsky/Freud), and the poetical (Mallarmé/Celan) dimensions of the testimony. Neither dimension, taken in itself, however, truly captures the complexity of what the testimony is, since this complexity, as we have seen, always implies, in one way or another, the coexistence of all three dimensions and their mutual interaction. The Holocaust testimonies in themselves are definitely, at least on their manifest level, as foreign to "poetry" as anything can be, both in their substance and in their intent. Yet many of them attain, surprisingly, in the very structure of their occurrence, the dimension of discovery and of advent inherent to the literary speech act, and the power of significance and impact of a true *event* of language—an event which can unwittingly resemble a poetic, or a literary, act. The very real, overwhelming and as such, traumatic aspect of these narratives engages, on the other hand, both the clinical and the historical dimensions of the testimony. The clinical and the historical dimensions are implied, as well, by Celan's poetry. What makes Celan's poetry crucially poetic (even in its postesthetic, anti-poetic stage) is, as we have seen, its formal insistence on the unpredictability of its own rhythm. In thus insisting on the unpredictability of its own music and its "turns of breath,"[9] Celan's poetry insisted, in effect (as did Mallarmé's), on the risky unpredictability of the endeavor of the witness, who does not master—and does not possess—his testimony or his "message in the bottle," which may or may not reach a "you." I would suggest, indeed, that both the mystery and the complexity of the endeavor of the testimony and of its compelling power drive, precisely, from this element of unpredictability, from what is unpredictable, specifically, in the effects of the exchange and the degree of interaction between the historical, the clinical and the poetical dimensions of the testimony.

For the first time in the history of my teaching, I decided, therefore, to have recourse to the archive—to move on, as it were, from poetry into reality and to study in a literary class something which is *a priori* not defined as literary, but is rather of the order of raw documents—historical and auto-biographical. It seemed to me that this added dimension of *the real* was, at this point, both relevant and necessary to the insight we were gaining into testimony. Intuitively, I also knew that the transference, the shift in medium from text to video—from the literary to the real and from the textual to the visual—would have an impact that would somehow be illuminating, and that the interpenetration of historical and literary testaments would turn out to be quite crucial to the understanding—and the process—of this class.

### THE DETERMINATION TO SURVIVE

I watched a number of testimonies at the Fortunoff Video Archive, and I selected, for the purpose of the class, two videotapes whose singular histori-cal narration seemed to contain the added power of a figure, and the unfold-ing of a self-discovery: the testimonies of one woman and one man.

The woman's story is the story of a catastrophic, overwhelming *loss* which leads, however, to an insight into the joint mystery of *life* and of the need for *testimony*. The testimony is, precisely, to the experience of the narrator's repetitious crossing of the line dividing life from death. Starting at age fifteen, the testifier had to live through the successive deaths of nearly all members of her family—her father, her mother, her youngest brother, her sister-in-law, and a baby (the last three dying in her presence, in her arms). The sole survivor of her family is her newly wedded husband, himself lost during the war but miraculously refound after liberation. Each one of them is, in turn, the only one to survive his or her own family. Although estranged at the time of their reunion, they stay together after the war because, she says, "he knew who I was":

The man I married and the man he was after the war were not the same person. And I'm sure I was not the same person either . . . but somehow we had a need for each other because, he knew who I was, *he was the only person who knew.* . . . He knew who I was, and I knew who he was. . . . And we're here, we're here to tell you the story. (Fortunoff, T58)

What is unique about the story of this woman is her conscious determination to survive precisely at the most abysmal and most devastating moment of her confrontation with death. Her determination to survive, her decision to live paradoxically springs out of her most intimate and close attendance of the actual dying of her youngest brother, a boy of thirteen, who, asphyxiated in the transport wagon, literally expires in her arms:

He was going to be thirteen. . . . And you know, when my brother died in my arms, I said to myself, "I'm going to live." I made up my mind to defy Hitler. I'm not going to give in. Because he wants me to die, I'm going to live. This was our way of fighting back.

After I was liberated . . . a Russian doctor examined me and said, "Under normal circumstances you would not have survived. . . . It's just a medical miracle that you survived." But I told you, I really wanted to live, I said to myself, "I want to live one day after Hitler, one day after the end of the war. . . . And we are here to tell you the story."

The woman's testimony is, therefore, a testament to how she survived in order to give her testimony. The story of survival is, in fact, the incredible narration of the survival of the story, at the crossroads between life and death.

### LIBERATION FROM SILENCE

The second videotaped testimony screened to the class narrates the story of a man who was a child survivor, one of the two children to remain alive of the four thousand children incarcerated in the Plashow concentration camp. In 1942, his parents decided to smuggle him out of the camp because they learned that all the children would shortly be rounded up for examination. At the age of four he was thus instructed by his parents to leave them, to run away and head toward a refuge place, which at the time he took to be a hospital, but which turned out to have been—as he later learned—a high-class brothel, hospitable to marginal people like himself. As his stay there became in turn risky, he had to leave and make it on his own as a member of a gang of children of the streets, who stayed alive by begging and by stealing. In moments of distress, he would turn to—and pray to—a student ID picture of his mother, given to him by her at the time of his escape, with the promise that she and his father will come to look for him after the war and will find him wherever he will be. The promise of the picture and his trust in their future reunion gave him both the strength and the resourcefulness to endure and to survive the war.

In effect, after the war, he did miraculously find his parents, but the people who returned from the camp—dressed in prison garb, emaciated and disfigured—bore no resemblance either to the mother's picture or to the parents he had been waiting for and dreaming of. He could not accept these strangers, could not address them as "Mom" and "Dad," but instead insisted upon calling them "Mr." and "Mrs." It was during the years that followed the war, when he was finally safe, that he disintegrated, could not sleep, developed fears, and started having nightmares. Haunted, he nonetheless could not talk about the war experience. For thirty-five years he kept his silence:

> This was not a subject brought up in my father's household. It was always . . . something you have to forget. . . .
>
> I was unable to read any books. . . . I didn't read a word about the Holocaust. . . . It just wasn't there. . . .
>
> For the past thirty-five years I've been trying to convince myself that it never happened, that . . . maybe it happened, but I wasn't affected. I walked under the rain without getting wet. . . .
>
> But I never realized that I never talked about it, neither with my wife nor with my children. (Fortunoff, T152)

It is not without dread nor without conflict that he decides to give his testimony, after having first refused to do so. Once he resolves to testify, however, his own dreams—which he recounts—bear witness to the fact that he experiences his own decision to speak up as profoundly *freeing*: his own sudden realization of the magnitude of his burden of silence and its dead weight on himself and on his loved ones comes to him, surprisingly, at once as an exhilarating, unexpected liberation from his nightmares—a liberation that allows him for the first time to experience feelings both of mourning and of hope—and as a transfiguring illumination, a transforming insight into the extent to which this burden—and this silence—has in fact affected, and reshaped, his whole life:

> The thing that troubles me right now is the following: if we don't deal with our feelings, if we don't understand our experience, what are we doing to our children? . . .

We are what we are . . . we can change some, but we will never be able to eradicate . . . what happened. . . . The big question is: Are we transferring our anxieties, our fears, our problems, to the generations to come? And this is why I feel that we are talking here not only of *the lost generation*—like the term they coined after World War I—this time we are dealing with *lost generations*. It's not only us. It's the generations to come. And I think this is the biggest tragedy of those who survived.

# VII

## THE CLASS IN CRISIS

These reflections of the child survivor on the liberating, although frightening, effects of his own rebirth to speech in the testimonial process, on the value of his own emergence from a life of silence not just for himself, but for his children, for the conscious and unconscious legacy that history and memory—unwittingly or lucidly—leave for the forthcoming generations, were meant, in this way, to conclude the course with the very eloquence of life, with a striking, vivid, and extreme *real example* of the *liberating, vital function of the testimony.*

But the eloquence of life—coupled with the eloquence of literature (with the testimonial eloquence of Albert Camus, Fyodor Dostoevsky, Sigmund Freud, Stephane Mallarmé, and Paul Celan)—carried the class beyond a limit that I could foresee and had envisioned. The unpredictability of the events that took place at this point in the class indeed confirmed, once more, in an unanticipated manner, the unpredictability of testimony. Something happened, toward the conclusion of the class, which took me completely by surprise. The class itself broke out into a crisis. And it was this crisis which made this class unique in my experience, this crisis which determined me to write about it.

That turn of events took place after the screening of the first Holocaust videotape, recounting the story of the woman. The tapes were screened in the informal privacy of an apartment, with the students sitting on the carpet, all over the floor. During the screening some were crying, but that in itself was not an unusual phenomenon. When the film was over, I purposely left the floor to them. But even though this class, throughout the course, had been particularly literate and eloquent, they remained, after the screening session, inarticulate and speechless. They looked subdued and kept their silence even as they left. That in itself is not unusual either. What was unusual was that the experience did not *end* in silence, but instead, fermented into endless and relentless talking in the days and weeks to come; a talking that could not take place, however, within the confines of the classroom but that somehow had to *break the very framework of the class* (and thus emerge outside it), in much the same way as the writers we examined somehow all *broke through the framework* of what they had initially set out to write.

I realized that something strange was going on when I started getting phone calls from the students at my home at all odd hours, in a manifest wish to talk about the session, although they did not quite know what to say. As I later learned from my colleagues, the students of my class who met in other classes could only talk about the session and could focus on no other subject. Friends and roommates of my students later wrote me letters, to tell me of the interest they had developed in my class, by virtue of their having become, as one letter puts it, the "coerced listeners" to these outside proceedings of the class and to the frantic talking of my students, who apparently could talk of nothing else no matter where they were, in other classes, study rooms or dorms. They were set apart and set themselves apart from others who had not gone through the same experience. They were obsessed. They felt apart, and yet not quite together. They sought out each other and yet felt they could not reach each other. They kept turning to each other and to me. They felt alone, suddenly deprived of their bonding to the world and to one another. As I listened to their outpour, I realized the class was entirely at a loss, disoriented and uprooted.

I was myself in turn taken by surprise, and worried by the critical dimensions of this crisis which the class was obviously going through, and which was gathering momentum. I realized, at the same time, that the unpredicted outcome of the screening was itself a psychoanalytical enhancement of the way in which the class felt actively *addressed* not only by the videotape but by the intensity and intimacy of the testimonial encounter throughout the course. Since the class viewing of the archive films had been in effect planned in the presence of the psychoanalyst who was, specifically, the interviewer of the two Holocaust survivors and the conceiver of the very idea of the archive, Dr. Dori Laub, I turned to him for counsel.

After we discussed the turn of events, we concluded that what was called for was for me to reassume authority as the teacher of the class, and bring the students back into significance. I therefore called the students who had failed to contact me, to discuss with each one his or her reactions to the "crisis-session." Next, I prepared a half-hour lecture as an introduction to the second screening in the form of an address to the class which opened, in effect, the next and final session. This address was divided into two parts: the first part summarized, and returned to the students, in their own words, the importance and significance of their reactions; the second part attempted to articulate for them an integrated view of the literary texts and of the video-tapes—of the significance of all the texts together, in relation to their own reactions.

The following are excerpts from this introduction.[10]

### THE ADDRESS TO THE CLASS

We have in this second screening session quite a task before us: the task of surviving the first session. I would like to begin by reviewing with you your responses to the first Holocaust testimony. Your reactions helped me, started in me a process of thinking in dialogue with your responses. As I told many of you over the phone, I consider this class in general and the videotape sessions in particular, as a kind of process which, as such, has an existence in time, a process that implies both a working out, and a working through, of our subject.

What your responses most of all conveyed to me was something like an *anxiety of fragmentation*. People talked of having the feeling of being "cut off" at the end of the session. Some felt very lonely. It struck me that Celan's words were very accurate to describe the feeling of the class:

> A strange lostness
> Was palpably present.      (Celan, 1980a, 139)

There was a sort of *panic* that consisted in both emotional and intellectual disorientation, *loss of direction*. One person told me that he literally "lost the whole class," that the emotion of the first videotape was so overwhelming that everything he thought he had acquired in the previous classes got somehow "*disconnected.*"

On the other hand, a number of people said that they suddenly realized how much this class counted for them, and the way in which it counted seemed crucially important, though unsettling. The videotape viewing was described as "a shattering experience"; it was felt that the last session "was not just painful, but very powerful," so powerful that it was "hard to think about it analytically without trivializing it." Most people said that they were much more affected twenty four hours after the session, and as time went on, than on the spot. Some felt a need to write down their reflections and emotions. They kept diaries of every word thought or said. Some kept diaries of their dreams.

There was a great *need to talk* about the class experience, and everybody mentioned that. People frantically looked for interlocutors, but expressed their frustration at the fact that everything that they could say to an outsider to convey a sense of the event was just fragments: they could not convey the whole experience. "I was compelled," said one student, "to speak about the Holocaust testimonies, the class, etcetera, to friends who were not disinterested but who were perhaps a bit surprised. This speaking was at best fragmentary, dissolving into silence: at moments, lapsing into long, obsessive monologues. It was absolutely necessary to speak of it, however incoherently. It was the most fragmented of testimonies. At times, I felt that I would simply have to abduct someone and lock them up in my room and tell them about the '*whole*' thing."

One person suggested an analytic view of the whole situation. "Until now and throughout the texts we have been studying," he said, "we have been talking (to borrow Mallarmé's terms) about '*the testimony of an accident.*' We have been *talking* about the accident—and here all of a sudden *the accident happened* in the class, happened *to* the class. The accident *passed through* the class."

In trying to address the fragmentation in the class and bring it back into significance, the first articulate response that I, in turn, could offer, was to *reread* to them again a text that we had read together in the course: an excerpt from Celan's "Bremen Address," about what happened to the act of speaking, and to language, after the Holocaust. In setting out, however, to re-cite this text again, I now referred it to the resonances of what happened in the class:

> I will suggest that the significance of the event of your viewing of the first Holocaust videotape was, not unlike Celan's own Holocaust experience, something akin to *a loss of language*; and even though you came out of it with a deep need to talk about it and to talk it out, you also felt that language was somehow incommensurate with it. What you felt as a "*disconnection*" with the class was, precisely, an experience of *suspension*: a *suspension*, that is, *of the knowledge* that had been acquired in the class: you feel that you have lost it. But you are going to find it again. I will suggest it is this *loss* Celan precisely talks about, this loss that we have all been somehow made to live. You can now, perhaps, relate to this loss more immediately, more viscerally, when you hear the poet say that *language was "all that remained."* Here again is Celan's language, that remains: lost and regained again through the videotape experience.

> Within reach, close and not lost, there remained, in the midst of the losses, this one thing: language.

This, the language, was not lost but remained, yes, in spite of everything. But it had to *pass through its own answerlessness*, pass through a frightful falling mute, pass through the thousand darknesses of death-bringing speech. It passed through and yielded no words for what was happening—*but it went through those happenings*. Went through and could come into the light of day again, "enriched" by all that. (see Felstiner, 1982, 23)

This, I would suggest, is also what has happened now precisely to the language of the class: it *passed through its own answerlessness*.

Another possible response to the answerlessness through which the class is passing now, can be given in the context of our thought about the *significance of testimony*. You remember the very impressive moment in the first videotape, where the woman-survivor speaks about her husband whom she lost during the war, but with whom she reunited after liberation. As if to explain the necessity—and the significance—of this miraculous and improbable reunion, she says: "*He knew who I was*." You will remember Dr. Laub's comment right after we viewed the tape, suggesting, with elliptical abruptness, that " *'who she was' was precisely her testimony*." "Who she was," in other words, is here implicitly expressed by the survivor as a radical and irretrievable *loss*, one of the most devastating losses—dispossessions—inflicted by the Holocaust, one of those "answerlessnesses," of those answerless questions, through which the Holocaust inexorably made one pass. The narrator herself does not know any longer who she was, except *through her testimony*. This knowledge or self-knowledge is neither a given before the testimony nor a residual substantial knowledge consequential to it. In itself, this knowledge *does not exist*, it can only *happen* through the testimony: it cannot be separated from it. It can only unfold itself in the process of testifying, but it can never become a substance that can be possessed by either speaker or listener, outside of this dialogic process. In its performative aspect, the testimony, in this way, can be thought of as a sort of signature. And I would suggest, now, that this signatory value of the testimony is engaging in exactly a *reverse process* to the Nazi process—and endeavor—of standardization of the people sent to death. What constitutes the outrage of the Holocaust—the very essence of erasure and annihilation—is not so much death in itself, as the more obscene fact that *death itself does not make any difference*, the fact that death is radically *indifferent*: everyone is leveled off, people die as numbers, not as proper names. In contrast to this leveling, to testify is to engage, precisely, in the process of *re-finding one's own proper name*, one's *signature*.

As the next step in the course, I want to ask you to write a paper for next week. I would like you to think about this paper in relation with, and as a function of, the *timing* of this act of writing. The writing is designed to be, in other words, an essential element of your working through this experience. And as such, it needs precisely to encroach on your reactions to the first screening session. Many of you, indeed, quite literally said that you felt you *did not count* after the first session, that, had you been there in the camps, you are certain that you would have died. And I am inviting you now to testify to that experience, so as to accept the obligation—and the right—to repossess yourselves, to take, in other words, the *chance to sign*, the *chance to count*.

I invite you thus to write a paper on *your* experience of the testimony, and on your experience of the class. To do that, you need to think of the Holocaust videotapes in the context of the significance of the entire course, and in relation to the other texts we studied. I want you to work on precisely what you said was so difficult for you to achieve: you felt a disconnection, and I want you to look, on the contrary, *for the connections*. What has this experience taught you in the end? What did it change in your perception of those other texts? *What difference* did it make in your global perception of the class?

What I am suggesting is, in other words, that you view this paper as *your testimony to this course*. I admit that it would be a *precocious testimony*: I know you feel you are not ready. But perhaps the testimony *has* to be precocious, perhaps there is no other way. I wish to remind you of the fact that the writers we have read also, and quite often, give expression to the feeling that their testimony is precocious. Mallarmé, you will remember, says: "Il convient d'en parler *déjà*," "It is appropriate to talk about it *now already*"—

> It is appropriate . . . to talk about it *now already*, much like an invited traveler who, without delay, in breathless gasps, discharges himself of the testimony of an accident known, and pursuing him. . . .
>
> Should I stop here, and where do I get the feeling that I have come relatively to a subject vaster and perhaps to myself unknown —vaster than this or that innovation of rites or rhymes; in order *to attempt to reach this subject, if not to treat it*. (Mallarmé, 1945, 643–44)

Celan in turn puts an emphasis on the precocity of testimony:

> I have gotten ahead of myself (not far enough, I know). (Celan, 1978, 33)

But after all, literature, too, often shoots ahead of us. *La poésie, elle aussi, brûle nos étapes.* (ibid., 34)

I am inviting *you*, in turn, to "shoot ahead of yourselves" precisely in this way and to give, in turn, *your* precocious testimony.

Upon reading the final paper submitted by the students a few weeks later, I realized that the crisis, in effect, had been worked through and overcome and that a resolution had been reached, both on an intellectual and on a vital level. The written work the class had finally submitted turned out to be an amazingly articulate, reflective, and profound statement of the trauma they had gone through and of the significance of their assuming the position of the witness.

## VIII

### PEDAGOGICAL TRANSVALUATION

I have since had the occasion—and the time—to reflect upon what I have learned from that class and to attempt to think out and rethink the nature of what took me then so completely by surprise. Because what happened then happened as an accident—an unpredictable vicissitude of teaching—without the full control of my deliberate and conscious understanding, I am recounting it (to borrow Mallarmé's words once again), as my own *testimony to an accident*. And yet, I would submit that the very singularity, the very idiosyncracy both of the accident and of my testimony to it (like the idiosyncratic and yet archetypal status of the Irma dream) comprises a generic story, and the validity of a generic pedagogical event and thus of a generic lesson.

I would venture to propose, today, as the accidental and yet generally valid lesson I have learned from that class, that teaching in itself, teaching as such, takes place precisely only through a crisis: if teaching does not hit upon some sort of crisis, if it does not encounter either the vulnerability or the explosiveness of an (explicit or implicit) critical and unpredictable dimension, it has perhaps not truly taught: it has perhaps passed on some facts, passed on some information and some documents, with which the students or the audience—the recipients—can for instance do what people during the occurrence of the Holocaust precisely did with information that kept coming forth but that no one could *recognize*, and that no one could therefore truly *learn*, *read* or *put to use*.

Looking back at the experience of that class, I therefore think that my job as teacher, paradoxical as it may sound, was in fact that of creating in the class the highest state of crisis that it could withstand, without "driving the students crazy," without compromising the students' bounds.

## THE EVENT OF TEACHING

In the era of the Holocaust, of Hiroshima, of Vietnam—in the age of testimony—teaching, I would venture to suggest, must in turn *testify*, make something *happen*, and not just transmit a passive knowledge, pass on information that is preconceived, substantiated, believed to be known in advance, misguidedly believed, that is, to be (exclusively) a *given*.

There is a parallel between this kind of teaching (in its reliance on the testimonial process) and psychoanalysis (in its reliance on the psychoanalytic process), insofar as both this teaching and psychoanalysis have, precisely, to *live through a crisis*. Both are called upon to be *performative*, and not just *cognitive*, insofar as they both strive to produce, and to enable, *change*. Both this kind of teaching and psychoanalysis are interested not merely in new information, but, primarily, in the capacity of their recipients to *transform themselves* in function of the newness of that information.

In the age of testimony, and in view of contemporary history, I want my students to be able to receive information that is *dissonant*, and not just *congruent*, with everything that they have learned beforehand. Testimonial teaching fosters the capacity to witness something that may be surprising, cognitively dissonant. The surprise implies the crisis. Testimony cannot be authentic without that crisis, which has to break and to transvaluate, precisely, previous categories, and previous frames of reference. "The poem," writes Celan, "takes its position at the edge of itself" (1978). In a post-traumatic age, I would suggest that teaching, equally, should take its position at the edge of itself, at the edge of its conventional conception.

As far as the great literary subjects are concerned, teaching must itself be viewed not merely as *transmitting*, but as *accessing*: as accessing the crisis or the critical dimension which, I will propose, is inherent in the literary subjects. Each great subject has a turning point contained within it, and that turning point has to be met. The question for the teacher is, then, on the one hand, how to access, how *not to foreclose* the crisis, and, on the other hand, how to *contain it*, how much crisis can the class sustain.

It is the teacher's task to recontextualize the crisis and to put it back into perspective, to relate the present to the past and to the future and to thus reintegrate the crisis in a *transformed* frame of meaning.

### TEACHING AS TESTIMONY

In much the same way as psychoanalysts, in their practice of dream interpretation, will register as literally as they can the manifest dream content and the incoherent flow of dream associations, so did I take down, word by word, the emotional upheaval of my students' statements and the spectrum both of their responses and of their literal expressions. This documentation and this written record served as the material basis upon which interpretation—in the guise of a returned testimony—could indeed begin to be articulated.

In much the same way as the psychoanalyst serves as witness to the story of the patient, which he then interprets and puts together, so did I return to the students—in their own words—the narrative I had compiled and formed of their own reactions. When the story of the class—the story I am telling now—was for the first time, thus, narrated to the class itself in its final session, its very telling was a "crisis intervention." I lived the crisis with them, testified to it and made them testify to it. My own testimony to the class, which echoed their reactions, returning to them the expressions of their shock, their trauma, and their disarray, bore witness nonetheless to the important fact that their experience, incoherent though it seemed, *made sense*, and that *it mattered.* My testimony was thus both an echo and *a return of significance,* both a repetition and an affirmation of the double fact that their response was *meaningful,* and that it *counted.*

In working through the crisis that broke the framework of the course, the dynamics of the class and the practice of my teaching exceeded, thus, the mere concept of the testimony as I had initially devised it and set out to teach it. What was first conceived as a *theory* of testimony got unwittingly *enacted,* had become itself not theory, but an *event* of life: of life itself as the perpetual necessity—and the perpetual predicament—of a learning that in fact can never end.

### EPILOGUE

In conclusion, I would like to return to my students' words and to quote two excerpts from two papers that were written as the last assignment of the class, both to illustrate the way in which the students met the challenge of *emerging* from the crisis, and to highlight the words and the significance that they in turn returned to me.

The first excerpt, written by a Chinese woman, reflects on the testimony of the child survivor.

The testifier seemed to be a man of great compassion. He wondered aloud what sorts of testimony one leaves to one's children, when one does not confront the past. I thought at first, what sorts of burdens will I pass on to *my* children, in the unlikely event that I have any. And then, I thought of my father, who lived through the Chinese Civil War, and four years of incarceration as a political prisoner on the Island of Taiwan. What sorts of burdens has he passed on to me? . . .

In an odd sort of way, I feel a strange sort of collectively has been formed in the class. This, of course, is a most frightening thing. As I mentioned above, my mode of interaction with those whom I do not know, has always been one of radical differentiation, rather than of collectivization. My autonomy has been rendered precarious, even fragile. Somehow, though, I have managed to survive, whole and a bit fragmented at the same time; the same, but decidedly altered. Perhaps this final paper can only be testimony to that simple fact, that simple event.

The second paper was, in contrast, written by a man (a man who—I might mention in parenthesis—was not Jewish).

Viewing the Holocaust testimony was not for me initially catastrophic—so much of the historical coverage of it functions to empty it from its horror. Yet, in the week that followed the first screening, and throughout the remainder of the class, I felt increasingly implicated in the pain of the testimony, which found a particular reverberation in my own life. . . .

﹍ Literature has become for me the site of my own stammering. Literature, as that which can sensitively bear witness to the Holocaust, gives me a voice, a right, and a necessity to survive. Yet, I cannot discount the literature which in the dark awakens the screams, which opens the wounds, and which makes me want to fall silent. Caught by two contradictory wishes at once, to speak or not to speak, I can only stammer. Literature, for me, in these moments, has had a performative value: my life has suffered a burden, undergone a transference of pain. If I am to
✓continue reading, I must, like David Copperfield, read *as if for life*.

## Notes

This essay was originally published in *American Imago* 48, no. 1 (1991); it was reprinted, in modified form, in Shoshana Felman and Dori Laub, M.D., *Testimony: Crises of Witnessing in Literature, Psychoanalysis, and History* (1992), Routledge, New York. The essay here conforms to the version in the book and is reprinted by permission of the publisher.

1. "J'apporte en effet des nouvelles. Les plus surprenantes. Même cas ne se vit encore. Ils ont touché au vers. Il convient d'en parler déjà, ainsi qu'un invité voyageur

tout de suite se décharge par traits haletants du témoignage d'un accident su et le poursuivant." "La Musique et les lettres." Subsequent quotations from Mallarmé will refer to this French edition. The English version of all cited texts from Mallarmé is here in my translation.

2. "Les gouvernements changent: toujours la prosodie reste intacte: soit que, dans les révolutions, elle passe inaperçue ou que l'attentat ne s'impose pas avec opinion que ce dogme dernier puisse varier."

3. Free verse, in effect, has both declassified and mingled poetry and prose, both of which are henceforth equally infused with poetic inspiration. Prose, in Mallarmé's perspective, is essentially *poeticized* through the accidenting of the verse, and is thus no longer separate, no longer formally distinct from poetry. "Verse is all there is (le vers est tout)," says Mallarmé, "from the moment there is writing. There is style, versification, wherever there is rhythm, and this is why every prose . . . has the weight of a ruptured verse. . . . This is indeed, the crowning of what was formerly entitled *prose poem*" (Mallarmé, 1945, 664).

4. "Faut-il s'arrêter là et d'où ai-je le sentiment que je suis venu relativement à un sujet plus vaste peut-être à moi-même inconnu, que telle rénovation de rites et de rimes; pour y attendre, sinon le traiter. . . . Le conscient manque chez nous de ce qui là-haut éclate."

5. On the belated knowledge of "the accident," and the significance of this belatedness for an understanding of the relation between trauma and history, see Caruth, 1991.

6. "Tu remarquas, on n'écrit pas, lumineusement, sur champ obscur . . . l'homme poursuit noir sur blanc."

7. "Ecrire—L'encrier, cristal comme une conscience, avec sa goutte, au fond, des ténèbres . . . écarte la lampe."

8. "The Meridian," speech given by Celan in 1960, on the occasion of receiving the prestigious Georg Büchner Prize (by the German Academy for Language and Literature).

9. "Literature: that can signify a turn-of-breath. Who knows, perhaps literature travels its path—which is also the path of art—for the sake of such a breath-turning?" (Celan, 1978, 35).

10. Given and tape recorded on December 4, 1984, and consequently transcribed.

# References

Adorno, Theodor. 1973. *Negative Dialectics.* Trans. E. B. Ashton. New York: Continuum.

———. 1982. *The Essential Frankfurt School Reader.* New York: Continuum.

Camus, Albert. 1972. *The Plague.* Trans. Stuart Gilbert. New York: Random House.

Canetti, Elias. 1974. *Kafka's Other Trial.* New York: Schocken.

Caruth, Cathy. 1991. "Unclaimed Experience: Trauma and the Possibility of History." *Yale French Studies* 79 (Jan.).

Celan, Paul. 1978. "The Meridian." Trans. Jerry Glenn. *Chicago Review* 29, no. 3: 29–40.

———. 1980a. *Poems*. Trans. Michael Hamburger. New York: Persea.

———. 1980b. *Prose Writings and Selected Poems*. Trans. Walter Billeter. Paper Castle.

Dostoevsky, Fyodor. 1961. *Notes from the Underground*. Trans. Andrew MacAndrew. New York: Signet.

Felstiner, John. 1982. "Translating Celan's Last Poem." *American Poetry Review* (July–Aug.).

Fortunoff Video Archive for Holocaust Testimonies. Yale University. Founded in 1981.

Freud, Sigmund. 1900 (1953–58). *The Standard Edition of the Complete Psychological Works of Sigmund Freud*. Vol. 4–5. Translated under the editorship of James Strachey in collaboration with Anna Freud, assisted by Alix Strachey and Alan Tyson. 24 vols. (1953–74). London: Hogarth.

———. 1910. *The Standard Edition*. Vol. 11.

Johnson, Barbara. 1979. *Défigurations du language poétique*. Paris: Flammarion.

Mallarmé, Stéphane. 1945. *Oeuvres complètes*. Paris: Gallimard.

Wiesel, Elie. 1977. *Dimensions of the Holocaust*. Evanston: Northwestern University Press.

———. 1984. "The Loneliness of God." In *Dvar Hashavu* (Tel Aviv).

# TRUTH AND TESTIMONY:
# THE PROCESS AND THE STRUGGLE

DORI LAUB

I would like to propose some reflections on the relation of witnessing to truth, in reference to the historical experience of the Holocaust. For a long time now, and from a variety of perspectives, I have been concretely involved in the quest of testifying and of witnessing—and have come to conceive of the process of the testimony as, essentially, a ceaseless struggle, which I would like here to attempt to sketch out.[1]

## I

### MY POSITION AS A WITNESS

I recognize three separate, distinct levels of witnessing in relation to the Holocaust experience: the level of being a witness to oneself within the experience, the level of being a witness to the testimonies of others, and the level of being a witness to the process of witnessing itself.

The first level, that of being a witness to oneself, proceeds from my autobiographical awareness as a child survivor. I have distinct memories of my deportation, arrival in the camp, and the subsequent life my family and I led there. I remember both these events and the feelings and thoughts they provoked in minute detail. They are not facts that were gleaned from somebody else's telling me about them. The explicit details (including names of places and people), which I so vividly remember, are a constant source of amazement to my mother in their accuracy and general comprehension of all that was happening.

But these are the memories of an adult. Curiously enough, the events are remembered and seem to have been experienced in a way that was far beyond the normal capacity for recall in a young child of my age. It is as though this process of witnessing was of an event that happened on another level, and was not part of the mainstream of the conscious life of a little boy. Rather, these memories are like discrete islands of precocious thinking, and feel almost like the remembrances of another child, removed, yet connected to me in a complex way.

This essay is based in part on this enigma of one child's memory of trauma. The remembrances of yet another child survivor, known to me quite intimately (from having been his later interviewer and friend) and therefore subtly related to my own in the quality of their precociousness, will serve as a connecting, reemerging thread in the latter part of the essay.

The second level of my involvement in the process of witnessing is my participation, not in the events, but in the account given of them, in my role as the interviewer of survivors who give testimony to the Video Archive—that is, as the immediate receiver of these testimonies. My function in this setting has been that of a companion on the eerie journey of the testimony. As an interviewer, I am present as someone who actually participates in the reliving and reexperiencing of the event. I also become part of the struggle to go beyond the event and not be submerged and lost in it.

The third level is one in which the process of witnessing is itself being witnessed. I observe how the narrator and myself as listener alternate between moving closer and then retreating from the experience—with the sense that there is a truth that we are both trying to reach, and this sense serves as a beacon we both try to follow. The traumatic experience has normally long been submerged and has become distorted in its submersion. The horror of the historical experience is maintained in the testimony only as an elusive memory that feels as if it no longer resembles any reality. The horror is, indeed, compelling not only in its reality but even more so, in its flagrant distortion and subversion of reality. Realizing its dimensions becomes a process that demands retreat. The narrator and I need to halt and reflect on these memories as they are spoken, so as to reassert the veracity of the past and to build anew its linkage to, and assimilation into, present-day life.

### THE IMPERATIVE TO TELL

Toward the end of her testimony at the Fortunoff Video Archive for Holocaust Testimonies at Yale, one woman survivor made the statement:

"We wanted to survive so as to live one day after Hitler, in order to be able to tell our story" (Fortunoff, T58).

In listening to testimonies, and in working with survivors and their children, I came to believe the opposite to be equally true. The survivors did not only need to survive so that they could tell their stories; they also needed to tell their stories in order to survive. There is, in each survivor, an imperative need to *tell* and thus to come to *know* one's story, unimpeded by ghosts from the past against which one has to protect oneself. One has to know one's buried truth in order to be able to live one's life.

This imperative to tell and to be heard can become itself an all-consuming life task. Yet no amount of telling seems ever to do justice to this inner compulsion. There are never enough words or the right words, there is never enough time or the right time, and never enough listening or the right listening to articulate the story that cannot be fully captured in *thought*, *memory*, and *speech*. The pressure thus continues unremittingly, and if words are not trustworthy or adequate, the life that is chosen can become the vehicle by which the struggle to tell continues. The above-mentioned survivor, for example, constructed her life in such a fated way, that it came to be a testimony to her loneliness and bereavement, in spite of the fact that her world was filled with living people and in spite of her remarkable gifts— her creativity, her warmth, her generosity, her eloquence, and her love of life.

Hers was a life in which the new family she created, the children she bore, had to give continuance and meaning, perhaps provide healing and restitution, to the so suddenly and brutally broken family of her childhood— parents, brothers, and children, several of whom died while she was holding them in her arms. In her present life, she relentlessly holds on to, and searches for, what is familiar to her from her past, with only a dim awareness of what she is doing. Her own children she experiences with deep disappointment as unempathic strangers because of the "otherness" she senses in them, because of their refusal to substitute for, and completely fit into, the world of parents, brothers, and children that was so abruptly destroyed.

Yet hers is a story that could never be told in the way she chose to tell it, that is, by structuring her whole life as a substitute for the mourned past, because there could not be an audience (even in her family) that was generous, sensitive, and self-effacing enough to obliterate its own existence and be nothing but the substitutive actors of her unexplicated memory. Her specific attempt to tell her story by the very conduct of her life led to an unavoidable dead end, in which the fight against the obliteration of the story could only be won at the cost of the obliteration of the audience.

## THE IMPOSSIBILITY OF TELLING

In this case as in many others, the imperative to tell the story of the Holocaust is inhabited by the impossibility of telling, and therefore, silence about the truth commonly prevails. Many of the survivors interviewed at the Fortunoff Video Archive realize that they have only begun the long process of witnessing now—forty years after the event. Some have hardly spoken of it, but even those who have talked incessantly, feel that they managed to say very little that was heard. None find peace in silence, even when it is their choice to remain silent. Moreover, survivors who do not tell their story become victims of a distorted memory, that is, of a forcibly imposed "external evil," which causes an endless struggle with and over a delusion.[2] The "not telling" of the story serves as a perpetuation of its tyranny. The events become more and more distorted in their silent retention and pervasively invade and contaminate the survivor's daily life. The longer the story remains untold, the more distorted it becomes in the survivor's conception of it, so much so that the survivor doubts the reality of the actual events.

This power of distortion in present-day life is demonstrated by the loss of a sense of human *relatedness* experienced by one woman survivor I interviewed. She described herself as "someone who had never known feelings of love." This feeling of *lack* encompassed all the people in her life. Her family, including her children, were never able to thaw her heart, or penetrate the bars of her "self-imprisonment." Because of this self-inflicted emotional imprisonment she found herself surrounded by hatred and disdain for and from all those closest to her. Ironically, throughout those years she spent all her free time, and still does, caring for the terminally sick and the old. But these anguished people she cares for, make her feel precisely that she cannot love them enough.

As a teenager during the war, she had lost most of her family and witnessed many awesome events. Among them was the choking to death of a small baby who had cried too loudly, as well as the burning alive of several of her close relatives. These relatives had been put into a boarded-up wooden shack that was set afire. Toward the end of the war, she participated as a partisan in the hunting down and killing of local collaborators. During this period, her fellow partisans captured and turned over a seventeen-year-old German youth to her. She was given free hand to take revenge. After all that she had witnessed and lived through, this woman bandaged the German's wounds and turned him over to the POW group. When asked why she had done this, she replied: "How could I kill him—he looked into my face and I looked into his."

Had she been fully able to grasp the truth about herself, and not perceived herself as someone "with a heart of stone" but as a compassionate, loving person, she might have lived her life differently. Her previous inability to tell her story had marred her perception of herself. The untold events had become so distorted in her unconscious memory as to make her believe that she herself, and not the perpetrator, was responsible for the atrocities she witnessed. If she could not stop them, rescue or comfort the victims, *she* bore the responsibility for their pain. In other words, in her memory of her Holocaust experience, as well as in the distorted way in which her present life proceeded from this memory, she failed to be an authentic witness to herself. This collapse of witnessing is precisely, in my view, what is central to the Holocaust experience.

## II

### AN EVENT WITHOUT A WITNESS

On the basis of the many Holocaust testimonies I have listened to, I would like to suggest a certain way of looking at the Holocaust that would reside in the following theoretical perspective: that what precisely made a Holocaust out of the event is the unique way in which, during its historical occurrence, *the event produced no witnesses*. Not only, in effect did the Nazis try to exterminate the physical witnesses of their crime; but the inherently incomprehensible *and* deceptive psychological structure of the event precluded its own witnessing, even by its very victims.

A witness is a witness to the truth of what happens during an event. During the era of the Nazi persecution of the Jews, the truth of the event could have been recorded in perception and in memory, either from within or from without, by Jews, or any one of a number of "outsiders." Outsider-witnesses could have been, for instance, the next door neighbor, a friend, a business partner, community institutions including the police and the courts of law, as well as bystanders and potential rescuers and allies from other countries.

Jews from all over the world, especially from Palestine and the United States could have been such possible outside witnesses. Even the executioner, who was totally oblivious to the plea for life, was potentially such an "outside" witness. Ultimately, God himself could be the witness. As the event of the Jewish Genocide unfolded, however, most actual or potential witnesses failed one-by-one to occupy their position as a witness, and at a certain point it seemed as if there was no one left to witness what was taking place.

In addition, it was inconceivable that any historical insider could remove herself sufficiently from the contaminating power of the event so as to remain a fully lucid, unaffected witness, that is, to be sufficiently detached from the inside so as to stay entirely *outside* of the trapping roles, and the consequent identities, either of the victim or of the executioner. No observer could remain untainted, that is, maintain an integrity—a wholeness and a separateness—that could keep itself uncompromised, unharmed, by his or her very witnessing. The perpetrators, in their attempt to rationalize the unprecedented scope of the destructiveness, brutally imposed upon their victims a delusional ideology whose grandiose coercive pressure totally excluded and eliminated the possibility of an unviolated, unencumbered, and thus sane, point of reference in the witness.

What I feel is therefore crucial to emphasize is the following: it was not only the reality of the situation and the lack of responsiveness of bystanders or the world that accounts for the fact that history was taking place with no witness: it was also the very circumstance of *being inside the event* that made unthinkable the very notion that a witness could exist, that is, someone who could step outside of the coercively totalitarian and dehumanizing frame of reference in which the event was taking place, and provide an independent frame of reference through which the event could be observed. One might say that there was, thus, historically no witness to the Holocaust, either from outside or from inside the event.

What do I mean by the notion of a witness from inside? To understand it one has to conceive of the world of the Holocaust as a world in which the very imagination of the *Other* was no longer possible. There was no longer an other to which one could say "Thou" in the hope of being heard, of being recognized as a subject, of being answered (cf. Buber, 1953).[3] The historical reality of the Holocaust became, thus, a reality that extinguished philosophically the very possibility of address, the possibility of appealing, or of turning to, another. But when one cannot turn to a "you" one cannot say "thou" even to oneself. The Holocaust created in this way a world in which one *could not bear witness to oneself.* The Nazi system turned out therefore to be fool proof, not only in the sense that there were in theory no outside witnesses but also in the sense that it convinced its victims, the potential witnesses from the inside, that what was affirmed about their "otherness" and their inhumanity was correct and that their experiences were no longer communicable even to themselves, and therefore, perhaps never took place. This loss of the capacity to be a witness to oneself and thus to witness from the inside is perhaps the true meaning of annihilation, for when one's history is abolished, one's identity ceases to exist as well.

### THE SECRET ORDER

Survivors often claim that they experience the feeling of belonging to a "secret order" that is sworn to silence. Because of their "participation" in the Holocaust they have become the "bearers of a secret (*Geheimnisstraeger*)" never to be divulged. The implications of this imaginary complicity and of this conviction of their having been chosen for a secret mission are that they believe, out of loyalty, that their persecution and execution by the Nazis was actually warranted. This burdensome secret belief in the Nazi-propagated "truth" of Jewish subhumanity compels them to maintain silence. As "sub-humans," a position they have accepted and assumed as their identity by virtue of their contamination by the "secret order," they have no right to speak up or protest. Moreover, by never divulging their stories, they feel that the rest of the world will never come to know the *real* truth, the one that involved the destruction of their humanity. The difficulty that prevents these victims from speaking out about their victimization emphasizes even more the delusional quality of the Holocaust. This delusion, fostered by the Holocaust, is actually lived as an unconscious alternate truth, by executioners, victims and bystanders alike. How can such deadlock be broken?

### THE EMPEROR'S NEW CLOTHES

It is in children's stories that we often find the wisdom of the old. "The Emperor's New Clothes" is an example of one such story about the secret sharing of a collective delusion. The emperor, though naked, is deluded, duped into believing that he is seated before his audience in his splendid new clothes. The entire audience participates in this delusion by expressing wonderment at his spectacular new suit. There is no one in the audience who dares remove himself from the crowd and become an outcast by pointing out that the new clothes are nonexistent. It takes a young, innocent child, whose eyes are not veiled by conventionality, to declare the emperor naked. In much the same way that the power of this delusion in the story is ubiquitous, the Nazi delusion was ubiquitously effective in Jewish communities as well. This is why those who were lucid enough to warn the Jewish communities about the forthcoming destruction either through information or through foresight, were dismissed as "prophets of doom" and labeled traitors or madmen. They were discredited because they were not conforming by staying within the confines of the delusion. It is in this way that the capability of a witness alone to stand out from the crowd and not be flooded and engulfed by the event itself, was precluded.

The silence about the Holocaust after the war might have been, in turn, a continuation of the power and the victory of that delusion. As in the story of "The Emperor's New Clothes," it has taken a new generation of "innocent children," removed enough from the experience, to be in a position to ask questions.

## III

### ACROSS THE GAP

Because the event that had no witness to its truth essentially did not exist, and thus signified its own death, its own reduction to silence, any instance of its survival inevitably implied the presence of some sort of informal discourse, of some degree of unconscious witnessing that could not find its voice or its expression during the event.

And indeed, against all odds, attempts at bearing witness did take place; chroniclers of course existed and the struggle to maintain the process of recording and of salvaging and safeguarding evidence was carried on relentlessly. Diaries were written and buried in the ground so as to be historically preserved, pictures were taken in secret, messengers and escapees tried to inform and to warn the world of what was taking place. However, these attempts to inform oneself and to inform others were doomed to fail. The historical imperative to bear witness could essentially *not be met during the actual occurrence.* The degree to which bearing witness was required, entailed such an outstanding measure of awareness and of comprehension of the event—of its dimensions, consequences, and above all, of its radical *otherness* to all known frames of reference—that it was beyond the limits of human ability (and willingness) to grasp, to transmit, or to imagine. There was therefore no concurrent "knowing" or assimilation of the history of the occurrence. The event could thus unimpededly proceed *as though* there were no witnessing whatsoever, *no witnessing that could decisively impact on it.*[3]

The experience of encountering today the abundance of the retrospective testimonies about the Holocaust is thus doubly significant and doubly moving. It is not by chance that these testimonies—even if they were engendered during the event—become receivable only *today*; it is not by chance that it is only now, *belatedly*, that the event begins to be historically grasped and seen. I wish to emphasize this *historical gap* which the event created in the collective witnessing. This emphasis does not invalidate in any way the power and the value of the individual testimonies, but it underscores the fact that these testimonies were not transmittable, and integratable, at the time. It is all the more imperative to recognize and to enhance today the value and the momentous contributions of the testimonies and the witnesses who preserved evidence often by risking their lives. The ultimate historical transmission of the testimonies beyond and through the historical gap, emphasizes the human will to live and the human will to know even in the most radical circumstances designed for its obliteration and destruction.

The perspective I propose tries to highlight, however, what was ultimately missing, not in the courage of the witnesses, not in the depth of their emotional responses, but in the human cognitive capacity to perceive and to assimilate the totality of what was really happening at the time.

## WITNESSING AND RESTORATION

Yet it is essential for this narrative that *could not be articulated* to be *told*, to be *transmitted*, to be *heard*, and hence the importance of endeavors like the Fortunoff Video Archive designed to enable the survivors to bear witness, to enable, that is, the act of bearing witness (which the Holocaust invalidated) to take place, belatedly, as though retroactively.

Such endeavors make up for the survivors' need for witnesses, as well as for the historical lack of witnessing, by setting the stage for a reliving, a reoccurrence of the event, in the presence of a witness. In fact, the listener (or the interviewer) becomes the Holocaust witness *before* the narrator does.

To a certain extent, the interviewer-listener takes on the responsibility for bearing witness that previously the narrator felt he bore alone, and therefore could not carry out. It is the encounter and the coming together between the survivor and the listener, which makes possible something like a repossession of the act of witnessing. This joint responsibility is the source of the reemerging truth.

The Video Archive might, therefore, be thought of as helping to create, after the fact, the missing Holocaust witness, in opening up the historical conceivability (the retrospective condition of possibility), of the Holocaust witness. The testimony constitutes in this way a conceptual breakthrough, as well as a historical event in its own right, a historical recovery which I tend to think of as a "historical retroaction."

What ultimately matters in all processes of witnessing, spasmodic and continuous, conscious and unconscious, is not simply the information, the establishment of the facts, but the experience itself of *living through* testimony, of giving testimony.

The testimony is, therefore, the process by which the narrator (the survivor) reclaims his position as a witness: reconstitutes the internal "thou," and thus the possibility of a witness or a listener inside himself.

In my experience, repossessing one's life story through giving testimony is itself a form of action, of change, which one has to actually pass through, in order to continue and complete the process of survival after liberation. The event must be reclaimed because even if successfully repressed, it nevertheless invariably plays a decisive formative role in who one comes to be, and in how one comes to live one's life.

## IV

### THE ICON

To illustrate the importance of the process of witnessing and of giving testimony and the struggle involved in it, I would like to relate the story of a man who is currently a high ranking officer in the Israeli army and whom I interviewed during a sabbatical year he spent at Yale University (Fortunoff, T152).

As a little boy of about four years old, he lived with his parents in the Krakow ghetto. A rumor, which eventually materialized, began spreading that all children were going to be rounded up for extermination. The parents started to make plans to devise ways to save their son by smuggling him out of the ghetto. They would talk about it at night when he should have been asleep, but he overheard them. One night, while the guards were being distracted, they indeed managed to get him out of the gate. His mother wrapped him up in a shawl and gave him a passport photograph of herself as a student. She told him to turn to the picture whenever he felt the need to do so. His parents both promised him that they would come and find him and bring him home after the war. With that, and with an address where to go, he was sent out into the streets. The address was a whorehouse, a marginal institution itself and therefore, more hospitable to the homeless. He was received with open arms. For years he used to speak of the whorehouse as a hospital, with the color white featuring predominantly in his memory, because the first thing he was given on arrival was a white glass of milk, and, in his imagination, the place could not be anything but a helping hospital. Eventually, his hideout became too dangerous and he had to leave. He roamed the streets, joined other gangs of boys, and found refuge in the homes of generous, gentile families who took him in for periods of time. The task of making it from day to day preoccupied him completely and in moments of solitude he would take out his mother's picture and talk to her.

In one of the gentile houses he stayed in (living on the papers of a child that had died), the family was in the habit of praying together every evening. When everybody knelt and prayed to the crucifix, the lady of the house, who may have suspected he was Jewish, was kind enough to allow him to pray to whomever he wished. The young boy would take out the photograph of his mother and pray to it, saying, "Mother, let this war be over and come and take me back as you promised." Mother indeed had promised to come and take him back after the war, and not for a moment did he doubt that promise.

In my interpretation, what this young vagabond was doing with the photograph of his mother was, precisely, creating his first witness, and the creation of that witness was what enabled him to survive his years on the streets of Krakow. This story exemplifies the process whereby survival takes place through the creative act of establishing and maintaining an internal witness, who substitutes for the lack of witnessing in real life.

This early internal witness in turn played a crucial role not only in his actual physical survival but also in the later adult testimony the child survivor gave to himself and to others by augmenting his ability to create a cohesive, integrated narrative, of the event. This testimony to himself came to be the story of the hidden truth of his life, with which he has to struggle incessantly in order to remain authentic to himself.

## A PASSAGE THROUGH DIFFERENCE OR THE BROKEN PROMISE

Knowing one's real truth, however, can also be very costly, as is demonstrated by what happens to the little vagabond boy after liberation. He manages miraculously to find his parents, but when he and his parents are reunited, they are not the people he remembers: they no longer even resemble the image he has carried in his mind for so long. His mother does not look like the person in the photograph. His parents have come back as death camp survivors, haggard and emaciated, in striped uniforms, with teeth hanging loose in their gums. Their return does not bring back the lost safety of childhood the boy has so ardently prayed for. He finds that he can only address them as Mr. and Mrs., not as Mom and Dad. I read this story to mean that in regaining his real mother, he inevitably loses the internal witness he had found in her image. This loss of his internal witness to whom he has addressed his daily prayers causes the boy to fall apart. He begins to have a nightmare that will recur all his life. In it he finds himself on a conveyor belt moving relentlessly towards a metal compactor. Nothing he can do will stop that conveyor belt and he will be carried to his end, crushed to death by the machine. Every time he has this dream, he wakes up, totally disoriented and utterly terrified. Because he has lost the life-sustaining internal witness he found in his mother's image, after the war, he becomes, paradoxically enough, a mere "child victim" deprived of the holding presence of a witness. Many of the things he consequently does, as he grows up to be a man, are desperate attempts to subdue the abandoned child victim within himself. As a high-ranking officer in the Israeli army he becomes known for repeated acts of bravery, risking his life, as he rescues wounded soldiers under heavy fire. In speaking about these brave acts, he will later state, however, that he did not consider them brave at all. They simply partook of his feeling of being invulnerable. He was convinced he could walk in a hail of bullets and not be hit. In my understanding, this conviction is part of a psychological construction which centered his life on the denial of the child victim within himself. He becomes instead an untouchable and self-sufficient hero. Because he had lost his inner witness and because he could not face his horrors without a witness, he was trapped. He could neither allow himself to experience the horrors nor could he move away from the position of the child victim, except by relentlessly attempting to deny them.

It was years later that I happened to meet him and invite him to give his testimony to the Archive at Yale. This provoked a crisis in him. At first he refused. A prolonged struggle with himself ensued.

> My initial reaction was, "NO." My wife said, "Why don't you think it over? . . . What are you afraid of?" I said, "I'm scared that everything will come back, my nightmares, and so on. . . ." She said, "You've been living with this thing for thirty-five years after the war, and you're still afraid. You never talked about it. Why don't you try the other way?" We spent a lot of time talking about it; I began to see the logic. This particular night

we went to bed very early in the morning, because we had talked very far into the night, and the next night I had my nightmares again. But this time it was different. It was again the conveyor belt, it was again the rolling presses; it was again the feeling of helplessness and of terrible anxiety. But for the first time in my life, I stopped the conveyor belt. I woke up, still feeling anxious, but the anxiety was turning into a wonderful sense of fulfillment and satisfaction. I got up; for the first time I wasn't disoriented. I knew where I was; I knew what happened. . . . I feel strongly that it has to do with the fact that I decided to open up. (Fortunoff, T152)

Once the link to the listener has been reestablished in his mind, once no longer alone and without a witness, he is able to stop the death machine in his dream without having to wake up. Coincidentally he expresses the fact that for the first time in his life he was able to experience feelings of fear as well.

As is evident in the example of this child survivor, the act of bearing witness at the same time *makes* and *breaks* a promise: the promise of the testimony as a realization of the truth. On the one hand, the process of the testimony does in fact hold out the promise of truth as the return of a sane, normal, and connected world. On the other hand, because of its very commitment to truth, the testimony enforces at least a partial breach, failure and relinquishment of this promise. The mother that comes back not only fails to make the world safe for the little boy as she promised, but she comes back different, disfigured, not identical to herself. She no longer looks like the mother in the picture. There is no healing reunion with those who are, and continue to be, missing, no recapture or restoration of what has been lost, no resumption of an abruptly interrupted innocent childhood. The testimony aspires to recapture the lost truth of that reality, but the realization of the testimony is not the fulfillment of this promise. The testimony in its commitment to truth is a passage through, and an exploration of, difference, rather than an exploration of identity, just as the experience it testifies to—the Holocaust—is unassimilable, because it is a passage through the ultimate difference—the otherness of death.

Yet it is this very commitment to truth, in a dialogic context and with an authentic listener, which allows for a reconciliation with the broken promise, and which makes the resumption of life, in spite of the failed promise, at all possible. The testimony cannot efface the Holocaust. It cannot deny it. It cannot bring back the dead, undo the horror, or reestablish the safety, the authenticity and the harmony of what was home. But neither does it succumb to death, nostalgia, memorializing, ongoing repetitious embattlements with the past, or flight to superficiality or to the seductive temptation of the illusion of substitutions. It is a dialogical process of exploration and reconciliation of two worlds—the one that was brutally destroyed and the one that is—that are different and will always remain so. The testimony is inherently a process of facing loss—of going through the pain of the act of witnessing, and of the ending of the act of witnessing—which entails yet another repetition of the experience of separation and loss. It reenacts the passage through difference in such a way, however, that it allows perhaps a certain repossession of it.

It is the realization that the lost ones are not coming back; the realization that what life is all about is precisely living with an unfulfilled hope; only this time with the sense that you are not alone any longer—that someone can be there as your companion—knowing you, living with you through the unfulfilled hope, someone saying: "I'll be with you in the very process of your losing me. I am your witness."

> To stand in the shadow
> of the scar up in the air.
>
> To stand-for-no-one-and-nothing.
> Unrecognized,
> for you
> alone.
>
> With all there is room for in that,
> even without
> language.                                    (Celan, 1980, 181)

## Notes

This essay was originally published in *American Imago* 48, no. 1 (1991); it was reprinted, in modified form, in Shoshana Felman and Dori Laub, M.D., *Testimony: Crises of Witnessing in Literature, Psychoanalysis, and History* (1992), Routledge, New York. The essay here conforms to the version in the book and is reprinted by permission of the publisher.

1. As the cofounder of the Fortunoff Video Archive for Holocaust Testimonies at Yale; as an interviewer of the survivors who give testimony; as a psychoanalyst who treats Holocaust survivors and their children, and as a child survivor myself.

2. As an example for the core of this delusion, I shall quote the interpretation

made by a psychoanalyst to a survivor patient: "Hitler's crime was not only the killing of the Jews, but getting the Jews to believe that they deserved it."

3. Had there been such effective, material witnessing, the event would have had to change its course and the "final solution" could not have been carried out to the extent that it was, in full view of the civilized world.

## References

Buber, Martin. 1953. *The I and the Thou.* Edinburgh: T. and T. Clark.

Celan, Paul. *Poems,* trans. Michael Hamburger. New York: Persea, 1980.

Fortunoff Video Archive for Holocaust Testimonies, Yale University. Founded in 1981.

# Trauma and Aging:
# A Thirty-Year Follow-Up

## Henry Krystal

In 1963 I found myself in a unique position, as the psychiatric examiner of claims for restitution in the area under the jurisdiction of the German Consul General in Detroit. Since I have been doing it for more than 30 years, at various points I was tempted to stop and reflect on what I have learned about the parties involved (Krystal, 1966, 1968, 1978a, 1978b, 1984, 1985). At the same time I tried to observe the effect this activity had on me, and on one occasion I even undertook to compare the statistics of the evaluation of the applicants by the various restitution offices in Germany and compare the diagnoses and the percentages of disability of the applicants (1971). On this occasion I found quite impressive consistency within each of the offices, but very little agreement between any two offices (218–23).

On November 22, 1990, I read a paper to the Boston Society for Gerontological Psychiatry, which I would like to reprint "unretouched."

### General Remarks

The difficulties of the Holocaust survivors, which Niederland (1961) described twenty years ago, have continued to be studied (Eitinger and Strom, 1973; Eitinger, 1980; Chodoff, 1980). These patients have continued to suffer from depression, sleep disturbances, repetitive dreams, various chronic pain syndromes, and chronic anxiety (Eitinger, 1980), as well as characterological difficulties. Eitinger's follow-up of the entire Norwegian population of former concentration camp inmates led him to the conclusion that "the greater morbidity among survivors is not restricted to any special diagnosis. The differences between ex-prisoners and the controls vary somewhat from diagnostic group to diagnostic group, but there are more ex-prisoners than controls suffering from the various illnesses" (ibid., 155).

Eitinger further observed that "the ex-prisoner's sick periods and hospitalization periods were about three times as long as those of the controls, and the average member of sick leaves per person, sick days per person and sick days per sick leave was greater for the ex-prisoners than for the controls" (ibid.). Chodoff's review of his experiences showed the continuing unhappiness within "ill-advised marriages" and described the survivors as living in "withdrawn depression, uninfluenced by any available measures" (1980, 208). Among the aftereffects of the Holocaust that made psychotherapy very difficult for the survivors was the destruction of their "basic trust," their inability to re-experience and describe some of their harmful experiences, their retroactive idealization of their childhood problems of (survivor) guilt feelings, which he described as "intractable to psychotherapy" (209), their continuation of the camp-regressively-induced disturbances in the body image, and finally, the problems of continuing aggression of an intensity that could not be handled in psychotherapy and the tendency to deal with this aggression through a rigid religiously oriented superego.

My own follow-up contacts with the population of about a thousand concentration camp survivors have consisted of those who were requested to come in for a follow-up interview by the German restitution authorities, and the people who sought consultations because of difficulties in their lives. About a dozen of these patients, who are as old as seventy-eight years, have been in psychoanalytic psychotherapy with me. Basically, my findings coincide with those reported by others. Problems of chronic depression, masochistic life patterns, chronic anxiety, and psychosomatic disease continue. With retirement, and the reexamination of one's life, some dormant problems are reactivated and produce exquisite pain. Such are, for instance, the self-reproaches of the individuals who lost a child or mate during the Holocaust. Their "survivor" guilt becomes severe, and some of these individuals assume a depressive or penitent lifestyle. Similarly, some other specific acts or wishes during the persecution may become the focus of a depressive preoccupation.

*Rather than reviewing the problems of technique, I want to focus my discussion on the relation of certain post-traumatic constellations to the old-age reevaluation of one's life.* Old age poses a question of diminishing gratification, and in this population, with serious to severe anhedonia being a common finding, we could expect special difficulty. The progressive loss of gratification, support, and distraction limits the choices to the two alternatives: *integration* of one's life or living in despair. I shall try to show that the major task of senescence is identical with the one of psychoanalysis or psychoanalytic psychotherapy. In old age, as in treatment, we come to the point where our past lies unfolded before us, and the question is, What should be done with it? The answer is that it must be accepted or one must keep waging an internal war against the ghosts of one's past. The influences in this task consist of the elements in one's life story that continue to generate painful affects, the nature of the affective processes, and the nature of the hedonic level maintained by the given individual. For this reason, I will be forced to take a long digression in order to provide a background by reviewing the nature of anhedonia and alexithymia.

## The Affective and Hedonic Sequelae of Trauma

Long-term follow-up of a large group of concentration camp survivors for thirty-five years after their liberation has given me a chance to observe certain aftereffects of massive psychic traumatization. In the process of working with these patients, I found that the economic conception of psychic trauma was inadequate to explain, and unsuited to deal with, the problem. In my previous publications, I have described some of the aftereffects of the concentration camp experience that were separate from the consequences of survivorship of the Holocaust, such as survivor guilt (Krystal, 1978a). Among these findings were certain disturbances of affective and cognitive patterns, which are now known as "alexithymia" (Krystal, 1971). Immersed in my attempts to understand the problems of survivorship and trauma, I was shocked and surprised to find that these patterns of emotional responses were also quite common and conspicuous among substance-dependent individuals. About the same time, a group of Paris psychoanalytic researchers was describing the same pattern in psychosomatic patients (Marty and de M'Uzan, 1963). Researchers in Boston have also been working on this phenomenon, publishing it since Sifneos' paper (1967) in which he coined the term "alexithymia."

The reconciliation of these far-flung observations turned out to be both simple and productive. I had earlier reported a very high rate of psychosomatic diseases among the concentration camp survivor group—as high as 30 to 70 percent (Krystal, 1971). Working with these data, I realized that we were dealing with a pattern of regression in affect expression. This conception in turn made it possible to recognize the genetic developmental story of affects and their basic developmental lines, consisting of verbalization, desomatization, and differentiation (Krystal, 1974). The regression in the affect form produces the main aspects of alexithymia. A concurrent finding is that of "operative thinking"—an overly exaggerated emphasis upon the mundane details of the "things" in one's life, and a severe impairment in the capacity for wish-fulfillment fantasy. While the etiology and meaning of these difficulties is still being studied, I feel that I have demonstrated to my satisfaction that when alexithymia is post-traumatic, it is accompanied by some, often a severe degree of, anhedonia (Krystal, 1978a, 1978b).

## Infantile Trauma

In order to consider the connection between the diminution in the capacity for pleasure, joy and happiness and psychic trauma, I must step back again and retrace my work on psychic trauma. The recognition that affects themselves undergo a developmental change made it possible to separate the pattern of infantile psychic trauma from the adult catastrophic type. Because of the primitive nature of the infantile affect forerunners—in that they are mostly somatic, and undifferentiated—they can become overwhelming and cause a response that I define as the infantile trauma pattern.

The infantile gross stress, or "alarm," pattern is basically that behavior most likely to prevent the separation from the mother, though it may be brought on by any distress or discomfort. Since separation from the mother quickly becomes a matter of life and death, the whole affective apparatus of the child is mobilized, the infant becomes frantic and noisy and assumes a search pattern—as permitted by his motor skill development. At its highest point, the infant searches for its mother in concentric circles of increasing radius, vocalizing in a way as to provoke pity and caring responses. Periodically, the infant gives in to exhaustion and apathy and becomes stationary, whimpering piteously. "Freezing" and immobility represent another basic response pattern. In contrast to the adult state of catastrophic trauma, which may lead directly to psychogenic death, in the young there is *a safety valve whereby the child will go to sleep* for a while, only to awaken with a start and resume the frantic search. At the same time, the child in this traumatic state is in a frenzy of "total excitement." The whole organism is in an alarm and mobilization state. The child's emotional responses represent an activation of affect precursors, or ur-affects, and with it the activation of entire emotional brain and centers for pleasure, pain, and the hedonic regulators. The affect forerunners are general; that is, there is but one pattern in all states of distress and one for well-being and contentment. In the course of normal development, this global response pattern becomes gradually differentiated, and, through verbalization and desomatization, assumes the affective patterns known to adults. However, the affect precursors, which constitute the infantile pattern, include the as-yet-undifferentiated pain responses as well, since there is neither the neurological nor the psychological development to localize and identify pain experiences. That is why the infantile mass response can be imagined to mobilize the entire limbic system, with a number of specialized areas that later become involved with pain, pleasure, distress, and even orgasm regulation.

If this infantile emergency pattern goes on for an appreciable period of time, there is a modification of the child's pleasure and pain regulatory centers, including those for vital functions. For if this state continues too long, or is repeated too often, it leads to a failure to thrive: marasmus, hospitalismus, anaclitic depression, and eventually death. This pattern has been found and described for all mammals. The question is not nutrition but the necessary affective support of mothering. If there is not prompt resumption of adequate mothering—but enough care is available to make survival possible—anhedonia sets in.

## Adult Catastrophic Psychic Trauma

In contrast to the infantile traumatic state, which is caused by the nature of the affect pattern, the adult catastrophic trauma state is determined by the presence of *unavoidable danger.* Adults are capable of experiencing affect storms without being overwhelmed by them. In fact, intense stimulation is frequently sought as a source of thrills or trances. Adult psychic trauma is *not* caused by the intensity of stimuli (Krystal, 1970). The adult traumatic state is initiated by the recognition of inevitable danger, and the surrendering to it. Thereupon the affective state changes from the signal of avoidable danger (anxiety) to a surrender pattern which is the common pattern of "freezing," "playing possum" or "panic inaction" which is common throughout the animal kingdom (see Seligman, 1975; Tyhurst, 1951; Cannon, 1942).

With the surrender to what is perceived as inevitable, inescapable, immediate danger, an affective process is initiated, which Stern (1951) has called "catatonoid reaction." Briefly, it consists of a paralysis of initiative, followed by *varying degrees of immobilization leading to automatic obedience. At the same time, there is a "numbing" process by which all affective and pain responses are blocked,* leading to what Eugene Minkowski (1946)called "affective anaesthesia," and Robert Lifton (1967) extended the idea to "psychic closing off."

The broader conception is useful, because the next aspect of the traumatic process is the *progressive construction of cognitive processes, including memory and problem solving, until a mere vestige of self-observing ego is preserved. This process may culminate in psychogenic death.*

On the other hand, it is possible for this process to stay at the point where a degree of "psychic closing off" has been accomplished, which permits a certain automatonlike behavior, which is necessary for survival in situations of subjugation, such as prison and concentration camps (Krystal, 1968; Krystal and Niederland, 1971).

I am especially interested in emphasizing the "specific" aftereffects of catastrophic adult psychic trauma, that is, those aftereffects that represent a continuation of the traumatic process. These disturbances consist of (1) a continuation of cognitive constriction in various forms of dullness, obtuseness, or inability to function as parents; (2) episodic "freezing" when under stress. The result may be an inability to act assertively or aggressively. The general picture is of either passivity or blundering (as caricatured by the "Inspector Clouseau" character). There may also be a variety of "surrender" patterns that are perpetuated in characterological or stress-related behaviors; and (3) pseudophobia, usually related to some memory or affect representing a traumatic screen and, therefore, dreaded and avoided. Repetitive dreams also represent the trauma as their dreaded by expected destiny. It may also be *but ?* said that these individuals, who experienced catastrophic psychic trauma in adult life, show signs of continuation of the trauma patterns, hypervigilance, anxiety dreams, sometimes a driven need to talk about the events of the traumatic period, at other times a need to avoid doing so. By contrast, the survivors of infantile trauma have often no recollection or even suspicion of their traumatic history and no direct pattern of behavior traceable to the traumatic process.

This brings us to the two problems *shared* as sequelae of infantile and adult type of psychic trauma—they are, as mentioned already, *anhedonia and alexithymia.* In other words, anhedonia is a characteristic and quite reliable mark of post-traumatic states, whether they took place in infancy or later life. Alexithymia, however, represents a broader range of problems, and can be found in certain hereditary (Heilberg and Heilberg, 1977), psychosomatic, addictive states as well as in reactions to acute life-endangering illness (Freyberger, 1977). Next, I will consider the impact of alexithymia and anhedonia on the problems of aging, and particularly on the psychotherapy with the aged.

## Alexithymia, Anhedonia, and the
## Achievement of Integrity in Old Age

One need not belabor the many reasons why aging involves a gradual diminution in the potential for pleasure and gratification. If the process runs its full course, one is left to enjoy nothing but one's vegetative functions. As the attrition proceeds, one can observe easily that people vary in regard to their hedonic potential, and that some individuals enter old age with an already diminished hedonic capacity (Meehl, 1975). Additional and independent factors on opposite poles of this capacity are the ability to play (Krystal, 1981) and problems of masochism and guilt. Hedonic potential needs to be carefully evaluated with every aged person, as there is a marked difference among people from similar populations. Individuals with a good hedonic capacity can enjoy practically anything, even if it's only inhaling and exhaling, and are known for their "sunny disposition" since childhood. This function has been identified as a personality factor (Meehl et al., 1971) and has been called "surgency," a term coined by R. B. Catell (1955). But, regardless of where on this spectrum of capacity for pleasure, joy, and happiness one falls, there is no way to avoid the progressive ravages to the hedonic span with age. Particularly severe losses are accrued to the things one *does*, in all spheres of activity, from sexual through occupational, avocational to recreational. These losses force a shift from doing to thinking, from planning to reminiscing, from preoccupation with everyday events and long-range planning to reviewing and rethinking one's life.

Simply being forced to recall and remember is in itself frightening and stressful to survivors of the Holocaust. They have spent most of their time "fighting off" their memories. Many go to great lengths to avoid any historical material. When I asked such patients to associate to Thematic Apperception Test cards 1, 3, and 5, their responses were usually limited to one or two sentences predicting a dismal future for everyone in the picture. Some patients even volunteered the observation that they are so afraid of "make-believe" that they do not want to view or read any fictional stories. A patient who had had some psychotherapy commented—when she realized that she kept describing the cards in terms of her own life—"The past is always catching up to the present in my mind." The reasons for "running away from one's history" have been kenningly described by G. S. Klein (1976) as resulting from the "sensitivity to cleavage and dissonance," which "reaches its crest . . . in the twilight years when irreversible finitude is finally to be faced and the effort to bring together past, present, and the shrinking future into a self-justifying meaning is especially poignant and difficult" (231).

Old age, with its losses, imposes the inescapable necessity to face one's past. This development determines that one either accepts one's self and one's past or continues to reject it angrily. In other words, the choice is, as Erik Erikson put it (1959), integration or despair. But integration means that one has to accept, acquiesce to the "accidental coincidence of but one life cycle with but one segment of history" (98). Erikson further explained that to achieve integrity one has to *accept* "one's own life cycle and . . . the people who have become significant to it as something that had to be, and that, by necessity, it accepted no substitutions." This task can also be said to represent the very goal and essence of all psychoanalytic psychotherapy.

The heart of the work of psychoanalysis can be reviewed in two parts: (1) the expansion of the *consciously* acknowledged self and object representations, and (2) the acceptance of the inevitability and necessity of every event which was part of one's life as having been *justified by its causes*. It may be said that the challenge in the acceptance of one's old age and the completion of psychoanalytic work is the same—to acquiesce and embrace what has happened and to renounce continuing anger about it. But, in regard to this task, the psychotherapy for post-traumatic states encounters special difficulties.

For the survivors of the Holocaust to accept that what happened to them was *justified by its causes* implies an acceptance that Hitler and Nazism and the bizarre events they experienced were also justified by their causes, and such an acceptance is too closely reminiscent of the *submission* to persecution. The process of making peace with one's self becomes impossible when it is experienced as bringing back the helplessness and the *shame* of the past. Hence, many survivors would experience this self-healing as granting Hitler a posthumous victory, and they therefore angrily reject it. To them, self-integration appears antithetical to the only justification of their survival—that they are obligated to be angry witnesses against the outrage of the Holocaust.

Moreover, to give up the infantile wishes—including the omnipotence, the quest for perfection, the entitlement to ideal parents—to accept the negative aspects of one's self, including these very angry and vengeful feelings, requires a capacity for effective grieving. However, in order to be able to mourn, one has to have available to him the adult-type affects, which is just what (by definition) the alexithymic patients are lacking. In addition, the "operative thinking" characteristic of alexithymia interferes further with the capacity for symbolization, transference elaboration, and achievement of changes and sublimations. Finally, one must have good affect tolerance (Krystal, 1975a) to carry out the process of mourning without it snowballing into a maladaptive state of depression. In fact, the chronic depressive state in which these people and similar ones live can be defined by the mourning that needs to be accomplished but that is precluded. These patients keep berating and accusing themselves, indicating a low opinion of themselves, and yet fail to lower their high self-expectations. The belated discovery of one's own anhedonia is the last blow, and causes a bitter rejection of one's lifelong reparative efforts for having failed to produce the long yearned-for pleasure and well-being. There is a feeling of depression resulting from the failure to produce gratification. One is also faced with the tragic choice between continuing the "hate addition" and turning against one's self in contempt for having missed the point of life.

A common finding with survivors of the Holocaust is that even in the relative absence of alexithymia and impairment in affect tolerance, there is a limitation to how much an individual can absorb through grieving and achieve integrity and good-natured acceptance of the past. There seems to be an absolute limit to how much an individual is able to give up through grieving. The limitation is a double one—first there is only so much a person can grieve over *at one time*; for example, if one is severely burned and loses a spouse at the same time, one may not be able to deal with the object loss while attending to the corporeal losses. I am referring to cases reported from the Coconut Grove disaster (Lindemann, 1944). Second, there is an absolute or lifetime limit to what a given person can absorb in terms of either loss or accepting the negative qualities of one's self. There are both qualitative and quantitative factors in the limitations on what can be dealt with through mourning. The quantity or the quality of losses may be beyond one's capacity to integrate, for example, when in the case of the Holocaust one's entire people and civilization perished. But even if we were to discount these difficulties, which could fill volumes, we still come back to the simplest, most basic fact—that there are limitations to the kind of losses an individual may be able to deal with through mourning. The loss of a child by parents is an example of one that may not be capable of completion, and various forms of denial, idealization, and introject "walling off" may become necessary. An example of a negative quality within one's self that cannot be accepted but must be compensated for is Joseph Conrad's story *Lord Jim* (1900); the hero has to sacrifice his life to show that he is not, after all, a coward.

In addition, the survivor of a genocidal holocaust stands the risk of having the object and self-representations polarized into victim and per-petrators. The anhedonia and alexithymia propel him into continuing the victim identity and, with it, the longing to change places with the aggressor. But, the identification with the aggressor must remain unconscious or else it will flood the self-representation with psychotic rage. This unsolvable di-lemma was best perceived by Robert Shaw and portrayed in his novel: *The Man in the Glass Booth* (1967). The story, which was subsequently turned into a play (and movie) involves a spectacularly successful, but very unhappy and unstable survivor. There is a question of identity; is this Goldman the former prisoner—or his cousin SS Colonel Dorff of the Einsatz (mass-murder) commandoes and death camps?

Paradoxically, while it may be very painful and difficult for an individual who has endured serious psychic traumatization to achieve interpsychic integration, this is what he needs most of all. One of the most devastating aftereffects of trauma is that it causes widespread use of repression, denial, and psychic splitting. Much of the psychic representation of the "enemy" or "oppressor" or even impersonal elements such as "fate" and clearly personal attributes like one's own emotions come to be experienced as outside the self-representation. *Thus the post-traumatic state is characterized by an impoverish-ment of the areas of one's mind to which the "I" feeling of self-sameness is extended, and a hypertrophy of the "not-I" alienated areas.* The symptoms of "pseudophobia," fear of one's dreams and of one's own emotions, are all the result of this post-traumatic depletion of the consciously recognized spheres of selfhood.

Moral and ethical judgment is often substituted for self-healing. It seems virtuous to "feed" righteous indignation, and treasonous to stop the rage. In this respect, it is useful to consider it a masochistic perversion that the survivor should be promoting the continuation of these pains within himself. Rather, to the extent possible, he should soothe himself and gain peace through self-acceptance.

Robert Lifton (1979) addressed himself to the issue of post-traumatic integration but has focused on the confrontation with death rather than the reaction to loss of love objects. As he sees it, "Death tests everyone's integrity; the dying person's immediate survivors, and the attending healers contribute to a collective psychic constellation within which issues of continuity, dis-continuity, self-completion and disintegration are addressed" (109). Empha-sizing the confrontation with "absurd" death, mass destruction leads Lifton to understand that the survivors' "life review" is derailed by "psychic numb-ing, desymbolization, deformation" (or "decentralization"), and an inability to restore a feeling of intimacy because of a suspicion of "counterfeit nurturance" (69). In effect, then, Lifton's observations coincide with the above expressed view that the difficulties that become conspicuous in the survivors in old age may be considered a paradigm of many of the major difficulties in the attempts at post-traumatic self-healing and mastery of the intrapsychic injuries. My major emphasis is that, whereas mourning and grieving work requires the availability of adult-type affects, alexithymia becomes a specific obstacle—but by no means the only one found under these circumstances.

Survivors of the Holocaust show early aging and early high death rates from all causes (Eitinger and Strom, 1973). This loss of vitality should not be viewed as separate or independent from the alexithymia or anhedonia. S. Rado long ago stressed the importance of the "pleasure economy" (1969). He believed that a "deficiency in welfare emotions (joy, pleasure, happiness, love, affection, etc.) alters every operation of the integrative apparatus. No phase of life, no area of behavior remains unaffected" (24). My observations and the findings of Eitinger (1980) prove the validity of Rado's ideas. In survivors, we have a combination of anhedonia, a problem of special guilt, quite possibly an attachment to pain (Valenstein, 1973), and a fear of joy and happiness. But in addition, psychotherapeutic work with the survivors has been ineffective because they fear their emotions; that is, they have a post-traumatic impairment of affect tolerance because they experience their own emotions as heralds of trauma (Krystal, 1975a, 1979). Getting past that, one encounters the problems of alexithymia. These patients do not *recognize* their emotions, because they experience them in an undifferentiated way, poorly verbalized, and because they have very poor reflective self-awareness. As a result, they tend to complain of symptoms, such as pain, palpitations, or insomnia, rather than forming complete emotions and recognizing them as "feelings." The tendency is to try to block the distress through medication and to keep "proposing a physical illness" (Balint, 1964) instead of utilizing one's emotions as signals.

But the underlying problem of depression and guilt still requires integration through mourning, lowering of narcissistic expectations of one's self, and acceptance of the necessity of what happened. For instance, survivors of the Holocaust still suffer from a feeling of shame over the idea that they did not fight back enough. Presently, renewed effort is being made to create a mythology about the heroic resistance, which is intended to stop the shame. The futility of this effort by certain groups on behalf of the Jewish people illustrates the task and challenge of integration in the life of every aging person. Whatever one is ashamed of has to be lovingly accepted as part of one's life that was unavoidable. Every pain aroused in the process of reviewing one's life as an individual or history of a group merely marks an area deprived of the self-healing application of the feeling of identity, self-sameness, and selfhood. One feels anger, guilt, or shame whenever one is unable (refuses) to accept the necessity and unavoidability of what happened. The trouble is that, in this process of reviewing one's life, as the memories are restored to the self-representation, and owned up to (in other words, in the process of the return of the repressed), pain is experienced. This is, in fact, (the very pain in mourning) what so puzzled Freud (1917). Freud said that he could not explain why mourning was so "extraordinarily painful" "*in terms of economics*" (emphasis mine) (245). But in terms of the task which goes on in senescence one can see many reasons why mourning must be so painful. I will stress only one, however, for the purpose of our discussion. The successful completion of mourning, and/or the successful integration of one's life bring one to the position of being able to own up to all of one's living as his own, including one's object representations. This state gives us a chance to discover that in ordinary living we maintain our object representations in a type of *repression through externalization*, in the sense that we maintain our mental representation of them in a nonself status.

Thus in mourning, if we do it to the point of owning up to the self-sameness of our object representations, there is a kind of return of the repressed. The illusion of externality that we maintained toward our object representations achieved a kind of analgesia for us, and when self-integration is achieved, this analgesia is "worn off." I see the motivation for the "externalization" to be in the dealing with infantile aggression. I feel that infantile trauma and the resulting ambivalence results in a distortion of the self-representation, wherein vital and affective aspects of one's self are attributed to the object representation, which is rigidly "walled off"—thus rendering one's capabilities for self-care functionally inaccessible (Krystal, 1978a).

Because mourning and integration must include the affective components (just as Freud and Breuer, 1893, 37f, first discovered that recollection did not do anything for hysteria if it was devoid of the emotions), affect tolerance becomes a major issue. That is also the reason why normal, adult-type, mostly cognitive, and signallike affects are necessary for the completion of mourning. Otherwise, in the presence of alexithymia, the undifferentiated, mostly somatic, unverbalized affect responses are so intense, threatening, and painful that one must ward them off by self-deadening, or else abort the process by escape into denial.

Another related subject is that of religiosity. The French say that when the Devil gets old he becomes pious. Desperate attempts are made by many survivors to restore and maintain their faith in God. However, the problems of aggression and the destruction of basic trust resulting from the events of the Holocaust (Krystal, 1978a) make *true faith and trust in the benevolence of an omnipotent God impossible.* So the yearning for the comfort of religion only results in a piling up of rituals. People who are unable to complete mourning and people troubled by their religious ambivalence have another tendency in common: the building of monumental and ecclesiastic edifices and this can be observed in the survivor group.

In addition, one has to keep maintaining intrapsychic barriers against the ambivalence, against the doubts, guilt, and rage. As a result, one observes a widespread constriction of fantasy—both in actual imagination and in transference reactions (Krystal, 1979).

The point that impressed me as I follow a large number of survivors of the Holocaust who are *not* in psychotherapy is that, in reaching old age, they are confronted with certain choices and tasks identical to those offered in analytic treatment. With the diminution of preoccupation with work, and gratification of the senses, there is a turning of the mind's activities inward and toward one's past. The choices are of *integration* of one's self and one's past, or denial, self-acceptance or depression, and depletion. The depressions are not necessarily consciously recognized or complained of. More commonly, the problems are handled by constriction of interest, by avoidance of both pleasure and excitement. The dread of one's affects extends from anxiety to any *sense of aliveness.* At last, the diminution in the tonic aspect of affect produces a retardation. The retardation may affect primarily the psychomotor sphere, but more commonly results in an alteration in life-preserving functions such as immune responses or other health-maintaining processes. There is a rapidly accumulating body of evidence that despair is an important predisposition for illness.

In conclusion, I have to admit that my attempts to engage aging survivors of the Holocaust in psychoanalytic psychotherapy have been for the most part unsuccessful. I have been able to effect a variety of supportive measures to make their life more bearable, among them, improving their "management," i.e., acceptance of their distressful affective states. But in regard to their capacity to work through their losses, and problems of guilt and shame with the aim of accomplishing integrity in aging, I have always run into the problem of the necessity for effective grieving (Wetmore, 1963). Effective mourning requires total emotional responses, which are felt and recognized as such.

Beyond being unable to complete mourning and achieve integration, the alexithymic becomes early prey to the most devastating pre-occupation of old age: "Who loves me?," "Who *cares* if I live?" With these individuals, the problem is a particularly difficult one because of their regression in affect, and other aspects of alexithymia. They neither experience love, nor do they have the kind of empathy that would permit them to sense their object's affection for them. One has to feel love to be able to believe in its existence. Most of all, one has to feel love in order to be able to accept one's own self and one's own past.

### Alter

In mir ist Orpheus noch, ein Aufgehren
ein Draengen nach Gestalt, Gesang, Gebot
ein hoch sich Baeumen und ein Wildes Wehren,
ein Wettlauf mit der Zeit und mit dem Tod.

Eurydike ist tot. Das Ideal entschwand
fuer immer in das Grabtuch meiner Klage.
Die letzten Blicke gehen unervandt
den Weg zu Gott. Dem ich mein Schweigen sage.

(Hoppe, 1982)

### Age

In me is Orpheus, a covetousness,
a longing for form, poetry, command,
a high prancing and a wild resisting,
a race with time and with death.

Eurydice is dead. The ideal vanished
forever into the shroud of my elegy.
The last glance goes steadfastly
the road to God. I tell Him my silence.

## The Ultimate Follow-up

Since the operation of the restitution activities, we had one practical rule; once the German Restitution Authorities established the degree of industrial disability, and consequently the disability pension, there was no point in submitting any reexamination of individuals suffering from psychological damages, because they were not subject to reconsideration. We knew that we would just be wasting our and the patients' time. For reasons not known to me, that policy was changed sometime in the fall of 1992. I was informed by patients who discovered that, if survivors of the Holocaust sent a report from their doctor claiming that their disability caused by the emotional aftereffects of the persecutions has increased, the chain of communications was activated, resulting in the patient receiving a letter from the Consul General's office, instructing him (her) to contact me for a "neuropsychiatric reexamination" by me. Thus, unexpectedly, I found myself interviewing patients I had seen just about thirty years earlier, that is, about fifty years after the major systematic extermination was at its height.

The patients were all in their later sixties, and seventies. A recently published study by a sociologist indicated that the Holocaust survivor population was considerably above average of the general population of the United States in terms of measures of family life, criminal record (absence of), and other sociological criteria of adjustment. A reporter for the *New York Times* interviewed me about that book. Of my responses to him, he quoted two sentences: "It seems that Holocaust survivors look a lot better to sociologists than they do to psychiatrists," and in another context, he attributed to me the following statement: "As we see it, the state of the survivors who are functional can be best understood by their having learned to live with a great deal of pain." This indeed turns out to be my repeated experience with the follow-up cases. When they come to see me and I look at their charts, I generally make a comment about the time that has elapsed since I first saw them. About half the people express amazement and assert that they do not have any recollection of ever having seen me before under any circumstances prior to this encounter.

I then ask, in an offhand way, how they are getting along. The answer is generally that they are much worse than ever, that their condition is very bad, as they were just telling their doctor recently. "What is the matter?" I inquire. The answers usually come in the following order: they are very nervous, everything upsets them, they are not able to be alone. Some complain of dysphoric affects with agoraphobia (which usually means that they cannot be in a car alone).

Next is the problem with sleep. Most commonly the complaint is, "I can not sleep at all." After some discussion and clarification, we settle for a compromise description. Perhaps they fall asleep for a couple of hours but then wake up, often in pain, and spend most of the night waking and walking around. In the morning, before dawn, they may sleep a little more. Some people then complain of many and terrible dreams, which, generally, they cannot remember. But they have the feeling that they are of a persecutory nature, sometimes referring to, but not reliving or repeating, the Holocaust experiences.

Next, we generally get into the subject of pain, which most of the time is introduced as, "I have pains everywhere." Again, in clarifying the generalization, we establish that most patients have pain in many joints, their back, and many muscles, but generally one or two places at a time, and particularly intensely at night. Of course, a high percentage turn out to suffer from arthritis and rheumatism, diabetes mellitus, and psychosomatic diseases such as asthma (many have a history of gastritis, peptic ulcer, reflux esophagitis, hypertension, and colitis). In a word, all possible psychosomatic diseases can be found.

So far, the interview goes easily and efficiently, and I expect that if I showed an interest, every one of the patients could recall a number of additional complaints and illnesses. But I am trying to do a psychiatric examination, and I start inquiring about the members of their family and how they get along with them. This part becomes very difficult. Regarding spouses, I can usually find out about the condition of their health and, if retired, whether they are able to participate in some activities outside the house. Some do participate in synagogue activities, some attend senior programs sponsored by the Jewish Community Center, cultural, and on occasion physical activities. Participation in physical activities requires an enormous effort, particularly when they are depressed or, more accurately, experience the mixed dysphoric state common among these alexithymic patients.

I can easily find out how many children they have, how many of those are married, and how many grandchildren they have. Sometimes they will comment that the grandchildren make it "all worth while." But a remarkable percentage of the patients do not follow up the grandchildren count with a statement of how delightful or "above average" they are. Usually they do complain about those grandchildren who live out of town, what an unbearable situation that is, since the grandparents cannot travel and are physically or emotionally unable to host their whole families. I do not know whether their failure to comment has some element of a fear of "evil eye" bringing on some misfortune, but there is a notable element of anhedonia; the patients are able to communicate that their grandchildren are doing very well, and sometimes even that the existence of this generation makes survival worthwhile, for it proves that Hitler did not succeed in his genocidal design; however, I rarely hear a description of the joy of grandparenthood.

I must explain that this new sample of survivors I have reexamined, under the new provisions that permit reapplication for individuals whose originally recognized persecution-connected problems have become much worse, is but a minute part of the two thousand survivors I examined when we were engaged in the restitution work. However, in this group I find a certain weariness in telling their problems in detail, in openly and with some trust relating how they feel and how much they suffer. There is a tendency to tell me a certain stereotyped story, and some patients actually refuse to go into the details of their complaints and their misery, even if I explain to them that unless they do so their application is not likely to be considered favorably. Some just become defiantly silent.

It is easy to obtain a litany of the patients' physical complaints, but it is very difficult to establish a relationship in which they can entrust me with an accurate picture of their present psychological state and family relations. They seem to be so bitter, and disappointed with the world at large, that they seem to have retreated into a sullen state. I have the feeling that there may be an organic reaction as part of it. I feel that this condition is similar to pseudodementia, in which individuals are so hurt, so deeply wounded beyond the possibility of recovery through grieving, that they constrict their mental functions, and function as if they were partly demented.

In particular, it is difficult to get beyond references to lost relatives and remembrances of the past that have become institutionalized structures, which I call Holocaust Memorials.

In fact, as part of the U.S. cultural education about the Holocaust, some survivors volunteer to go to schools to tell their stories. It happened in the case of one man, who was exceptionally young to survive Auschwitz, that he was sheltered by a group of men from his hometown, with whom he remains friendly. He has had many years of psychotherapy. We discovered, accidentally, that he did not actually remember some of the stories he was telling but learned them from his fellow survivors.

As I mentioned, my reports on the survivors are sent by the restitution office in each state, for a reevaluation, to the equivalent of the chairman of the department of psychiatry in the state university of that "land." His evaluation of the case and estimation of the degree of persecution-connected disability are generally accepted by the compensation officers in charge. Early in the development of the restitution procedures and laws, we (American psychiatrists) used to disagree with some opinions and appeal them. In fact, the concept of mental and emotional damages was evolved by the interaction of these appeals and the work of a number of outstanding German psychiatrists who undertook to change the prevalent organic-descriptive orientation prevalent in Germany at the end of the Second World War

(Pross, 1988). A number of American psychoanalysts, such as W. G. Niederland, M. Schur, K. Eissler, and others, have written many such appeals. Some American lawyers, notably M. Kestenberg, have also labored in this process.

However, most Holocaust survivors are not aware of this piece of our history and have a strong aversion to learning about it. Consequently, when I interview them, they experience me as acting as a representative of the German authorities. For the most part, they do not trust me unless they know me personally, and even then, there is a discernible transference reaction that forces them to be very careful about the statements they make to me. I learned from a social worker who treated a child of survivors that, as she was growing up, I was the local "bogeyman." If she was "bad," her mother would threaten her: "Dr. Krystal will come and get you!"

During our early work, there were many issues that we struggled with, while in Germany, there was much trouble not only with the psychiatric issues but also with the idea of compensating the victims of Nazi oppression, while German soldiers, even those returning from many years' incarceration in Soviet camps, were not afforded the same treatment. Besides the political and psychiatric problems, we had difficulty resulting from the fact that the Holocaust survivors, liberated in an uprooted state, discovering that most of them were alone, were not quite ready to resume a normal life. Many died after liberation, some had what I call a postliberation psychosis, during which they would run away and hide in the forests for some time after they were free. However, most managed to get to displaced persons' camps established by the United Nations' Authority (at that time called UNRRA) and proceeded to try to reconstruct their families by hasty, and often inappropriate, marriages.

They became so busy with the tasks of survival that their symptoms remained in denial for a long time. Frequently, they would be at ease enough to reflect on their condition when they were examined by a charity clinic affiliated with a resettlement service in this country. This development gave the appearance of a "latent period" after liberation, when no symptoms were registered, and this phenomenon again created an obstacle to the recognition of some claims. The early writings of Scandinavian psychiatrists, including the work of L. Eitinger, indicating that they were studying the survivors with skull X-rays, expecting that if there were going to be mental aftereffects they would likely be secondary to brain injuries and starvation, and they found some cases suggestive of brain atrophy.

But finally a rather wide literature developed on our findings on Holocaust survivors. The early writings combined the description of symptoms, many of which eventually became part of the general definition of post-traumatic states, as well as the psychodynamics of survival and the forensic aspects of the problems. Niederland's (1961) classic paper, "The Problem of the Survivor," was an inspiring example of this kind of work (for a review, see Hoppe, 1971). K. Eissler (1967) voices his reaction to the process in an article entitled "Perverted Psychiatry"; the long title, expressing his full outrage, appeared in German and is virtually untranslatable.

But there is (and has been for many years) a mass-transference reaction, in which the survivors expect me to "give them a pension," and if they are refused by the German authorities, no matter how it is explained to them, they feel that I am the embodiment of the Judenrat, the Jewish administrative body of the Nazi era that carried out the Nazis' bidding, even to the final step, having earlier registered all the Jews in the ghetto, of supplying, on demand, regular quotas of people for transport to the death camps. (The SS joke was that, as each ghetto was liquidated, the Jewish Judenrat and their families were loaded into a covered cattle car and shipped off to the same destiny.)

But Holocaust survivors, who have to maintain the Judenrat transference, are not ignorant people. This illustration is brought up here because the entire interview with any of them is dominated by this type of transference, even though some were sophisticated enough to have first had contact with the restitution offices in Germany, and even to have retained lawyers to represent them in Germany. No, this transference phenomenon is just one example of the survivors' identification with the opposite pole in the victim-oppressor polarization, the most difficult wound to heal.

Theoretically, every patient who was recognized as suffering from emotional damage was entitled to request an authorization from the German authorities for psychotherapy, a request that was rarely refused. Generally, the authorized treatment was once a week for a year. But the number of patients who availed themselves of it could be counted on the fingers of one hand. Two women came into treatment mainly because of headaches that they developed after they gave Bar Mitzvah parties for their sons, which caused them chronic headaches related to nor-adrenergic hyperactivity, from which they suffered anyway (van der Kolk et al., 1984), so it took them some time to recover. In the meantime, although they were lying on the couch, they were able to relate to me only the trivial events that took place since they last saw me—in chronological order. Another woman would come to see me off and on mainly because she wanted to talk to me about her son, who was an addict.

However, when her authorization for psychotherapy came through, she did not care to enter into "regular" treatment. A number of years later, when her son was creating an unbearable situation for her, she came to see me again. After a couple of visits, she asked me to get the treatment authorized "from Germany," because she could not afford it. I reminded her that she had refused to use it when it was granted before, but she had completely forgotten that incident.

I still have two Holocaust survivors in analysis after a number of years, both of whom are men, who were taken to Auschwitz at about age thirteen, and so it is remarkable that they survived. One of them happened to remain in Auschwitz I with his father and a number of men from his hometown. The entire male Jewish population from his hometown, a City in Silesia not far from Oswiecim (Auschwitz), were brought to the swampy area to build the camp. The patient arrived in Detroit as a young fellow, and through circumstances that are not clear to me, started seeing a psychiatrist, who was a full-time psychotherapist in the Detroit regional Veterans' Administration Office. The patient suffered from extreme depression, anxiety, and a mixture of dysphoric affects and pain. He remained in treatment for close to twenty years, until the psychiatrist retired and left town. He got along without treatment and continued to suffer periodic severe symptoms, until about a year after his wife died, when he came to me for a consultation, and we resumed psychotherapy.

Some time later, perhaps coincidentally, he became seriously interested in a divorced woman with a couple of teenaged children and was quite conflicted about the idea of remarrying. Up to this time, he had been doing quite well regarding his mourning the loss of his wife and managing his family and business. While planning a cruise with his new friend, he developed a severe physiological reaction, and we consulted a biological psychiatrist, who put him on a small dose of Tofranil. The patient took it for a while, while he continued psychotherapy with me on a weekly basis. Eventually, he did marry the woman. Early in his marriage we had the opportunity to work on his anhedonia, and his relationship with the people around him changed significantly. Twice he complained of emotional symptoms: once anger, later guilt, but they were not physiological problems or mixed dysphoria.

In the first year of his marriage he had problems with rage against his stepson and second wife, which, however, he "kept inside" and saved for his sessions with me. Although we talked about some aspects of his learning, after his liberation, that his father had died in another camp shortly before the camp was liberated, and we did on occasion discuss his relation to his first psychiatrist, we were not able to work with the transference in an effective analytic way, nor was there any notable period of mourning.

A week or so after he was honored by his synagogue, he had another dysphoric reaction, which we interpreted as his fear that success would be followed by disaster. We talked of his feeling that he should not "rock the boat." This patient wakes up every morning "feeling terrible"; the best he can explain is that he feels he cannot make it through the day. He forces himself to get up, goes to the health club, where he jogs maybe a couple miles, has a cup of coffee, and goes to his business, where he functions well the rest of the day.

My other patient is a man about whom I had heard before he came to see me. There are two remarkable things about him. He has a talent for making table-sized sculptures of death camp scenes, which he distributes for free to all the major local Jewish institutions. I also frequently saw his name in announcements of the meetings of various groups (especially women's clubs), where he would give a lecture entitled: "Never Forgive, and Never Forget." One day he made an appointment to see me and brought his wife with him. Straight away he explained his problem: he had had a number of near misses in the car. He was sure the next time he would get killed. Also, he wanted me to give him papers so he could get a Social Security disability pension. At first I did not know if he was joking or making fun of me. This man was a trained engineer who had done very well at his job but who quit because he felt that he was being discriminated against. At present, he was a successful insurance agent, but his work involved making house calls to potential clients, especially in the evening. Talking to his wife made me suspect that he had sleep apnea.

It turned out that he had such a tremendous hypertrophy of all the lymphatic tissues on his pharynx that, as his laryngologist explained to him, when he fell asleep and the tissues relaxed there was hardly any opening left for air to pass through. He had an operation, which included the removal of his uvula. After that he could not sleep because his mouth would become unbearably dry, a problem which he solved by inventing a device to hold a wet sponge in his mouth. He made another commercially successful invention, which was successfully merchandised. He gave me copies of two books he wrote about his Holocaust experience and his interpretation of the meaning of many events. For instance, he claimed that he survived because he made up his mind that he would: while he was in the camp, he visualized opening the door to his house. After liberation, he did return and opened the door of his house as he had visualized.

This patient has many serious family and other problems. At present, he feels he cannot remain in Detroit; he must move to an area where the temperature and humidity are higher. Indoors, he requires a temperature of 78 degrees Fahrenheit, whereas his wife is unable to bear to be in a room warmer than 72 degrees, which creates a difficult logistical problem. While this individual has many remarkable talents, his problems of alexithymia diminishes his ability to deal with his family empathically.

## Summary

In reviewing and restudying the paper I wrote in 1980 that tried to anticipate the effect of massive Holocaust trauma on the survivor's aging process, I find that, unfortunately, my anticipation has proven correct: unable to grieve effectively, most survivors become severely depressed, become ill, and die early. While they are alive, they live in constant pain. When I started to reexamine patients I had examined thirty years earlier, I discovered that they experienced a negative transference, mistook me as a Jewish Quisling, and could not share their psychological problems with me. If, after we had put together a report to the German restitution authorities, they were refused a raise in their pension, they invariably blamed me.

On the other hand, survivors were treatable if we could work patiently for many years—or in exceptional cases, if they were especially endowed with literary or artistic talents that permitted them to develop or reconstruct damaged functions. This is something we have to do with severely or early (infantile) traumatized individuals before they can utilize psychoanalytic psychotherapy. These exceptional ones can recover from their post-traumatic problems, can integrate, and can heal themselves to a significant degree.

## References

Balint, M. 1964. *The Doctor, His Patient, and the Illness.* New York: IUP.

Cannon, W. 1942. "Voodoo Deaths." *American Anthropologist* 44:169–81.

Catell, R. 1955. "Preservation and Personality: Some Experiments and a Hypothesis." *Journal of Mental Science* 81:115–67.

Chodoff, P. 1980. "Psychotherapy with the Survivor." In *Survivors, Victims, and Perpetrators*, ed. J. Dimsdale. Washington, D.C.: Hemisphere.

Conrad, J. 1900 (1961). *Lord Jim.* New York: Dell.

Eissler, K. 1967. "Perverted Psychiatry." *American Journal of Psychiatry* 123:11–34.

———. 1980. "The Concentration Camp Syndrome and Its Late Sequelae." In *Survivors, Victims, and Perpetrators*, ed. J. Dimsdale.

Eitinger, L., and A. Strom. 1973. *Mortality and Morbidity of Excessive Stress.* New York: Humanities Press.

Erikson, E. 1959. *Psychological Issues.* Vol. 1. New York: IUP.

Freud, S. 1917 (1957). "Mourning and Melancholia." In *The Standard Edition of the Complete Psychological Works of Sigmund Freud.* Vol. 14. Translated under editorship of James Strachey in collaboration with Anna Freud, assisted by Alix Strachey and Alan Tyson. 24 vols. (1953–74). London: Hogarth.

Freud, S., and J. Breuer. 1893 (1955). "On the Psychical Mechanism of Hysterical Phenomena: Preliminary Communication." *SE* 2.

Freyberger, H. 1977. "Supportive Psychotherapeutic Technique in Primary and Secondary Alexithymia." *Psychother. Psychosom.* 28:337–42.

Heilberg, A., and A. Heilberg. 1977. "Alexithymia and Inherited Trait?" *Psychother. Psychosom.* 28:221–25.

Hoppe, K. 1971. "The Aftermath of Nazi Persecution Reflected in Recent Psychiatric Literature." In *Psychiatric Traumatization,* ed. H. Krystal and W. Niederland. Boston: Little, Brown.

———. 1982. "Age." In *Reflections and Images, 1979–1987.* Published by the author.

Klein, G. 1976. *Theory of Psychoanalysis.* New York: IUP.

Krystal, H. 1966. "Psychic Sequelae of Massive Psychic Trauma." *Proceedings of the Fourth World Congress of Psychiatry.* Madrid, Sept. 5–11.

———. 1968. *Massive Psychic Trauma.* New York: IUP.

———. 1970. "Trauma and the Stimulus Barrier." Paper prepared for the annual meeting of the American Psychoanalytic Association, San Francisco.

———. 1971. "Trauma: Consideration of Severity and Chronicity." In *Psychic Traumatization,* ed. H. Krystal and W. Niederland. Boston: Little, Brown.

———. 1974. "The Genetic Development of Affects and Affect Regression." *Annual of Psychoanalysis* 3:179–219.

———. 1975a. "Affect Tolerance." *Annual of Psychoanalysis.*

———. 1975b. Letter to the Editor. *Midstream* 29:3–4.

———. 1978a. "Self-Representation and the Capacity for Self-Care." *Annual of Psychoanalysis* 6:209–46.

———. 1978b. "Trauma and Affects." *Psychoanalytic Study of the Child* 33:81–116.

———. 1979. "Alexithymia and Psychotherapy." *American Journal of Psychotherapy* 33: 17–31.

———. 1981. "The Hedonic Element of Affectivity." *Annual of Psychoanalysis* 9:93–113.

———. 1984. "Psychoanalytic Views on Human Emotional Damage." In *Post-Traumatic Stress Disorder: Psychological and Biological Sequelae,* ed. B. van der Kolk. Washington, D.C.: American Psychiatric Press.

———. 1985. "Trauma and the Stimulus Barrier." *Psychoanalytic Inquiry* 5:131–61.

Krystal, H., and W. Niederland. 1971. *Massive Psychic Trauma.* New York: IUP.

Lifton, R. 1967. *Death in Life: Survivors of Hiroshima.* New York: Random House.

———. 1979. *The Broken Connection: On Death and the Continuity of Life.* New York: Simon and Schuster.

Lindemann, E. 1944. "Symptomatology and the Management of Acute Grief." *American Journal of Psychiatry* 101:141–49.

Marty, P., and M. de M'Uzan. 1963. "La Pensee operatoire." *Rev. Franc. Psychanal.* 527:1345–56.

Meehl, P. 1975. "Hedonic Capacity: Some Conjectures." *Bulletin of the Menninger Clinic* 30:295–307.

Meehl, P., D. Likken, W. Schafield, and L. Pellegen. 1971. "Recaptured Item Technique (RIT): A Method for Reducing Somewhat the Subjective Element in Factor Naming." *Journal of Experimental Research* 5:171–90.

Minkowski, E. 1946. "L'anastesie affective." *Annual of Medico-psychol.* 104:8–13.

Niederland, W. 1961. "The Problem of the Survivor." *Journal of Hillside Hospital* 10:233–47.

Pross, C. 1988. *Wiedergutmachung: Der Kleinkrieg gegen die Orfer.* Frankfurt am Main: Atheneum.

Rado, S. 1969. *Adaptational Psychodynamics: Motivation and Control.* New York: Science House.

Seligman, M. 1975. *Helplessness.* San Francisco: Freeman.

Shaw, R. 1967. *The Man in the Glass Booth.* London: Chatto and Windus.

Sifneos, P. 1967. "Clinical Observations on Some Patients Suffering from a Variety of Psychosomatic Disorders." *Proceedings of the Seventh Conference on Psychosomatic Research.* Basel: Karger.

Stern, M. 1951. "Anxiety, Trauma, and Shock." *Psychoanalytic Quarterly* 20:179–203.

Tyhurst, J. 1951. "Individual Reactions to Community Disasters." *American Journal of Psychiatry* 107:764–69.

Valenstein, A. 1973. "On Attachment to Painful Feelings and the Negative Therapeutic Reaction." *Psychoanalytic Study of the Child* 28:365–92.

van der Kolk, B., A. Boyd, J. Krystal, and M. Greenberg. 1984. In *Post-traumatic Disorders*, ed. B. van der Kolk. Washington, D.C.: American Psychiatric Press.

Wetmore, R. 1963. "The Role of Grief in Psychoanalysis." *International Journal of Psychoanalysis* 44:97–103.

# NOT OUTSIDE THE RANGE:
# ONE FEMINIST PERSPECTIVE
# ON PSYCHIC TRAUMA

---

**LAURA S. BROWN**

As I began to think about what a feminist therapist might contribute to a discussion of trauma, I turned to the description of trauma in the American Psychiatric Association's (1987) *Diagnostic and Statistical Manual* (DSM III-R), that bible of psychiatric diagnosis, and to the criteria for a diagnosis of post-traumatic stress disorder (PTSD), the psychiatric syndrome that arises out of the experience of trauma. The book opens almost by itself to the right page; I have been there so many times. Trauma is the one constant in the work that I do as a psychotherapist.

I read again the words at the beginning of the diagnosis, the words that define the necessary and sufficient conditions for embarking upon this diagnosis, the definition of a traumatic event which must have occurred for this diagnosis to be considered by the clinician: "The person has experienced an event that is outside the range of human experience" (250). Categories of symptoms follow: reexperiencing symptoms, nightmares, and flashbacks; avoidance symptoms, the marks of psychic numbing; and the symptoms of heightened physiological arousal: hypervigilance, disturbed sleep, a distracted mind. But first and foremost, *an event outside the range of human experience.*

Then I remember the words of a defense attorney cross-examining me in a case where I was the therapist of a young woman whose stepfather had sexually abused her for many years. My patient was suing her stepfather for damages, hoping in this way to have the funds to continue in therapy long enough to feel healed. This woman's trauma had been repetitive, continuous over a long period of time, as is true for many incest survivors. This was a woman suffering, in my opinion, from PTSD. She had all of the symptoms;

certainly incest was traumatic. But the attorney disagreed with me. How, asked this attorney, who represented the perpetrator, could my patient possibly have PTSD? After all, wasn't incest relatively common? I had myself testified only minutes earlier that as many as a third of all girls are sexually abused prior to the age of sixteen. Incest wasn't unusual, wasn't "outside the range of human experience." How could it be called a trauma? And thus wasn't my diagnosis (and by inference, everything else that I was saying about the damage done my patient) wrong? Perhaps I was well prepared to answer this question only because I had heard it so many times before. How could such an event which happens so often to women, so often in the life of one woman, be outside the range of human experience?

Diana Russell, in the book from which I had taken those statistics, called incest the "secret trauma" (Russell, 1986). For girls and women, most traumas *do* occur in secret. They happen in bed, where our fathers and stepfathers and uncles and older brothers molest us in the dead of night; behind the closed doors of marital relationships where men beat and sometimes rape their wives and lovers; in the back seats of cars, where women are forced into sex by their boyfriends, not knowing until years later that they can call this a rape; in the offices of physicians and therapists who sexually exploit patients, knowing that their status is likely to protect them (Brown, 1989). These experiences are not unusual, statistically; they are well within the "range of human experience." They are the experiences of most of the women who come into my office every day. They are experiences that could happen in the life of any girl or woman in North America today. They are experiences to which women accommodate; potentials for which women make room in their lives and their psyches. They are private events, sometimes known only to the victim and perpetrator.

This picture of "normal" traumatic events gives shape to my problem as a feminist therapist with the classic definitions of appropriate etiologies for psychic trauma. "Human experience" as referred to in our diagnostic manuals, and as the subject for much of the important writing on trauma, often means "male human experience" or, at the least, an experience common to both women and men. The range of human experience becomes the range of what is normal and usual in the lives of men of the dominant class; white, young, able-bodied, educated, middle-class, Christian men. Trauma is thus that which disrupts these particular human lives, but no other. War and genocide, which are the work of men and male-dominated culture, are agreed-upon traumas; so are natural disasters, vehicle crashes, boats sinking in the freezing ocean.

Public events, visible to all, rarely themselves harbingers of stigma for their victims, things that can and do happen to men—all of these constitute trauma in the official lexicon. Their victims are rarely blamed for these events; I have yet to encounter writing about the characterological pathology of people who seek out floodplains or tornado alleys to live in, nor do those who wage war or go down to the sea in ships that can sink come under the sort of scrutiny we find given to battered women or survivors of rape or incest. In the mental health disciplines, this distinction is meaningful; the "self-defeating" woman who's been in a battering relationship is treated quite differently (and less well) than is the survivor of a train wreck, even when the presenting symptoms are similar. The former is assumed to have contributed to her problem, in particular because of the interpersonal locus of her distress (Brown, 1986); the latter is almost always seen as the innocent victim of a random event.

One thesis that I will explore here is that a feminist analysis calls us to look beyond the public and male experiences of trauma to the private, secret experiences that women encounter in the interpersonal realm and at the hands of those we love and depend upon. We (by which I mean those in the mental health disciplines and behavioral sciences) must attempt to find the meanings of these different sorts of events that constitute an assault on the integrity and safety of those who are not members of the dominant classes if we are to fully comprehend the meanings and nuances of psychic trauma and its presence in the lives of all humans. When we do so, we must ask questions about how we have understood that which constitutes a traumatic event and how some experiences have been excluded and turned inward upon their victims, who are then blamed for what has happened to them.

We are also challenged by such a feminist analysis and the questions that emerge from it to examine our definitions of *human* and to observe how our images of trauma have been narrow and constructed within the experiences and realities of dominant groups in cultures. The dominant, after all, writes the diagnostic manuals and informs the public discourse, on which we have built our images of "real" trauma. "Real" trauma is often only that form of trauma in which the dominant group can participate as a victim rather than as the perpetrator or etiologist of the trauma. The private, secret, insidious traumas to which a feminist analysis draws attention are more often than not those events in which the dominant culture and its forms and institutions are expressed and perpetuated. Feminist analysis also asks us to understand how the constant presence and threat of trauma in the lives of girls and women of all colors, men of color in the United States, lesbian and gay people, people in poverty, and people with disabilities has shaped our society, a continuing background noise rather than an unusual event. What does it mean if we admit that our culture is a factory for the production of so many walking wounded?

Feminist therapy, the orientation to understanding human development and psychotherapy to which I subscribe, is a philosophy of psychotherapy that draws upon a feminist analysis to understand and intervene in human distress. Feminist therapists such as myself share certain assumptions. Among these is the thesis that personality develops in a complex web of interaction between the internal, phenomenological experiences of the individual and the external, social context in which that person lives (Lerman, 1986). The constant interplay between these two, in which context informs phenomenology and phenomenology in turn creates the lens through which context is observed and interpreted, requires equal attention to both aspects of human experience. In this regard, feminist therapy eschews the sort of dichotomous thinking that characterizes much of mainstream psychology in which there tends to be an overemphasis on one or the other perspective to the detriment of a more integrated view. This focus on the interplay between internal and external is particularly salient when, as feminist therapists, we attempt to understand the meaning of psychic trauma. Feminist therapy theory also attempts to make central the experiences of girls and women and to attend to the diverse and complex aspects of the gender in such theorizing, rather than comparing women to an androcentric norm based on white male experiences.

## What Do We Speak About When We Speak About Trauma?

What purposes are served when we formally define a traumatic stressor as an event outside of normal human experience and, by inference, exclude those events that occur at a high enough base rate in the lives of certain groups that such events are in fact, normative, "normal" in a statistical sense? I would argue that such parameters function so as to create a social discourse on "normal" life that then imputes psychopathology to the everyday lives of those who cannot protect themselves from these high base-rate events and who respond to these events with evidence of psychic pain. Such a discourse defines a human being as one who is not subject to such high base-rate events and conveniently consigns the rest of us to the category of less than human, less than deserving of fair treatment.

Consider for a moment my patient, a working-class white woman in her early forties now on disability from her job as a factory work. She was raised in poverty; her first child was born when she was in her late teens, and, unmarried, she lived on welfare and illegal, under-the-counter work until she married in her early twenties and bore a second child. Her husband turned out to be a batterer, and she left him when her first child became a target. Years of instability followed; she had no trade, so she found work where she could get it, at hours that allowed her to be home with her children when she could. Much of the work she gets is physically risky; she is exposed to sharp edges, toxic and caustic chemicals, hot grease, wet slippery floors. More than once she's been off work with a job-related injury. Finally, in her thirties, her life seems to pull together. She marries a good man, not abusive, a man with a steady job; she goes to trade school and learns enough to get good work, work that pays well, has benefits, work that she imagines will help her to finally have the steady and predictable life she has always yearned for.

A few months into the job, she is disabled with a repetitive strain injury. Unfortunately for her, this is before the world of occupational medicine discovers repetitive strain. Her problem is difficult to diagnose; she is accused of malingering, and begins to be the target of verbal and emotional abuse at the hands of a foreman who is penalized for each day she cannot return to her full work duties. She becomes depressed, unable to work because of her fear as much as because of the pain in her hands. The constellation of events is further tangled by the interventions of health care providers who tell her that she is faking, trying to get something for nothing. Her marriage shakes under the strain; she can no longer do any of her hobbies or even wash her own hair without pain.

I see this woman as traumatized; she has all of the symptoms of a trauma victim when she first walks into my office. Nightmares of her supervisor screaming at her, anticipatory terror of being reinjured in a work setting and being disbelieved again, psychic numbing and withdrawal, loss of hope, the feeling that her old, familiar self has gone, missing somewhere in a fog of endless evaluations of her capacity to go back and twist wires again. But the psychiatrist to whom she is sent by the employer's insurance company cannot see her experience as trauma; he refers to the DSM III-R definition, points out that being injured at work and hassled about it simply isn't that unusual, and can't possibly be traumatic. In his report, he excoriates those who would stretch the definition of trauma to include such daily occurrences. My patient, who functioned well and courageously through the hard times in her life, must, he insists have a characterological disorder, a predisposition to fall apart at the least little disruption in her life; her normal poor woman's history of spotty work is defined as a sign of pathology, as is her rage at her treatment by her employer when she first attempted to report her injury and have it treated. Her past experiences of being hurt on jobs with dangerous environments is read as evidence of a tendency to seek out danger and to develop somatic problems. She has not, he pronounces, been traumatized by her work; her emotional problems are her own, no responsibility of her employer.

I read the psychiatrist's vita, attached to his report. He is a white middle-class man; he went directly from undergraduate to a prestigious medical school, and has had an unbroken string of jobs in interesting settings since. He represents dominant culture in his life; in that culture, lives such as that of my patient simply do not happen. How would he respond, how would he cope, if presented with the set of circumstances that this woman must deal with every day? What effect would it have upon him to be a priori not believed whenever he said that something hurt, or was frightening? If he spent hours at the job each day fearing reinjury, the target of verbal abuse and humiliation, how might he feel?

To deny that this patient's, and many other women's experiences of trauma, are in fact traumatic, and to insist that only the disordered and diseased would respond to such treatment with severe distress, sends a message that oppression, be it based on gender, class, race, or other variables, is to be tolerated; that psychic pain in response to oppression is pathological, not a normal response to abnormal events. It is *not* seen as traumatic. Unfair treatment at work, sexual harassment in academia—annoying, yes; traumatic, no. More times than I care to count I have heard women who have survived such circumstances accused of overreacting; as one defender of a sexual harasser said, "Well she wasn't raped, was she?" To admit that these everyday assaults on integrity and personal safety are sources of psychic trauma, to acknowledge the absence of safety in the daily lives of women and other nondominant groups, admits to what is deeply wrong in many sacred social institutions and challenges the benign mask behind which everyday oppression operates. A collusion of the mental health professions with this oppressive dominance can be found in the rigid insistence that these events, regardless of their felt and lived impacts, cannot be "real" trauma.

Another function of these rigid parameters for the definition of genuine traumatic events is to maintain the myth of the willing victim of interpersonal violence, a myth that serves to uphold power relationships in a hetero-patriarchal society between women and men, between people of color and white people, between poor people and those with wealth. Again, I have yet to find literature on the supposed preexisting personality traits of mugging victims that may render them prone to being the targets of such violence; mugging is one of the few high base-rate types of interpersonal violence that is an equal opportunity crime. But look for a moment at gay-bashing; roughly the same behaviors can happen as in any mugging, except that the victim is clearly being targeted because he or she is believed by the assailants to be gay or lesbian. Articles on the so-called "propensity" of gay men to be assault or murder victims *do* exist and were cited by such legislative homophobes as Jesse Helms and William Dannemeyer when attempts were first made to include sexual orientation as a category of analysis for hate crimes as evidence that gays and lesbians bring such violence upon ourselves (Berrill and Henek, 1990).

And while remarkable strides have been made in the past two decades toward altering this sort of analysis of the survivors of gender-based violence such as wife abuse, incest, and rape, we currently find ourselves in a regressive period, in which a new perspective on victim-blame, the codependency movement, has entered the public mind as a way to pathologize the victims (Brown, 1990). Battered women are not, from the frame of a codependency analysis, the victims of random violence, rendered phenomenologically helpless by the relentless behaviors of their abuser. Rather, they are "relationship addicts," perpetually ill and forever in need of treatment, who seek out such relationships because of their illness (Norwood, 1985). Incest survivors who have problems with intimacy as adults are not manifesting survival skills honed during long years of repetitive assault; they are "sex addicts," no different from this analytic framework, than those who assaulted them (Kasl, 1989).

If we maintain the myth of the willing victim, who we then pathologize for her presumed willingness, we need never question the social structures that perpetuate her victimization. It is far easier to say that a woman sexually harassed on the job has returned to work every day (and thus to the clutches of the harasser) because she somehow enjoyed it or was drawn to being harassed by her preexisting characterological pathology than it is to ask what will become of this woman if she complains or leaves to try to find other work. When we ask, we are disconcerted by the answers, by learning that this woman may never again find a job or may be cast out into the outer reaches of her workplace, where she can be edged out, made superfluous.

Similarly, if we continue to blame nonparticipating mothers for their husbands' incestuous attacks on their daughters by engaging in long discourses on how these women must have set up their daughters, or were triangulated with them, or had abdicated their mother role (or you can fill in the blank), we are excused from asking what kind of culture continues to reproduce fathers who rape their own children. We develop a diagnosis of "self-defeating personality disorder" to describe the victims, defining the expressions of their psychic trauma as their own inherent pathology (American Psychiatric Association, 1987). We do not, instead, ask ourselves whether we perhaps need to expand and make more complex our definitions of psychic trauma and its wake.

My feminist therapist colleague, Maria Root, has begun to develop the concept of "insidious trauma" (Root, 1989, 1992). By this, she refers to the traumatogenic effects of oppression that are not necessarily overtly violent or threatening to bodily well-being at the given moment but that do violence to the soul and spirit. Her model suggests, for instance, that for all women living in a culture where there is a high base rate of sexual assault and where such behavior is considered normal and erotic by men, as it is in North American culture, is an exposure to insidious trauma. Most women in North America today are aware that they may be raped at any time and by anyone. All of us know someone like ourselves who was raped, more often than not in her own home by a man she knew. In consequence, many women who have never been raped have symptoms of rape trauma; we are hypervigilant to certain cues, avoid situations that we sense are high risk, go numb in response to overtures from men that might be friendly—but that might also be the first step toward our violation.

Often the only way we avoid these manifestations of trauma is to assiduously rely upon the defenses of denial and minimization: "it will never happen to me." Insidious rape trauma is a part of everyday life for those women whose denial structures are less well padded. And each day, new assaults upon that denial greet us; the much-publicized rape of the Central Park jogger has killed forever the myth that you can run away if you're strong enough. For each nondominant group in this society, similar phenomena operate: the African-American who must constantly anticipate a Howard Beach, the lesbian or gay man who must walk in fear of being murdered for whom they love, the person with a disability never knowing when she or he will be dropped, perhaps fatally, through the cracks of the social so-called safety net. All of these people encounter insidious trauma.

How then, do we understand the woman whose symptoms of psychic trauma have occurred entirely at secondhand, as it were, through the mechanism of insidious trauma? Mainstream trauma theory has begun to recognize that post-traumatic symptoms can be intergenerational, as in the case of children of survivors of the Nazi Holocaust. We have yet to admit that it can be spread laterally throughout an oppressed social group as well, when membership in that group means a constant lifetime risk of exposure to certain trauma. When we do so, and start to count the numbers of those for whom insidious trauma is a way of life, we must, if we have any morality, question a society that subjects so many of its inhabitants to traumatic stressors.

## Life in the Expanded Range

If we begin to admit the feminist perspective on psychic trauma, and to include as traumatic stressors all of those everyday, repetitive, interpersonal events that are so often the sources of psychic pain for women, then our worldview changes as well. When trauma is unusual, we can pretend safety, engage in the daily self-deceptions that allow us to believe ourselves beyond the reach of the unusual. We can be spectators, titillated by the thrill of risk, safe behind our imaginary psychic barriers; or we can watch in horror as trauma happens to others but reassure ourselves that we are not next because we are safe so long as we do not protest, do not stick out our necks and "make" ourselves into the target. We can ignore the institutions of the society that appear to privilege us as long as we pretend that we will not be next (Pharr, 1988).

But when we admit to the immanence of trauma in our lives, when we see it as something more likely to happen than not, we lose our cloak of invulnerability. A feminist analysis, illuminating the realities of women's lives, turns a spotlight on the subtle manifestations of trauma, allows us to see the hidden sharp edges and secret leghold traps, whose scars we have borne or might find ourselves bearing. We are forced to acknowledge that we might be next. We cannot disidentify with those who have already been the victims of a traumatic stressor when we hold in consciousness our knowledge that only an accident may have spared us thus far. "It could have been me, but instead it was you, and it may be me, dear sisters and brothers, before we are through," sings Holly Near, in a poetic expression of what it means to know deeply that we are all vulnerable. And when we make this identification, admit that we can all be on the receiving end, we rest much less easily with those institutions of the society which might eventually make us their target.

A feminist perspective on trauma requires us to move out of our comfortable positions—as those who study trauma, or treat its effects, or categorize its types—to a position of identification and action. When we do so, we must be prepared for the scorn of some of our colleagues at our loss of so-called objectivity; we must anticipate the diagnostic inferences regarding our own pathology, which will emerge when we approach the study of trauma as a step in challenging and changing those social institutions that wound and keep wounds open rather than as another interesting topic that engages only the intellect and not the soul. Such action emerges from a feminist analysis, from a feminist vision of right relationship, in which mutuality and respect are the norm rather than power and dominance (Heyward, 1989). I have found, in my work as a specialist in the treatment of survivors of inter-personal violence, the assumption by many colleagues that I must myself be such a one; how else, they reason, to explain my apparent preoccupation wtih the subject, my insistence that understanding trauma and its effects is essential for the practical of ethical psychotherapy. I have been diagnosed from afar as having issues to be worked through, whose resolution would be manifested by the end of my activism on this topic.

In fact, I have so far been spared all but the "normal" insidious traumata of being a woman, a Jew, and a lesbian; I only must deal with the small violences to the spirit that any such as I encounter in daily life. I am cush-ioned by my white skin, my upper-middle-class status, my education and access to language and resources. No one has *yet* beaten or raped me, or torn me from my home or taken my job or threatened my life. This is not to say that no one ever will. By insisting that the personal is political, a holy truth of the feminist vision, it is impossible to remove myself and my experiences from my understanding of the etiology, meaning, and treatment of psychic trauma. I must be willing to face its presence and potential in my life, to understand the political and social realities in which I am situated and which will wound me no matter how adamantly I deny it. And thus it is impossible to not attempt to ameliorate the problem at its source, in the larger society. If I, if any of us who work in the field of trauma are not to be numbed psychically, we must hear our patients, our research participants, ourselves into speech and action to change that which would wound again.

A feminist analysis thus raises different questions, moves us to reevaluate our approach to working with the survivors of trauma. How, rather than de-sensitizing survivors to symptom triggers, a currently fashionable approach to the treatment of post-traumatic symptoms, can we help them to recon-struct their worldviews with the knowledge that evil can and does happen? Rather than teaching trauma survivors ways to attain their pretrauma levels of denial and numbness, how can we facilitate their integration of their painful new knowledge into a new ethic of compassion, feeling with, struggling with the web of life with which they relate? How can those of us who do the work of therapy with survivors become, not traumatized by our exposure to these stories of pain, but heightened in our sensitivity, exquisitely aware of how life needs to be fine-tuned, moved to be the changer and the changed?

In understanding post-traumatic symptomatology, a feminist analysis leads us to factor in the effects of long-standing insidious trauma. Rather than looking to biological vulnerability, or to the presence of previous pathology, to explain severity and intensity of symptoms (van der Kolk, 1987), we might begin instead to ask how many layers of trauma are being peeled off by what appears initially to be only one traumatic event or process? Simple bereavement may not be simple if this death happens after too many others; job loss may be traumatic when occurring in the context of extreme economic scarcity. Yet currently both of these events are specifically excluded from the set of potentially traumatic stressors by the authors of the DSM III-R. To steal from Stein, from Gertrude Stein, a trauma is not a trauma is not a trauma. Social context, and the individual's personal history within that social context, can lend traumatic meaning to events that might be only sad or troubling in another time and place.

Ultimately, a feminist analysis of the experience of psychic trauma requires that we change our vision of what is "human" to a more inclusive image and will move us to a radical revisioning of our understanding of the human condition. The mental health disciplines, assigned to the position of secular high priests, are faced with a choice. Do we, as did Freud a century ago, betray the truth of what we know of the immediacy and frequency of traumatic events in daily life (Masson, 1984)? Or do we follow the radical potential of psychoanalysis, which opened the doors to the unconscious and the irrational, to the next stage in which we retell the lost truths of pain among us? Do we act as handmaidens of the status quo, saying that only those already ill suffer from cultural toxicity? Or do we name as poisonous those institutions of society that might sicken anyone?

A feminist perspective, which draws our attention to the lives of girls and women, to the secret, private, hidden experiences of everyday pain, reminds us that traumatic events do lie within the range of normal human experience. Faced with this reality, we will be moved to include in our understanding of human responses those events that *are* unusual. A feminist perspective on the trauma of war is different because it includes a knowledge of the social context and because it factors the presence of daily and insidious trauma into an analysis of what is now the only "real" trauma (Brown, 1987). When we begin to acknowledge that reality, we make our professions revolutionary; we challenge the status quo and participate in the process of social change.

## Epilogue

As this volume goes to press, the definition of a traumatic stressor in the upcoming revision of the APA's DSM IV is undergoing change. In the past several years, many people who work with the survivors of interpersonal violence have been raising questions similar to those that I advanced in this chapter. Some of our concerns have been heard; Criterion A for post-traumatic stress disorder will no longer require that an event be infrequent, unusual, or outside of a mythical human norm of experience. There will be more reliance upon the person's subjective perceptions of fear, threat, and risk to well-being. There may be some acknowledgment, based upon the research field trials for the revision process, that certain sorts of traumatic events, such as rape and criminal victimization, are not only not unusual, but quite frequent. However, the definition falls short of encompassing many of the questions raised by a feminist analysis. While the debate is moving forward in the field of trauma, some of the questions raised by a feminist analysis about the nature and meaning of the continuum of trauma in a world where some people are never free of exposure to some sort of traumatic stressor continue to be salient and necessary. These revisions to the *Diagnostic and Statistical Manual* also continue to beg the question of whether all of the interpersonal and interpsychic effects of trauma can be adequately described with one diagnosis. The DSM IV revision has failed to provide us with a diagnosis to describe the effects of exposure to repetitive interpersonal violence and victimization.

One final note. I began this chapter with a description of my courtroom encounter with a lawyer questioning the traumatic nature of incest. I have since had the pleasure, as it were, of having lawyers read this work out loud to me in court in attempts to discredit my views. One attorney attempted to portray the title as suggesting that my ideas were "outside the range." Several others have tried to distort the references to insidious trauma as representing the view that all women have PTSD (inferring that I was wildly out of control in my application of this diagnosis). Still another read the personal descriptors referencing my membership in target groups to try to evoke homophobia in a jury (unsuccessfully, I might add, to judge by the outcome of the case). Such can be the results of joining in the scholarly discourse on trauma through a different, if not necessarily dissenting, voice. These are not results I shrink from but are evidence of the profound difficulties encountered when attempts are made to bring feminist analysis—and the feminist transformation of the personal into the theoretical—to bear on the nature and meaning of trauma.

## References

American Psychiatric Association. 1987. *Diagnostic and Statistical Manual of Mental Disorder.* 3d ed., rev. Washington, D.C.: APA.

Berrill, Kevin T., and Gregory M. Herek. 1990. "Violence against Lesbians and Gay Men: An Introduction." *Journal of Interpersonal Violence* 5:269–73.

Brown, Laura S. 1986. "Diagnosis and the Zeitgeist: The Politics of Masochism in the DSM-III-R." Paper prepared for the Convention of the American Psychological Association, Washington, D.C.

———. 1987. "From Alienation to Connection: Feminist Therapy with Post-Traumatic Stress Disorder." *Women and Therapy* 5:13–26.

———. 1989. "Victimization as a Risk Factor for Depressive Symptomatology in Women." Paper prepared for the Convention of the American Psychological Association, New Orleans.

———. 1990. "What's Addiction Got to Do with It? A Feminist Critique of Codependence." *Psychology of Women Newsletter* 17:1–4.

Heyward, Carter. 1989. *Touching Our Strength: The Erotic as Power and the Love of God.* San Francisco: Harper and Row.

Kasl, Charlotte D. 1989. *Women, Sex, and Addiction: A Search for Love and Power.* New York: Ticknor and Fields.

Lerman, H. 1986. *A Mote in Freud's Eye: From Psychoanalysis to the Psychology of Women.* New York: Springer.

Masson, Jeffrey. 1984. *The Assault on Truth: Freud's Suppression of the Seduction Theory.* New York: Farrar, Straus, Giroux.

Norwood, Robin. 1985. *Women Who Love Too Much.* Los Angeles: Tarcher.

Pharr, Suzanne. 1988. *Homophobia: A Weapon of Sexism.* Inveness, Calif.: Chardon.

Root, Maria P. P. 1989. "A Model for Understanding Variations in the Experience of Traumata and Their Sequelae." Paper prepared for the Eighth Advanced Feminist Therapy Institute, Banff.

———. 1992. "Reconstructing the Impact of Trauma on Personality." In *Personality and Psychopathology: Feminist Reappraisals,* ed. L. S. Brown and M. Ballou. New York: Guilford.

Russell, Diana. 1986. *The Secret Trauma: Incest in the Lives of Girls and Women.* New York: Basic Books.

van der Kolk, Bessel A. 1987. *Psychological Trauma.* Washington, D.C.: American Psychiatric Press.

# Freud: Frontier Concepts, Jewishness, and Interpretation

### HAROLD BLOOM

## I

Wittgenstein, memorably attacking Freud in conversation and in lectures, said of psychoanalysis that it was essentially speculation, not even reaching the level of hypothesis (1966). Like a related remark, in which Wittgenstein observed that Freud failed to distinguish between reasons and causes, such an attack has a dialectical undersong that unintentionally celebrates Freud while illuminating him. "A powerful mythology" was Wittgenstein's concluding judgment upon psychoanalysis, a judgment that can be interpreted antithetically as another involuntary tribute to Freud's mythologizing power. Perhaps it was not what he took to be Freudian muddles that most provoked Wittgenstein. Freud's peculiar strength was to say what could not be said, or at least to attempt to say it, thus refusing to be silent in the face of the unsayable. Freud is not philosophy, but then Montaigne also is not philosophy.

Speculation, rather than theory, is Freud's mode, as it was Montaigne's. It hardly matters that Montaigne cheerfully and knowingly also confused reasons with causes, or if it matters it is only to enrich his discourse. Freudian speculation may or may not be scientific or philosophical; what counts about it is its interpretative power. All mythology is interpretation, but interpretation only becomes mythology if it ages productively. Interpretation that dies young or ages barrenly is exposed as gossip. Montaigne, just short of Shakespeare, is the dominant mythologist of the later Renaissance. Freud, short of no one, is the dominant mythologist of our time, whatever our time turns out to have been.

In *The New Introductory Lectures on Psychoanalysis*, Freud boldly admitted that "the theory of the drives is, so to speak, our mythology" (Freud, 1933, 95). Drives (or "instincts," in Strachey's language in the *Standard Edition*) represent somatic demands upon the psyche, or as Philip Rieff elegantly phrased it, the drive is to Freud "just that element which makes any response inadequate" (1961, 32). Bodily demands upon the soul are difficult to distinguish from psychic demands upon the body. Demands made across the frontier between inwardness and outwardness are conceptually peculiar, yet are crucial always for Freud, whose prideful dualism is more at war with outwardness than is generally recognized. Frontier concepts therefore have a hidden importance in Freud's work. I want to examine two of them here: the status of the drives and their ambiguous relation to the mechanisms of defense; and the even more difficult notion of the bodily ego, with its baffling relation to the nonrepressive defenses of introjection and projection. Partly I want to clarify these border speculations, if I can, but I am only an amateur student of psychoanalysis, and so can make no contribution to it. But I am a professional student of literary interpretation, and I suspect that psychoanalysis and criticism alike are belated versions neither of philosophy nor of religion, but of certain ancient modes of speculation, Hebraic and Hellenic. Frontier speculation marks both the Hebrew prophets and the Greek sages, whether pre-Socratics or later Neoplatonists. To ask either psychoanalysts or critics to become prophets and sages may be absurd, but a prophet or sage in our time is unlikely to become either a philosopher or one of the religious.

Psychoanalysis, as a speculation, is itself an interpretation, rather than method of interpretation. Freud, in his later phases, found his prime precursor in Empedocles; I will show that he could have found another true forerunner in Jeremiah. Empedocles and Jeremiah hardly are models for contemporary literary criticism, though they have their affinities with some of the greater critics of the nineteenth century; with Coleridge, Carlyle, Emerson, Ruskin, and Pater, or again with Nietzsche and Kierkegaard. I am suggesting that Freud's possible relation to contemporary criticism differs only in degree, not in kind, from the possible relation to us of Emerson, Pater, and Nietzsche. Exploring Freud's dualism by way of his frontier concepts, we might come upon just what it is about interpretation that survives the extinction of particular meanings, or even the evanescence of the objects of interpretation.

## II

In London, during the summer of 1938, Freud outlined psychoanalysis for a last time in his unfinished *Abriss*. The second chapter states very boldly what Freud calls "the Theory of the Drives" (1940, 148). What is oldest in us, the "it" or id, contains the drives, which originate in the body and first psychically express themselves in the id *in forms unknown to us*. Behind the tensions, Freud asks us to assume the existence of forces that he chooses to call "drives." Freud's most surprising professed disciple, the late Jacques Lacan, charmingly said of the Freudian drive "that it has no day or night, no spring or autumn, no rise and fall. It is a constant force" (1977, 165). If anything resembles the drive, Lacan added, "it is a *montage*" (169). Drive, Lacan seems to have meant, cannot be actual, vital human force in any sense, cannot be natural. This raises the nice question of how Eros can be other than natural? What is not cyclic, not seasonal, not like the ocean *in* Eros *is* drive. Since we cannot know drive, it becomes the unknowable and unconscious element in Eros. I believe myself to be expounding Freud and not Lacan when I indicate as the first power of the concept of drive that it recaptures what high literature and life experience always tell us about Eros: *we are driven*, and most strongly against conscious desire. What the archaic Greeks called a god, Freud calls a drive, or again, what the Greeks called daemonic, Freud will also call daemonic. A good materialist, Freud was too good an observer not to know that we are driven by something beyond material knowledge.

But what exactly is the Freudian drive, if it is a bodily demand that makes every mental response inadequate? Nothing mythological could sustain that question, and to go back to Freud's own authority, in the *New Introductory Lectures*: "The theory of the drives is so to say our mythology. Drives are mythical entities, magnificent in their indefiniteness" (1933, 95). *Magnificent in their indefiniteness* is a marvelous formula, and not so humorous as it sounds. We are incessantly pushed and pressured by a shadowy splendor, which we recognize only through the tensions supposedly caused by its force. Aside from these tensions, all that we know about the drive is its nonlocation. It is neither in the body nor in the mind, but on the frontier between the outward and the inward. Yet that beautifully locates our tensions, which are neither bodily nor psychic but hovering on or near those ghostly demarcations, as our circumference flows in or out. Drive becomes the guarantee that the narcissistic omnipotence of thought is an illusion, but also that the universe of sense, the body, has only a wavering power over the mind.

I am suggesting that the ambiguous status of the drive is at once the key to, and the defense of, Freud's kind of dualism, a dualism neither Pauline nor Cartesian, neither Platonic nor Hegelian. Rather, it is precisely a speculative dualism, and thought it may seek to be Empedoclean, I would locate it, after all, in prophetic and normative tradition, that is to say, in Jewish thought and sensibility. Few questions of spiritual or intellectual history are as vexed as the Jewishness of Freud. It mystified Freud, more than he knew, and we go on weakly misreading it. We ought to judge it in relation to Freud's profound and unstated assumptions: convictions about time, memory, hierarchy, rationality, ethics, morality, continuity, above all ambivalence towards the self and towards others. Jewish dualism is neither the split between body and soul, nor the abyss between subject and object. Rather it is the ceaseless agony within the self against not only all outward injustice but also against what might be called the injustice of outwardness, or more simply, the way things are. The *Nevi'im* or prophets inherit the Torah's skeptical inwardness, a spirit that drove Abraham upon his original journey, and that fostered the Second Commandment's rejection of all outward appearances. What appears to be most original in Elijah and in all his descendants down through Malachi is the exaltation of skeptical inwardness as the true mode of preparing to receive the God-word. When a prophet says: "The God-word was to me," everything turns upon the meaning of that "me." It is not meaning, but will, that gets started when Yahweh speaks. Meaning is there already in the prophetic "me," which as an ego is far closer to what we might call "the psychoanalytic ego" than to "the Romantic ego" of nineteenth- and twentieth-century Western philosophy and literature. The Romantic ego is the product of, and the protest against, a double split in consciousness, between the adverting mind and its object in nature, and between the mind and the body it inhabits. But the psychoanalytic ego is indeed what Freud calls "the bodily ego"; as he says: "The Ego is first and foremost a bodily Ego." What this rather profoundly means is that the ego frames itself on the paradigm of the human body, so that all the processes of the ego frame themselves also upon the paradigm of the body's processes. Human sexual activity and human cognition alike thus model themselves upon the processes of eating, or excreting, of the stimulation of the genitalia. The consequence is that sexual intercourse and thinking can be assimilated to one another, and to the specific locations of mouth, anus, genitals.

To visualize the ego as a body is to admit the image that pictures the ego physically ingesting the object of the drive, the image of introjection or swallowing-up the object. In *The Ego and the Id* (1923), Freud told us that the bodily ego "is not merely a surface entity, but is itself the projection of a surface." Freud's remark, as he apparently recognized, is quite difficult, and he evidently authorized an explanatory footnote in the English translation of 1927, which, however, does not appear in any of the German editions. The footnote reminds us that the ego ultimately derives from bodily sensations, particularly sensations springing from the surface of the body. Is the bodily ego then a mental projection of the body's surface? Where would the frontier between body and psyche be in such a projection? Like the Freudian concept of the drive, the notion of the bodily ego seems to lie precisely upon the frontier between the mental and the physical. Presumably, we can know neither the body nor the bodily ego; we can know only the drives and the defenses. Freud implies that the drives and the bodily ego alike are constructed ambivalently, that is to say, from their origins they are dualistic. In both, the borders between the psychical and the somatic are forever in dispute.

I want to go back a long way in finding a similar vision of ambivalence. Freud, of course, was willing to go back to Empedocles and Heraclitus. I think Freud was closer even to Jeremiah, doubtless unknowingly. Ancient Jewish dualism does not oppose body to spirit, or nature to mind, but rather sets outwardness against inwardness. Jeremiah, rather than Freud, is the initial discoverer of the bodily ego, of an untraceable border between selfhood and the somatic. For the Romantic Ego, whether in Hegel or Emerson, the body is part of the Not-Me. But for Freud, as for Jeremiah, the body is uneasily part of the Me, and not part of the external world. The drive, which excites from within, and so menaces the ego, is a somatic demand upon the psyche, and is very different from an external excitation of any kind. When Freud speaks of the psyche's "surface," he means perception and consciousness, and he founds this meaning upon what we commonly try to mean when we speak of the "surface" of the body.

Freud could speak of the bodily ego or the drives or even the defense of introjection as *frontier* concepts only because his image of the ego was that of the body, of a living organism. A body can be attacked and penetrated from without; it has a demarcation that needs defense, and can be defended. The bodily ego could as well have been called the egoistic body, because Freud's crucial metaphor is that of *inwardness* itself. "Inwardness" is the true name of the bodily ego. The defensive disorderings of the drive, or the vicissitudes of instinct, are figures of *outwardness*, or of what the prophet Jeremiah might have called "the injustice of outwardness."

In Chapter 20 of Jeremiah, the prophet laments to God that God has enticed him, and has overcome him, so as to make Jeremiah a mockery. But if Jeremiah seeks to speak no more in God's name:

Then there is in my heart as it were a burning fire
Shut up in my bones,
And I weary myself to hold it in,
But cannot.

The burning fire or inwardness drives outward, in a movement that culminates in the magnificence of Chapter 31, where God speaks of the days coming when he will make a new covenant with the house of Israel, in which all outwardness will be abolished: "I will put My law in their inward parts, and in their heart will I write it." Call this the ancient Jewish negation of the outward, since it is a new perspective upon the genesis of the ego. Indeed, it is a privileged perspective that has no relation to the external world. The drive out from inwardness, from the Freudian id, takes the ego as its object; it does not generate the ego. Doubtless, a strict psychoanalytic reading of Jeremiah would say that he is manic, and stretches his own ego until it introjects God, or the ego ideal; whereas earlier, Jeremiah had been depressive and melancholic, projecting his own ego out of self-hatred and self-abandonment. But such clinical judgment, whether accurate or not, is less vital than the striking similarity between Jeremiah's negative dualism and Freud's. Both erase the frontier between psyche and body and in its place install a narcissistic ambivalence. The difficult concept of the bodily ego, in which an imaginary object is introjected as though it were real, is uncannily similar to the prophetic concept of the placing of the law in our inward parts. Surely we have underestimated the conceptual difficulties of the bodily ego. How after all can a thought become an object, when the bodily ego has introjected it? How can the law be inscribed upon our inward parts?

The movement from psyche to body, in Freud, or the thrust out from inwardness, is what presumably is conveyed by his fundamental myth or metaphor, the theory of the drives. But if the bodily ego is a tough notion, the drive is even more ambiguously located upon the interpretative frontier. No single metaphor in all of twentieth-century literature is as vital or troubling as Freud's late nineteenth-century image of the drive, transformed by him in 1919–20 into the crucial modern image of human force and desire, not the less crucial for all its crudely mechanistic aspects.

Even though Freud never identified his mechanistic models with the aspects of mind they represented, he evidently underestimated his own powers of representation. Or perhaps that underestimation itself was another strategy for enhancing rhetorical persuasiveness. Thus, the frontier concept of the drive is a remarkably devious representation, to the extent that it is unclear exactly what it is that the drive is intended to represent. The book of the drive (as the Lacanians call it) is the much-revised *Three Essays on the Theory of Sexuality*, where the drive initially receives the most ambiguous and baffling definition of any Freudian term:

> By "drive" is provisionally to be understood the psychical representative of an endosomatic, continuously flowing source of stimulation, as contrasted with a "stimulus," which is set up by *single* excitations coming from *without*. The concept of drive is thus one of those lying on the frontier between the mental and the physical. The simplest and likeliest assumption as to the nature of drives would seem to be that in itself a drive is without quality, and, so far as mental life is concerned, is only to be regarded as a measure of the demand made upon the mind for work. What distinguishes the drives from one another and endows them with specific qualities is their relation to their somatic sources and to their aims. The source of a drive is a process of excitation occurring in an organ and the immediate aim of the drive lies in the removal of this organic stimulus. (1905, 68)

This is Freud in 1915, revising earlier statements of 1905 and 1910, but doubtless remembering his still earlier distinction between internal and external excitations, the internal being those from which we cannot flee by repression. Unquestionably, Freud's polemical purpose in positing the nature of the drive was to dismiss any notion that the sexual drive had a particular object or a particular aim. But that purpose is less vital now than the curious location of the force of excitation that attacks us from within. Is it bodily? Is it psychic? What can Freud mean when he says that this force, this drive, lies on the frontier between the mental and the physical? How can the body be represented *within the psyche*? The metaphor is odd in itself. If the body sends an ambassador or delegate to represent it in the parliament of the psyche, as it were, then who else sits in that parliament? Are there other envoys there, and if so, whom do they represent?

I hasten to remind myself that this difficult metaphor is not mine, but indeed is Freud's own figure, the "psychical representative." Here is its crucial use in "Drives and their Vicissitudes":

> A drive appears to us as a borderland concept between the mental and the physical, being both the mental representative of the stimuli emanating from within the organism and penetrating to the mind, and at the same time a measure of the demand made upon the energy of the latter in consequence of its connection with the body. (Freud, 1915, 121–22)

Stimuli emerge from within us and then penetrate our minds in the form of a representation, and *that* representation is what Freud calls "the drive." But are we not again in the same dilemma we confronted in Freud's concept of the bodily ego? There, an imaginary object was introjected, which means that a thought can become an object, which is admirable science fiction, but hardly biology. Here, the drive can be known only through its psychical envoy, the ambassador that penetrates our mind. But what then is the drive? It is an entity always in exile, always wandering through one vicissitude or another, unavailable to consciousness except through those vicissitudes, which means that each vicissitude necessarily is psychical rather than physical. Since the vicissitudes sometimes can be characterized either as defenses *or* perversions, we have the further puzzle that defenses and perversions, and sado-masochism in particular, join the drive and the bodily ego as frontier concepts. But I have been discussing the Freud of the first theory of the mind, the Freud who did not yet have the vision of the death drive. What happens to frontier concepts in the new theory of the drive, the theory of aggression and sado-masochism set forth from 1919 to 1924?

Since the mind had been mapped anew, the perpetually strange frontier concept of the drive had to be thought through again also. In particular, the darkest wandering or exile of the drive, into the labyrinths of sado-masochism, required a very different chronicle from 1919 onwards than had been written in 1915, the year of the metapsychological papers. Narcissism was the concept whose development had precipitated Freud's self-revision, but I amend this now by emphasizing that the precise stimulus from intellectual change was the insight that narcissism, when severely wounded, transformed itself into aggressivity, both against the self and against others. Aggressivity however is one of those human qualities whose analysis Freud seems to have usurped forever, so that a non-Freudian vision of aggressivity, while possible, might be rather uninteresting. That raises again a problem this discourse hopes to help resolve: How are we to understand those Freudian speculations that have been able to exclude nearly all possible rivals, so that the Freudian theories have assumed the status of necessary postulates if thinking about the human is to prolong itself?

Is the drive still such an idea? In *An Outline of Psychoanalysis* (Freud, 1940), his final formulation, Freud is no more nor less overtly mythological in positing the drive than he was in the paper of 1915, "Instincts and Their Vicissitudes" (Freud, 1915). Twenty-five continuous years of revisionism did not alter Freud's fundamental fiction of the drive, though it thoroughly reoriented the drives from the dualism between self-preservation and erotic union, to the dualism between the erotic and deathly strife. Freud openly rejoiced, early and late, in the indefiniteness of his notion of drive, realizing as he did that the magnificence of the conception lay in its frontier nature, always hovering between the mind and the body. No response, psychic or somatic, can be adequate to the demands of the drive, for if the drive represents what the body demands of the mind (as Freud thought), the converse is curiously true also. The fantasies of defense, activated by the drive, come to represent initially what the mind demands of the body, which is that it cease the full force of its demands. Shall we say that defense can appear to be the mind's drive against the body, just as the drive proper can seem the body's defense against the mind? The drive, as Freud emphasized, is a constant force, to which I seek to add that defense is no less constant a force. Like Plato, St. Paul, and Descartes, Freud is indeed one of the greatest of Western dualists, not only accepting but in a way celebrating the mind-body division, making of it indeed a larger human issue than it is construed to be by philosophers. The exile of the drive into sadomasochism is the most dramatic Freudian story of just how the civil wars of the mind are modified by the endless wars between mind and body.

Freud's earliest thoughts on sadomasochism are recorded in the first edition (1905) of the *Three Essays on the Theory of Sexuality* and center themselves rather simply on the obvious truth that male sexuality "contains" aggressiveness (Freud, 1905). Sadism thus seemed prior to masochism in male sexuality, but Freud was too perceptive to accept that seeming, long before he came to see that masochism, not sadism, was primary and erotogenic. In 1905 he is capable of saying that the oppositional difference between sadism and masochism is not just due to aggressiveness, but also to bisexuality, so that necessarily sadist and masochist are one person (157–60). Since the contrast between active and passive in sadism and masochism is a universal characteristic of the sexual life, Freud is a touch misled by the ageless convention that the male is more active and so more sadistic. That he was not to be so very misled for very long is hinted by a brilliant footnote in the 1905 text (later to be removed), which locates one of the roots of presumably male masochism in the sexual overvaluation of the object.

Strong as it is in other aspects, the metapsychological paper of 1915 on the vicissitudes of the drive offers few insights that Freud himself could develop into an authentic theory of sadomasochism. What is curiously absent in 1915 is any attempt to uncover the origins of sadomasochism in the Oedipal fantasy. While the essay does consider, at its close, the pregenital sadistic-anal organization, it does not cross over into the context of what

Freud called the "family romance," which was true also of that book of the drive, the *Three Essays on the Theory of Sexuality*. Freud's first effort to bring together Oedipal ambivalences and the wandering of the drive into sado-masochism does not come until the extraordinarily dramatic paper of 1919, "A Child Is Being Beaten" (Freud, 1919). Here, in an essay that investigates a universal if unconscious sense of guilt, Freud prepares the ground concepts from which will spring, five years later, the most acute speculation upon the human "need for punishment" that any psychologist or theologian ever has written, "The Economic Problem of Masochism" (Freud, 1923, 157), with its dread and convincing analysis of "moral masochism," a kind of drive toward failure that has been a peculiar stigma of the spiritually and intellectually gifted in the Post-Enlightenment Western world.

Philip Rieff, introducing "A Child Is Being Beaten," remarked that the essay "contains some essential comparative material on the erotic develop-ment of male and female, with special emphasis on masochism" (1961, 9). Certainly, the material was essential for Freud's own emphasis upon the image of authority that fatherhood constitutes in the erotic life, but the developmental differences between male and female seem distorted, here as elsewhere, by the power the paternal image has in Freud's own imagination. Freud shared with Nietzsche the realization that, among Western images, only that of the father was neither origin nor end; or to state this most simply, that the West never speaks of "Father nature." Cave and ocean, earth and mountain, river and forest; all can be metaphors both of source and of finality. Only the sun, by being made a figuration of the father, becomes a natural image of what can keep origin and aim or end, apart. When we read an essay like "A Child Is Being Beaten," and are told that all beating-fantasies originate in the incestuous attachment to the father, on the part of both girls and boys, we wonder at first why Freud excludes the mother from such fantasies. The unconscious sense of guilt, we are informed, is punishment both for the genital relation fantasized to the father, and for the regressive substitutes that avoidance of the relation breeds in us, women and men alike. Freud, perhaps on one level, intended the literal or phallic father as the fantasy object, but the mythological profundity of the notion of the drive sets such literalism aside. The unconscious guilt is caused rather by our refusal of the mother, a refusal of origins made from the fear that to choose the origin is a choice also of the end, a choice of death by men and women alike.

If this interpretation itself seems fantastic, let us test it against the essay's incessant evasion of the image of the mother:

Who was the child that was being beaten? The one who was himself producing the phantasy or another? Was it always the same child or as often as not a different one? Who was it who was beating the child? A grown-up person? And if so, who? (1919, 181)

Freud's answer to that final question always is: the father of the child, who himself or herself produces the fantasy. Though Freud, here as elsewhere, is consistent in urging us not to sexualize the motive forces of repression, since only infantile sexuality can be such a force, he now verges on a curious remythologizing of his speculations upon infantile sexuality. The focus of fantasy in the Freudian story of the origins of sexuality was the mother's milk, but the fantasy that engenders sado-masochism leans itself against an aggressivity arbitrarily identified with what could be called the fathering force. What is perhaps most immediate in Freud's presentation is the rigor with which he analyzes all beating fantasies as having three distinct phases:

1) My father is beating the child (whom I hate). My father loves only me.
2) I am being beaten by my father (he does not love me).
3) Unknown boys (whether in girls' or boys' fantasies) are being beaten by a male teacher.

Of these three phases, Freud judges the first to be neither quite masochistic nor yet wholly sadistic, while the second is masochistic and the third still masochistic in gratification, since the sadistic element is merely formal. All three phases find their common origin, in both girls and boys, in the incestuous attachment to the father. But Freud adds that, in boys, the second phase should be rendered: "I am loved by my father," because a boy's beating fantasy is passive from the start "and is derived from a feminine attitude towards his father" (1919, 183–86). The Oedipus complex therefore dominates the origins of sadomasochism in both sexes. But why? It cannot be an accident that Adler, though unmentioned, receives his customary drubbing from Freud in the final paragraphs of this essay, where the conception of the masculine protest yet once more is dismissed as inadequate to meet the problem of the neuroses. Repression alone is the adequate conception, and the story of Oedipus becomes the story of Antigone also. And still, we must ask now: why is the image of the mother excluded by Freud from this account of the origins of the exile of the drive into masochistic gratifications?

I can find no answer in the text of "A Child Is Being Beaten" and move instead to the consideration of Freud's masterpiece on sado-masochism, "The Economic Problem in Masochism" (1923), one of those very brief essays (like "Negation" in 1925) that is Freud at his strongest. Where the economic stance is taken up, Freud deals always in the quantitative queries that measure force against force as being more than, equal to, or less than one another. Where the fathering force is that of the superego, driving the lesser force of the ego before it, then the economics of sadomasochism progress from "the unconscious sense of guilt" in "A Child Is Being Beaten" through "the need for punishment" and on to the extraordinary oxymoron of "moral masochism" in this essay. Freud has moved from exiling the drive, to what could be called a poetics of pain, in which the Oedipal imagination creates one of its masterpieces of ambivalence, akin to the intensity of the mythological taboos and the analytical transference. The simultaneous love and hatred of the psyche for itself brings a new middle-world into being, a world without origin or end, and so motherless, but with a father more dangerous even than the tyrant slain and devoured by the Primal Horde in *Totem and Taboo* (1912–13).

The economic problem in masochism presumably ought to be that in masochistic experience "the pleasure-principle is paralysed, the watchman of our mental life is to all intents and purposes himself drugged and asleep." This is eloquent, but like the opening of *Beyond the Pleasure Principle* (1920), it also may provoke an alert reader to some surprise. Once again, Freud allows himself to forget that his pleasure principle is primarily an unpleasure principle, since he has defined unpleasure as being too high an intensity of excitation. The drugged, sleeping watchman is therefore truly the un-pleasure/pleasure principle, which regards too much pleasure as painful anyway, and easily enough might experience the converse. Yet Freud might reply subtly that pleasure, in his view, depends upon the absence of stimulation, the release from the drive, whereas masochistic excitation could be judged to be a kind of perverse Sublime. As always, Freud's economic perspective is partly at fault, and yet remains true to the ironic complexities of male sexuality, where "normal" desire dies even as it is fulfilled. The more enduring desires of masochism, in males, trouble Freud, and perhaps prompt his remarkable distinctions between three types of masochism: *erotogenic, feminine*, and *moral.*

Erotogenic masochism, "the lust of pain," is said by Freud (1905) to underlie the other two forms. Moral masochism, which Freud judges the most important of the three, is closest to the unconscious. Feminine masochism Freud calls the least mysterious of these types, and so he begins with it. We can begin by observing that this "feminine" masochism is wholly a masculine phenomenon, as Freud proceeds to describe it, which is to say, he discusses it only in regard to men. Male masochists wish to be treated like naughty children, or to be "placed in a situation characteristic of womanhood." This situation remarkably is said to comprise being castrated, playing the passive part in coitus, or giving birth. And yet the description Freud gives makes abundantly clear that if "feminine" masochism castrates the father, it also minimizes the mother, even to the point of disavowal. There is no superego in the world of "feminine" masochism, but strictly speaking there is only a Platonized form of the bodily ego, in which thought returns completely to its altogether sexual past. Freud's "feminine" masochism turns out to be another frontier concept, another introjection by the body of an imaginary object, another ambassadorial mission sent by the body into the mind. We may say that the mental delegate of "feminine" masochism is the ultimate vicissitude of the drive, the final inability to know whether pain is physical or psychic, or even whether exile from oneself is more a somatic reality or a psychic delusion.

The dilemma of "feminine" masochism is a paradigm for every theoretical dilemma in Freud's map of the mind. Freud's scientism, his Helmholzean materialism and cruder dualism, commits him to outwardness as a version of the reality principle. But his passion for interpretation, his ultimately Jewish conviction that there is sense in everything, is truly a passion for inwardness, akin to Jeremiah's vision of God stamping the Law upon our inmost parts. Freud is driven to frontier concepts because his own conflict lies upon the frontier between an overdetermined outwardness and a prophetic inwardness. In such a conflict, the inward cannot fail to win, despite Freud's overt intentions, and the vicissitudes of the drive become nothing less than the injustices of all outwardness whatsoever.

Though I have questioned Freud's formulation of "feminine" masochism, albeit more in its name than in its nature, I know of no analysis of the entire phenomenon of masochism that approaches Freud's in scope, acuteness, and moral complexity. I want to complement Freud's account of masochism by speculating upon the relation of this exile of the drive to an unconscious sense of temporal loss, rather than to the unconscious sense of guilt. Literary representations of masochistic experience frequently emphasize a curious conviction of timelessness that comes upon tormentor and victim alike. More naive accounts frequently cite a paradoxical feeling of freedom, which seems to be the particular delusion of the victimized partner. Freud doubtless would relate such illusions of temporal freedom to the renewed childishness of masochistic experience, a regression hardly in the service of the ego. But there may be another kind of contamination of the drive with a defense also, one in which the drive encounters, not regression, but an isolating substitution, in which time is replaced by the masochist's body, and by the area around the anus in particular. Isolation is the Freudian defense that burns away context, and is a defense difficult to activate in normal sexual intercourse. When masochism dominates, isolation is magically enhanced, in a way consonant with Freud's description of isolation in obsessional neuroses. Writing two years after the paper on the economic problem in masochism, in the great book of 1926, *Inhibitions, Symptoms, and Anxiety* (1933), Freud described again what he had observed first in the "Rat Man" case, the defense that interposes an interval and so disrupts temporality. In the midst of a felt unpleasantness, active or passive, the obsessional neurotic creates a time span in which nothing further must happen, during which nothing is perceived and nothing is accomplished. Affect and associations alike fade away, and a magical compulsion concentrates the ego so as to remove it from all possibilities of contact with others or otherness. The perversion of masochism is not, for Freud, an obsessional neurosis but a vicissitude of the drive. And yet the defense of isolation, when it and the drive contaminate one another, is indistinguishable from erotogenic masochism. I venture that the thinking burned away by the isolating aspect of masochism is the thinking of temporality, the sense of loss and belatedness that an obsession with time brings about.

But what then happens to the proper and doubtless necessary Freudian distinction between the perversion of drive and the compulsive defense characteristic of obsession? I am venturing yet again the speculation that the border concept of the drive and the more empirical idea of defense have a more peculiar relation to one another in Freud's work than he himself realized. Their mutual contamination of one another constitutes Freud's implicit theory of temporality, in which time becomes the medium of exchange between the opposed dualities of body and mind. If drive is the somatic demand upon the mind, and so the body's prime defense against whatever in and about the mind is most antithetical to body, then defense may be the mind's drive against whatever that is bodily is inimical to mind. Each duality reads the other as time and so as change, and so at last as death. In such a vision the body and the mind never can be friends, and the necessity for conceptualizing a death drive becomes overwhelming.

I recall observing elsewhere that the superego, rather than the ego, let alone the id, is in some sense the most Jewish of the psychic agencies. Others have ventured that repression is in a complex way a peculiarly Jewish notion, related as it is to the programmatic sorrows of Jewish memory. I conclude this meditation though by venturing that Freud's most profound Jewishness, voluntary and involuntary, was his consuming passion for interpretation, a passion that led him into the wilderness of his frontier concepts. The psychical representative of the drive, not in the individual consciousness, but in human history, allegorically or ironically considered, is the image of a wandering exile, propelled onward in time by all the vicissitudes of injustice and outwardness, all the bodily oppressiveness that is inflicted upon the representatives of interpretation itself, as they make their way along the frontiers between mind and body, known and unknown, past and future.

## References

Freud, Sigmund. 1905 (1953). *The Standard Edition of the Complete Psychological Works of Sigmund Freud.* Vol. 7. Translated under the editorship of James Strachey in collaboration with Anna Freud, assisted by Alix Strachey and Alan Tyson. 24 vols. (1953–74). London: Hogarth.

———. 1912–13 (1955–58). *SE* 13.

———. 1915 (1957). *SE* 14.

———. 1919 (1955). *SE* 17.

———. 1920 (1955). *SE* 18.

———. 1923 (1961). *SE* 19.

———. 1926 (1959). *SE* 20.

———. 1933 (1964). *SE* 22.

Lacan, Jacques. 1977. *The Four Fundamental Concepts of Psycho-Analysis.* London: Hogarth.

Rieff, Philip. 1961. *Freud: The Mind of the Moralist.* New York: Anchor.

Wittgenstein, Ludwig. 1966. *Lectures and Conversations in Aesthetics, Psychology, and Religious Belief.* Berkeley: University of California Press.

# An Interview with
# Robert Jay Lifton

CATHY CARUTH

Robert Jay Lifton's work on Hiroshima, Vietnam, the Holocaust, the nuclear threat, and other catastrophic events of our age has had a tremendous impact on the consciousness of trauma in our era. On June 8, 1990, I met with him to discuss his vision of a psychology of life that gives death its due, that extends and modifies psychoanalysis around a full recognition of the centrality and import of traumatic experience.

## I. Trauma and Survival

*CC:* I would like to begin by discussing some of the implications, for trauma theory and therapy, of your notion of survival. In your essay "Survivor Experience and Traumatic Syndrome," you suggest that the experience of trauma can be approached through the psychology of the survivor (Lifton, 1979). And your discussion in the essay centers upon the notion of survival. Equally important in this essay is your emphasis on the view of trauma, which, as you say, "puts the death back into traumatic neurosis." This might seem to be something of a paradox: on the one hand the insistence on survival, on the other hand the insistence on death in the theory. I'd like you to comment on the significance of understanding trauma in terms of survival, and also on this apparent paradox.

*RJL:* Focusing on survival, rather than on trauma, puts the death back into the traumatic experience, because survival suggests that there has been death, and the survivor therefore has had a death encounter, and the death encounter is central to his or her psychological experience. Very simple point, but death gets taken out of most psychological thought very readily. Lots of people are sensitive to the idea of death, beginning with Freud, who was enormously sensitive to the idea of death; but he too felt it necessary to leave death out conceptually. So that the only place you really find death, conceptually, in Freud, is in the death instinct, which tells us about Freud's awareness of the pervasive influence of death, or some representation of death for us psychologically. But putting it in that sweeping instinctual structure has confused people ever since.

*CC:* When you talk about Freud's introduction of the notion of the death instinct, something that interests me is the fact that you don't immediately begin by talking about what Freud says *about* trauma or about death, but rather about the relation of the movement itself, of his theory and of his own movement, to trauma and survival:

> The impact of the traumas of World War I on Freud and his movement has hardly been recorded. The war's traumas to the movement must have been perceived as a struggle for survival. This psychoanalytic survival of World War I reactivated earlier death anxieties within the movement. The problem for Freud was to assimilate these experiences into his already well-developed theoretical system. (1979, 164)

One might say, on the basis of these lines, that you are characterizing psychoanalytic theory itself as a survivor. What does it mean to say that theory is a survivor? How does the notion of theory as a survivor change the nature of the knowledge it offers us, or what it knows and the way it knows?

*RJL:* The survival placed certain pressures upon, and brought certain questions to, the theory. The way Freud led psychoanalysis to survive World War I was to reintegrate that death experience into his instinctual theory. That meant in some degree sexualizing the death encounter through the focus, for instance, on narcissism, which is after all a sexual theory. Narcissism means, in strict psychoanalytic theory, the flow of libido into one's own body. So he sexualized the death experience to some extent, and he evolved the death instinct, which was in a way a means of responding to the death-saturated world he was living in, that he had encountered. His famous essay, written over the course of World War I, "Thoughts for the Times on War and Death," is an expression of a deepening of reflection on the part of a highly sensitive man faced with a new dimension of death saturation in his world. In that essay you can see one direction of his response, that is, to give death its due—which something in him wanted very much to do. I think that Freud was caught in a certain dilemma. He was always very sensitive to death, always aware of it, usually fearful of it in a personal sense. But it was never a central theme in the theoretical structure he built. And therein lay a conflict. He had to develop his theoretical structure in the way that he could. And therefore he had to bring his brilliant one-sidedness to what he created. Without that, it would be nothing. No theory, unless it is probing and one-sided, amounts to anything. The trick is to have that one-sidedness in creative tension with a certain amount of balance and fairness. But it has got to be one-sided. And his one-sidedness was in the direction of childhood sexuality, of libido theory. He therefore had to maintain his death awareness while minimally expressing it within his theory. And out came post–World War I psychoanalytic theory, the death instinct, and the key gambit that he engaged in was narcissism—really transforming death anxiety and the fear of disintegration into the idea of narcissism.

*CC:* It would appear from what you have just said, then, that the encounter between theory and death is a central source of insight, but that it appears indirectly, through a kind of distortion. In *The Broken Connection* you describe this process as psychoanalysis itself "putting up a protective shield" like a survivor, and thus warding off "the potentially transforming influence of death on theory." What is the potentially transforming influence of death on theory or, specifically, on the instinctual theory?

*RJL:* Let me begin with a personal anecdote. When [Jacques] Lacan came to Yale in 1975, there was one small dinner I was involved in, and as he began to express his ideas, I raised the following question. I said, "Well, Professor Lacan, with your enormous stress on symbolization, which I applaud, as it is very close to my own heart, why is it that you did not come to the broadest paradigm for symbolization, that is, death and life continuity, or that of a life-death parameter, rather than remaining in the model of Freud, which is instinct and defense or, essentially, sexuality and repression?" And he looked at me as only Lacan could, he didn't know me then, and he asked his right-hand woman of the time, "Who is that man?" And she said, "That's Robert Lifton." And he looked at me with those bright eyes and a smile and he said, "Je suis Liftonian." Now he was half mocking, you know, and then he said, "Yes, you're right. The logic of the situation would be a life-death parameter. I agree with you. However my own formation was the Other, so I stayed with it."

So, what is the transformative potential of death? Well, death potentially transforms anything and everything. It's the single consistent fact of existence. Everybody's said that in one way or another. But to take in death, that is, to be open to a death encounter, always means reassessing what is ultimate, significant, or as one of the people years ago in our study put it, "what counts." One asks the question of what really matters in one's life. It has to do with what is most powerful, most life affirming, and what can survive one's own death. Freud was always asking those questions, in terms of his theory. Any really serious theorist does. And there was never a more serious theorist than Freud, or a man more concerned with the lasting or, I would say, immortalizing aspects of his theory. However, he dismissed talk about immortality as denial of death. So the encounter with death for a theorist, and therefore for his or her theory, is a potential opening out; there are two possibilities, opening out or closing down. Freud did a little of both, as most of us do.

*CC:* If numbing is indeed, as you say, essential to the experience of confrontation, this seems to suggest that some of that closing down will take place in most theoretical formulations. There is a relation between that opening and that closing, that somehow they are going to occur together in a theory, when it's at its most powerful.

*RJL:* Yes, and that's an interesting point, to bring up the simultaneous process of closing and opening, and a key issue here is what Freud did with castration anxiety, or with death anxiety. Rather consistently, Freud said that the idea or fear of death is a displacement of castration anxiety. Once you say that, with the central role of castration anxiety in the Oedipus Complex for Freud's opus, for psychoanalysis, then you are relegating anxiety about death to a secondary phenomenon. That is, for me, a key aspect of covering over. I don't begrudge it—Freud is a great intellectual hero to me, and in a way one's capacity to step back from Freud and free onself from Freud to a degree enables one to appreciate him more.

I really see *The Broken Connection* as a continuous dialogue with Freud, and there were so many other people but in reworking the narrative over time, I found myself mostly cutting away the other thinkers or putting them in footnotes, because I wanted to get the flavor of what Freud had originally said. And I always found things that had been neglected. And yet I couldn't say them or didn't want to say them the way Freud did, because I saw myself always transmuting them into symbolizing theory, as opposed to instinctual theory. But it's very important for me that I understand myself as a child of Freud, as all of us are.

In a way I had several encounters with Freud. I began to read him in medical school and helped to organize a psychiatry club. And of course I read him on and off during my residency training and during psychoanalytic training. But I didn't really read him in a way that had full power until I separated myself from him and really wanted to understand what I could learn from him, relearn from him, take from him for these horrendous issues I was struggling with, especially Hiroshima. Because *The Broken Connection* really stems from the Hiroshima experience. And that was the main encounter. It opened me up a lot.

[Erik] Erikson was my connection with psychoanalysis and with Freud. Erikson's identity theory was a marvelous baseline for what I was encountering with the Chinese and their identity changes [during the writing of *Thought Reform*, 1969]. But from Hiroshima I had to go into other spheres, and it was really death-related spheres, and that didn't exist in Erikson, really. It was more in Freud, again, but in a very different way. I still remain enormously influenced by Erikson, to this day. But that second encounter with Freud really meant reexamining what I thought about the world, and what I was seeing in Hiroshima, and what I thought about my own life, and death. It was Hiroshima and Freud together, and *The Broken Connection* is in a way the result.

*CC:* So you're reading Freud through Hiroshima.

*RJL:* That's right, I'm reading Freud through my Hiroshima experience.

*CC:* You mentioned just now that confronting Freud again in a creative fashion, you were forced into talking about symbolization. Elsewhere, you say that the encounter between death and Freudian psychoanalytic theory "carries Freud beyond mere libido theory toward a concept of meaning . . . what one is willing or not willing to die for" (1979, 166). And this is what you are suggesting that you carry out in your own symbolization theory. What is the significance of focusing on meaning instead of instinct, specifically in a death-oriented psychology?

*RJL:* Instinct is not a psychological entity. If you believe in some kind of instinct, it's a kind of driving force. And Freud himself was always inwardly divided about whether instinct could be represented psychically. So Freud was inwardly divided whether or not something in *him* felt that instinct could not be represented. Anything that is psychological experience has to do with meaning. In that sense, meaning is the broadest kind of psychological entity. When one considers a life-death model or paradigm, it has to exist in relation to meaning, or in relation to how we symbolize our life process and our vitality, on the one hand, and our prospective end or individual death, on the other. And my path to a psychology of meaning is not via Lacan, but via [Ernst] Cassirer and [Susanne] Langer. What they taught us is that our central motivations, our central energies, come from actual or aspired-to meaning structures. How we want to understand, how we seek to understand something, how we want to see ourselves. I came to this as I came to think about the prospective element of the image. The first sentence of *The Broken Connection* is, "We live on images."

In a way, what I think happened with Freud, and I learned this partly from Erikson and very largely from Cassirer and Langer, as Freud struggled painfully to remain a scientist in the terms of his era, in the nineteenth-century terms of science, he often neglected the very thing that he had so importantly discovered, the aspect of experience, of psychological experience. He neglected it for theories of origin, which were primarily instinctual. And Erikson once called it—not so much talking about Freud as about his disciples perhaps—he called it "originology," in which you focus so much on the origin that you lose a sense of the flow of experience along the way. And one way to recover the importance of the flow of experience, as I came to see it, was to take imagery very seriously.

A very good example is in the dream, for instance. Here Erikson is wonderful. His paper on dream analysis may be the single greatest paper ever written on the dream, in my view anyhow. It's all about experience in the dream, while in no way abandoning Freud's theory of the dream. But in the quick return to childhood sexuality or the quick focus on issues of repression or ostensible sources of the dream in childhood psychopathology, the significance of the dream imagery can be underestimated. Image and meaning are inseparable. And really, in this kind of work, as in a lot of Erikson, there's a struggle to return to a focus on image, on meaning structure, and on the whole issue of form. That's why I speak of the formative process. And it's that quality of form and meaning that I think is central to human experience. Really, that's what literature tells us, as well as psychology, and when literary people embrace psychoanalytic theory, that's what they're doing—they are transmuting it into expressions of form and meaning.

*CC:* By talking about image and symbolization and meaning in terms of death, you seem to imply that all of that meaning at some point has a reference point in death rather than, say, in origination or in a causal model.

*RJL:* It's a complex matter for me. And I don't mean that death replaces instinct, I would rather say that symbolization replaces instinct. And therefore the causative principles become symbolizing principles, and issues having to do with symbols, images, and meanings. And what is causative from early on, is the struggle for vitality and, ultimately, for symbolic immortality, in my view. And that's why to me what I call death equivalents are crucial, because before you're about two or two and a half years old—and then it's just a glimmer of an image—you have lots of emotional experience that can relate to death equivalents: separation, fear of disintegration, or something like the experience of disintegration. And these connect with causative experience, but they're not instincts in my view, they are the precursors of imagery and symbolization. And that's where I find causation: in imagery, symbolization, and meaning. And in the end, imagery, symbolization, and meaning are in a life-death model or paradigm.

*CC:* I want to press you a little bit on the centrality of death in meaning, or the life-death continuum. There is a way in which your emphasis on meaning rather than on instinct—and meaning always in touch with a notion of death—helps us recognize something resistant or incomprehensible at the heart of traumatic experience. In your terms, this is what you call "numbing," "the experience of a decreased or absent feeling either during or after trauma," a "matter of feeling what should have been but was not experienced." You distinguish this numbing from repression, which excludes or forgets an idea; in numbing, rather, "the mind is severed from its own psychic forms, there's an impairment in the symbolization process itself." So it would seem in this case that a confrontation with death in trauma is a radical break with any kind of knowledge, or with what we normally think of as experience. But at the same time, you insist on the numbing experience as having potential for insight. How does one gain insight from such a radical break; or, what would be the relation between numbing and insight?

*RJL:* The insight begins with the shattering of prior forms. Because forms have to be shattered for there to be new insight. In that sense, it is a shattering of form but it is also a new dimension of experience. One of the great difficulties in all of the extreme situations I've studied is that people subjected to them had no prior images through which to connect with them, or very few. What in one's life would enable one to connect with Hiroshima? Here the assumption is that, and this is the radical insight of symbolizing theory, we never receive anything nakedly, we must recreate it in our own minds, and that's what the cortex is for. In creating, in recreating experience, we need some prior imagery in order to do that work, in order to carry through that process. And there was precious little prior imagery that could enable people to take in the Hiroshima experience, the event of a weapon apparently destroying an entire city.

So once they struggled with it and took it in, there was the capacity to enlarge on their own inner imagery, enlarge on their life experience. So that toward the end of all of my interviews, or of almost all of my interviews with people, with Hiroshima survivors and, say, survivors of Nazi camps, as different as they are, they talk about something they've learned. Some have amazed me and troubled me by saying they would not want to have missed the experience. People have said this to me about Nazi camps. And I felt strange at hearing that, because it was such a cool thing to say and think, cool toward themselves. But what they meant was, and they could only say it once it was over, that nonetheless they had experienced something that, when in some measure it was absorbed or even mastered to a degree, had enormous value for them, taught them something very important.

It was never very easy to say exactly what that was; it was often rather inchoate, as much in relation to extreme trauma tends to be. But it has to do with knowledge of death. It's related to the mythology of the hero, to a degree. The traditional psychoanalytic way of looking at the mythology of the hero is the confrontation with the father in the Oedipus Complex. That's not my way; though again, there are hints in psychoanalysis, in which the ordeal of the hero is a powerful confrontation with threat and death, and, really, the threat of annihilation. And he or she undergoes that ordeal: it's a call to greatness, it's the call that the hero experiences, and the ordeal is the struggle with death. And what the hero achieves is some degree of mastery in that struggle which he—it's usually a male hero—can bring back to his people. It's a knowledge of death and therefore a knowledge of life, to bring back. It's a profound new knowledge. So in that sense the survivor has lived out the mythology of the hero, but not quite. And that "not quite" is the tragic dimension of it, that you see, well, in the story of Primo Levi, who seemed to have mastered it to a degree that moved us, even thrilled us. And

135

then killed himself, as an elderly man, for reasons that we don't fully understand. But still in a way that tells us that he was still haunted by that experience.

*CC:* I would like to pick up on that "not quite" aspect of the survivor's experience, the sense that the survivor doesn't simply bring back a mastered knowledge of death. It seems to me to be connected with your comments elsewhere that death is "anticipatory" and from the beginning has an "absolute influence" on the human being: this would suggest that the confrontation itself might have that anticipatory quality of not being fully assimilated or known but projected into a future.

*RJL:* That's right. When I first began to talk about psychic numbing in relation to Hiroshima survivors, I learned that they required numbing, that is, the sudden cutting off of feeling, which couldn't be understood simply by repression [*Death in Life*, 1991]. It had elements of repression, elements of isolation, denial, almost any psychoanalytic defense mechanism you could name, but was primarily a cessation of feeling. And even those Hiroshima survivors who came to emerge as leaders, and who derived from their experience the greatest amount of learning or wisdom, or energy, had to make use of a certain amount of numbing, certainly at the beginning and subsequently in various subtle combinations with confrontation. So confrontation in the sense of letting in the death encounter is never total. It's always a mixture, of how much you can take in and how much you keep out. And I think that's important to understand and I probably haven't made that sufficiently clear in my work. Because it seems to hold out some ideal of absolute confrontation, which none of us is capable of. And going back to Freud's wisdom, you know Freud spoke of the protective shield, and he really saw the organism as constantly having to keep things out, as that being perhaps more a requirement of the psyche than taking things in, or at least as much a requirement. And it always was some combination thereof.

*CC:* This also seems linked to your notion of death as anticipatory, that is, as something you don't confront immediately, but is always there.

*RJL:* Yes, anticipatory in the sense that one brings to a death encounter one's own death imagery and one's own lifelong experience not only with death but with death equivalents, such as separation, and with the way in which these interact and become, in some sense, in some degree interchangeable

136

over the course of one's life, if it is an adult who has the traumatic experience. So these experiences always contribute to the self-process, which like all psychological experience, is anticipatory or prospective, moves forward.

In trauma one moves forward into a situation that one has little capacity to imagine; and that's why it shatters whatever one had that was prospective or experiential in the past. Whatever prospective consolations one brought to that experience. And being shattered, one struggles to put together the pieces, so to speak, of the psyche, and to balance that need to reconstitute oneself with the capacity to take in the experience. Something tells one, or one becomes partly aware, that if one doesn't take in some of it one is immobilized by the numbing, that the numbing is so extreme, in that kind of situation. But this is not a logical process, and it's not a conscious process primarily. So one is inwardly or unconsciously struggling with how to cohere and how to absorb and in some measure confront what one has had thrust upon one, what one has been exposed to. And that's what trauma is all about.

I also think about trauma in a new way that I've just begun to write about, in terms of a theory of the self. That is, extreme trauma creates a second self. What I mean by that is, as I came to think about role, and self, and identity: strictly speaking, in theory, there's no such thing as role. There's a lot of talk about role, but it can be misleading. Because to the extent that one is *in* anything there's a self-involvement. But in extreme involvements, as in extreme trauma, one's sense of self is radically altered. And there is a traumatized self that is created. Of course, it's not a totally new self, it's what one brought into the trauma as affected significantly and painfully, confusedly, but in a very primal way, by that trauma. And recovery from post-traumatic effects, or from survivor conflicts, cannot really occur until that traumatized self is reintegrated. It's a form of doubling in the traumatized person. And in doubling, as I came to identify it, there have to be elements that are at odds in the two selves, including ethical contradictions. This is of course especially true in the Nazi doctors, or people who doubled in order to adapt to evil. But in doubling in the service of survival, for life-enhancing purposes, as I think is true of people who undergo extreme trauma, as with Auschwitz survivors, as they say, "I was a different person in Auschwitz."

*CC:* Literally.

*RJL:* And it's almost literally true. So the struggle in the post-traumatic experience is to reconstitute the self into the single self, reintegrate itself. And it's in that combination of feeling and not feeling, that the creative aspect of the survivor experience, or the potentially illuminating aspect of the survivor experience, takes shape.

## II. A Perverse Quest for Meaning

*CC:* That brings us to my second major area of interest. You talk a lot about the notion of witnessing in trauma and the survivor mission, the impulse to bear witness, which is presumably part of the recovery process. But at the same time you talk about the possibility of what you call "false witness." And you say specifically, referring to incidents in Vietnam (My Lai), that atrocity is a "perverse quest for meaning, the end result of a spurious sense of mission, the product of false witness." What is the relation between witnessing and survival, and what are the implications for this process of the very possibility of false witnessing?

*RJL:* When one witnesses the death of people, that really is the process of becoming a survivor, and the witness is crucial to the entire survivor experience. The witness is crucial to start with because it's at the center of what one very quickly perceives to be one's responsibility as a survivor. And it's involved in the transformation from guilt to responsibility. There's a lot of discussion, and some of it very pained, about survivor guilt. I sometimes talk about the paradoxical guilt of survivors. I want to make clear, of course, that there can be self-condemnation in survivors or what we call guilt, but it's paradoxical in terms of ethical judgment, because the wrong person can castigate himself or herself in terms of what is ethically just. . . . But carrying through the witness is a way of transmuting pain and guilt into responsibility, and carrying through that responsibility has enormous therapeutic value. It's both profoundly valuable to society and therapeutic for the individual survivor. And it's therapeutic in the sense of expressing the responsibility but also because that responsibility becomes a very central agent for reintegration of the self. One has had this experience, it has been overwhelming, the self has been shattered in some degree; the only way one can feel right or justified in reconstituting oneself and going on living with some vitality is to carry through one's responsibility to the dead. And it's carrying through that responsibility via one's witness, that survivor mission, that enables one to be an integrated human being once more.

*CC:* What happens in false witness, then?

*RJL:* Yes, well in false witness there is a compensatory process that is very dangerous. Because one has the same need to bear witness, and to take on the survivor mission, but through various pressures or dependencies one can block out elements of the death encounter in a dangerous way. The example I mention at My Lai was a very painful one and a very extreme one, in which the members of the company were survivors of the deaths of other soldiers in the company, which were very painful to them, in a situation that was inherently confusing; and especially the life-death elements were terribly confusing, as were the elements of meaning. Why was one there, why were buddies and comrades dying? Nobody really knew. But the only thing one could do was to try to make sense of the dying that had taken place, to witness the death of their comrades by carrying on their work of killing the enemy; by carrying it on immediately, even though no enemy was readily available. And this was also a way for the soldiers to shut out their own death anxiety. One might think of it this way: the false witness at My Lai was a suppression or numbing towards certain elements of death, and the way that that happened was by converting very quickly, almost immediately, one's own death anxiety into killing. Other factors went into that, including factors of the war; certain circumstances of a situation can encourage false witness. False witness tends to be a political and ideological process. And really false witness is at the heart of most victimization. Groups victimize others, they create what I now call "designated victims," the Jews in Europe, the Blacks in this country. They are people off whom we live not only economically, as is often the case, but psychologically. That is, we reassert our own vitality and symbolic immortality by denying them their right to live and by identifying them with the death taint, by designating them as victims. So we live off them. *That's* what false witness is. It's deriving one's solution to one's death anxiety from extreme trauma, in this case in an extreme situation, by exploiting a group of people and rendering them victims, designated victims for that psychological work.

*CC:* So it's attempting to witness, although in a perverse way, our own relation to death, our own traumatic relation to death—*that's* what our relation to various groups represents.

*RJL:* Yes. You know, I find it useful to look at the broad survivor response to World War I. You cannot understand, as many historians have said, the second world war except as a survival of World War I. So that the Hitler movement centered on undoing World War I and on witnessing World War I by reversing its outcome. It's what the Rambo movies do for the Vietnam War. And to some extent, Pétain's role in World War II also had an element of survival from World War I. He was the hero of Verdun because he simply stopped the slaughter. And he was exhausted and also a little bit right wing by that time. But he didn't have the heart to fight or try to fight the German armies anymore; he surrendered very quickly, and ignominiously, one might say. And consistently then gave in, as head of the Vichy regime, to the Nazis. This could also be a certain kind of survivor reaction—to World War I. So that these survivor reactions color all kinds of individual and collective behavior. The false witness can be—you know it's partly a moral judgment on my part of course, but it also has to do with certain psychological currents one can tease out—the act of using, exploiting, certain groups violently for the sake of coping with one's own death anxiety.

*CC:* It is psychological specifically insofar as it is, as you say, "a perverse quest for meaning." And thus this false witnessing seems central, since your entire theory is about meaning, and this is a perversion of meaning. Can you explain, with an example such as Pétain or whatever example you choose, how meaning is created perversely in this case? What kind of meaning is created, let's say, by creating a victim, or in the My Lai incident?

*RJL:* What is perverse is that one must impose death on others in order to reassert one's own life as an individual and a group. And the problem is that the meaning is real. It's *perceived* as meaning. And it's perverse in the way that in all psychological judgment there has to be ethical judgment. There's no separation in an absolute way of ethical and psychological judgment. Nonetheless, one does one's best to get to the psychological dimension, as you're doing and I'm doing. So my view is that you cannot kill large numbers of people except with a claim to virtue, so that killing on a large scale is always an attempt at affirming the life power of one's own group. Now there's some interesting work by a sociologist named Jack Katz, who wrote a book called *Seductions of Crime.* And he talks about how even in individual violence, when say a man kills his wife or a woman kills her husband, there's a moment of what you might call moralism in carrying through the murder. "This woman deserved to die, because she is a bad mother to her children and an unacceptable wife." Or "This man must die, because he is a horrible husband and a terrible father." So the act of killing becomes a morally necessary act. It's a perverse act in the sense of having to reaffirm one's moral system or sense of self by destroying, violating, murdering another.

*CC:* So the perversion might be thought of as the following: instead of relating to your own death, that is, instead of making your life have meaning in relation to your own death, you make it have meaning in terms of another's death.

*RJL:* That's right, exactly, because full life power, or genuine life power, depends upon some degree of confrontation with the idea of death, some degree of death being part of one's life, and artists have always known this. You know my favorite quotation from Heinrich Böhl; he says that "The artist carries death within him like the good priest his breviary." That's a brilliant economical statement of what I'm after, and many people know this. So that death is constitutive in this sense for all of us. That's not the only thing it is, but if we're to be constitutive in our work we need death. And that goes for social theorists as well as for artists, writers, whatever. So in one sense the perversion is a literalization of our struggle with death also (just as suicide can be a literalization instead of a symbolization of the confrontation with death), which ordinarily uses its full metaphor, or uses its metaphor more fully. Instead, in some literal way, one attaches the taint of death to another in order to reassert life's power.

*CC:* This suggests then that, whereas what you were talking about before was that you cannot actually confront death fully in a trauma—that it remains, let's say, somewhat partial—the illusion of meaning here, the perversion of meaning, is the belief that you can know it directly, and the way it's known here is by the other being dead, by killing off the other. So not only are you trying to substitute the other's death for your own, but you're also attempting to confront it in a way that you can't really do.

*RJL:* You're attempting to confront it and claim a knowledge of it that you can't have, but you're also reasserting a denial of death, or a form of numbing. You're reasserting powerfully the very issue you are struggling to deal with. You're taking on death anxiety through a reassertion of numbing, so that the Nazi movement saw itself as conquering death and never dying. The "thousand-year Reich" is a biblical phrase, and the Nazis took on all kinds of Christian imagery even while attacking Christianity. So it's a claim to have mastered death while deeply denying it, and numbing oneself to it. That's another dimension of that false knowledge, or perverse witness.

*CC:* That puts it at the center of every politics. It is fascinating to think of politics, of political relations, as a kind of false witness.

*RJL:* Yes, it's very much there, all the time.

### III. Double Witness

*CC:* Since you also say that this issue is more generally connected with "ideology," what about therapy? Presumably, the therapeutic process would be a matter of helping some kind of true witness to take place. Is there a way in which therapy (of trauma survivors) can be itself perverted in some sense, as a form of false witness?

*RJL:* Oh yes, I think that therapy could become false witness in its own way. At any level, we could be capable of false witness, because the therapist does undertake a form of witness, witness through the patient's or client's own pain and death equivalents, let's say, especially if they are survivors. What becomes false witness, for instance, is the all-too-frequent experience in therapy of people who have undergone extreme trauma of having that trauma negated, as the source of psychological importance or significance. And I've heard accounts of this again and again in which the therapist insists that the patient look only at his or her childhood stress, or early parental conflicts, when that patient feels overwhelmed by Auschwitz or other devastating forms of trauma. Because, as I say, adult trauma is still a stepchild in psychiatry and psychoanalysis. Now less so than before, there is much more awareness of it than in the past, but really certain therapists and psychoanalysts can be so deeply entrenched in a style that quickly focuses on childhood stress or trauma, that they can find it difficult to give not just death, but the death immersion, its due.

*CC:* So in a way what you're saying is that the ideological moment is when the therapist draws on this paradigm—it is perhaps itself a kind of "originology"—the moment at which the trauma gets assimilated into that narrative of "you must have had a stress in your childhood."

*RJL:* That's the false witness.

*CC:* That would be the moment the false witness occurs in therapy, and that's the moment of ideological collapse.

*RJL:* Well, you see, it's the therapist's false witness to the survivor's trauma. And it's taking the survivor on a false path, or path of false witness, to his or her survivor experience. And it has to do with the absence of death on two levels. One is the numbing or denial of death in therapists, like everybody else, and the other related idea is the absence of death conceptually, which is very important. Because with the interest in death in the United States, in American culture, you know with a lot of concern about death, beginning with Evelyn Waugh's book on Hollywood, with various exposés of death-denial in the United States, and then various forms of focus on consciousness of death by many people in the social sciences and psychology, there has been a greater awareness of death—it's even called the death-awareness movement, sometimes—in this society. But there has been relatively little in the way of development of theory that includes death importantly. That's been harder to do. And that can very much affect therapy. Because therapy is affected by theory, even though many therapists work differently from what their theory may tell them to do, nonetheless theory is very important. So the absence of death or of a quality of knowledge about traumatic experience—its relationship to a struggle with death anxiety and what that entails—can lead to false witness in therapy.

*CC:* Then you're saying that it is not only the process of getting the traumatized person to witness, because also on some level the therapist has to be in a position of constantly witnessing for him or herself; in his or her encounter with a patient the therapist is also in a process of his or her own witness.

*RJL:* That's right. There's a double witness there. And really what a therapist does, what any psychoanalyst or psychiatrist does in listening to a patient or client, or what I do in listening to patients when I treated patients, but over more years in listening to research subjects and people I've interviewed, is to take in their stories, and to form imagery in my own mind about what they're saying. And as one forms that imagery, one is forming a narrative about their story. And the narrative involves elements of their pain, the causation of their conflicts, and also the source of their knowledge, the nature of their experience. It's all forming itself or being reconstructed, recreated in the symbolizing process of the therapist. That's why a therapist having, in the truest sense, an open mind, is crucial, but an open mind to death-related issues as well as sex-related issues. God knows we've developed open minds in relation to sex-related issues, or you'd be run right out of the psychoanalytic movement. But less so in relation to death-related issues, because they're a little less acceptable for the reconstituted imagery of the therapist.

*CC:* The therapist's own participation resists that.

*RJL:* Yes, because they're much less present in the theory of the therapist than for everybody else. I mean the psychological and psychoanalytic theory.

*CC:* So there's a gap between the theory and the experience of the survivor.

*RJL:* It's the problem again that the therapist faces. It's very similar to the problem Freud's followers faced after World War I. What do you do with the death imagery in relation to our theory? Freud did what I think was the wrong thing, but the understandable thing, given the fact of everything he was creating. In one sense, he took the death out of death imagery or death anxiety—yet not quite, because he did struggle with it in some ways, and ways that some of us could help recover, I think. But for contemporary therapists it could be even worse, because, you know, they took the death out of the death instinct, as I said, and had less death-related material to work from. And it has to do with the difficulty psychiatry and psychoanalysis have always had in addressing themselves to adult trauma. Believe me it is very painful to sit in one's office and hear the description from an Auschwitz survivor or a Hiroshima survivor, of what it was like, of the concrete details; you know a story has to have very concrete details. From Hiroshima survivors—the people, what they looked like, I wrote some of this in my book. Or from Auschwitz survivors—what people actually did, what the Nazis actually did, what it was like when you smelled, you know, the smells of the crematoria, or when you learned that your children or your parents had been killed. It is very hard, for anybody, but all the more so as a therapist or as a researcher, to sit in your office and let the details in to reconstitute them in one's own imagery. And it's such a temptation to push them away, leave them out; to take that patient or client back to childhood is much more comfortable, and we're used to that. Or anywhere but in that terrible, terrible traumatic situation.

*CC:* Do you feel a little bit yourself like you're going through the trauma as they talk, that you're participating in it?

*RJL:* More than a little bit. This is the significance of the encounter. Well, you know I didn't say it in my book *The Nazi Doctors* (1986), but there's no reason why I can't say it. It was an encounter with Elie Wiesel. Wiesel and I are old friends, and he had been very interested in my work on Nazi doctors and had supported it in various ways. And when I came back, when I first began to immerse myself in that work and began to read all the things I had to read, I had coffee with Elie once and sort of complained to him half humorously, but not entirely humorously, obviously, "It's OK if you're enthusiastic about my work, but I'm having terrible dreams. Dreams of being behind the barbed wire in those camps, and not just me, my wife and my children, and it's quite terrible." And he looked at me, with a look that was neither unkind, nor especially sympathetic, just looking at me, and then nodded and said, "Good. Now you can do the study."

What he was saying is that you must in some significant psychological way experience what they experience. You can never do that quite. But it's being a survivor by proxy, and the proxy's important. You're not doing what they did, you're not exposed to what they were exposed to, but you must take your mind through, take your feelings through what they went through, and allow that in. It's hard, it's painful, and yet you know you must do it as you come into contact with it, and the people who have done the best therapy with survivors and who have written the most importantly and movingly about survivors have had to do that.

*CC:* So there's a double survivor situation, but a survivor and a proxy survivor, and it's the meeting of those two that constitutes the witness.

*RJL:* It's an encounter, it's an encounter and a dialogue. With me it was very openly dialogue. I was never doing therapy with survivors of Hiroshima or of Auschwitz. It was a dialogue with them, and it was very powerful. I say it very briefly and very gently in the introduction to the book on Nazi doctors, that interviewing all the Auschwitz survivors was a spiritual balance or a spiritual counterpart—no, was a way of maintaining spiritual balance while interviewing Nazi doctors. It was a way of hearing about the experience from the mouths of those who have been victimized or subjected to it, and therefore hearing a deeper truth, than anything the Nazi doctors could tell me about what they had done to people. Because it's a false story you get in a certain way, sitting in their studies. You get their stories about their lives, and you've got to supplement them with other things, as I did. But if it were the only thing, it would be a very misleading story. So it was a dialogue with survivors that I had, and they were teaching me a great deal, and I think that they were learning some things from the dialogue as well, as we talked very frankly and openly. And it became extraordinarily intense for me because of what it was, and because many of the Jewish survivors, and they were the majority of the survivors I interviewed, were rather similar in their backgrounds to me. They were doctors, they were maybe ten years older than I, they or their families came from places not too far from where my grandparents came, emigrated from, and they happened to emigrate, you know, at the turn of the century, so √ my parents could be born, barely, in the United States, and I could be what's called a third-generation American. But just by some chance development in history, I was the third-generation American, who had had a privileged existence interviewing them, people who had had a less than privileged existence. And that made the encounter and the dialogue so intense. They understood it immediately, and we talked about such things, as my research interviews always have a certain amount of give and take, in which the psychoanalytically oriented interview is radically modified in the direction of dialogue. And taking it in the direction of dialogue of course means you take in more, because it's an exchange among equals, as opposed to therapy, which is something else.

*CC:* Do you feel that, in the dialogues of your work over the years, you were yourself attempting, in some sense, to bear witness?

√ *RJL:* In each study, I experience something of the event and upheaval I'm exploring, and of course there must be a certain element of witnessing in that. And there is also a sense of commitment to the idea that illumination, or some kind of insight, can help serve human purposes. I don't have any simple explanation for how I came to do this kind of work and follow this particular path. But over time, doing study after study, one develops a sense of what is right for one as a scholar and a human being. And for me it's extremely important to listen to one's own voice and to follow a path that one feels to be authentic, that allows one to have both involvement and detachment, and to be ethically committed. And listening to that voice, this is the path I have chosen to follow.

# References

Lifton, Robert Jay. 1979. *The Broken Connection: On Death and the Continuity of Life.* New York: Basic Books.

———. 1986. *The Nazi Doctors: Medical Killing and the Psychology of Genocide.* New York: Basic Books.

———. 1969. *Thought Reform and the Psychology of Totalism: A Study of "Brainwashing" in China.* Chapel Hill: University of North Carolina.

———. 1991. *Death in Life: Survivors of Hiroshima.* Chapel Hill: University of North Carolina Press.

# II

## Recapturing the Past

# INTRODUCTION

## CATHY CARUTH

At the heart of this volume is the encounter with a peculiar kind of historical phenomenon—what has come to be called "Post-Traumatic Stress Disorder" (PTSD)—in which the overwhelming events of the past repeatedly possess, in intrusive images and thoughts, the one who has lived through them. This singular *possession by the past*, as we have seen in Part I, extends beyond the bounds of a marginal pathology and has become a central characteristic of the survivor experience of our time. Yet what is particularly striking in this singular experience is that its insistent reenactments of the past do not simply serve as testimony to an event, but may also, paradoxically enough, bear witness to a past that was never fully experienced as it occurred. Trauma, that is, does not simply serve as record of the past but precisely registers the force of an experience that is not yet fully owned. The essays in Part II examine the implications of this paradoxical experience for the ways we represent and communicate historical experience. The phenomenon of trauma, as they suggest, both urgently demands historical awareness and yet denies our usual modes of access to it. How is it possible, they thus ask, to gain access to a traumatic history?

Perhaps the most striking feature of traumatic recollection is the fact that it is not a simple memory. Beginning with the earliest work on trauma, a perplexing contradiction has formed the basis of its many definitions and descriptions: while the images of traumatic reenactment remain absolutely accurate and precise, they are largely inaccessible to conscious recall and control. It is this curious phenomenon that challenged Freud in his confrontation with the "war neuroses" stemming from the First World War. The traumatic reliving, like the nightmares of the accident victim, seemed like a waking memory, yet returned, repeatedly, only in the form of a dream:

> [People] think the fact that the traumatic experience is forcing itself upon the patient is a proof of the strength of the experience: the patient is, as one might say, fixated to his trauma. . . . I am not aware, however, that patients suffering from traumatic neurosis are much occupied in their waking lives with memories of their accident. Perhaps they are more concerned with *not* thinking of it. (Freud, 1920, 13)

The traumatic nightmare, undistorted by repression or unconscious wish, seems to point directly to an event, and yet, as Freud suggests, it occupies a space to which willed access is denied. Indeed, the vivid and precise return of the event appears, as modern researchers point out, to be accompanied by an *amnesia* for the past, a fact striking enough to be referred to by several major writers as a *paradox*:

> There are a number of *temporal paradoxes* that occur in patients with PTSD. . . . [One is that] recall of the actual trauma may often be impaired, whereas patients may reexperience aspects of the trauma in the form of intrusive thoughts, nightmares, or flashbacks. (John Krystal, 1990, 6; emphasis added)

> Pathologies of memory are characteristic features of post-traumatic stress disorder (PTSD). These range from amnesia for part, or all, of the traumatic events to frank dissociation, in which large realms of experience or aspects of one's identity are disowned. Such failures of recall can *paradoxically coexist* with the opposite: intruding memories and unbidden repetitive images of traumatic events. (Greenberg and van der Kolk, 1987, 191; emphasis added)

The flashback, it seems, provides a form of recall that survives at the cost of willed memory or of the very continuity of conscious thought. While the traumatized are called upon to see and to relive the insistent reality of the past, they recover a past that encounters consciousness only through the very denial of active recollection.

The ability to recover the past is thus closely and paradoxically tied up, in trauma, with the inability to have access to it. And this suggests that what returns in the flashback is not simply an overwhelming experience that has been obstructed by a later repression or amnesia, but an event that is itself constituted, in part, by its lack of integration into consciousness. Indeed, the literal registration of an event—the capacity to continually, in the flashback, reproduce it in exact detail—appears to be connected, in traumatic experience, precisely with the way it *escapes* full consciousness as it occurs. Modern neurobiologists have in fact suggested that the unerring "engraving" on the mind, the "etching into the brain" of an event in trauma may be associated with its elision of its normal encoding in memory. This strange connection—between the *elision* of memory and the *precision* of recall—was already central to Freud's work, and was even earlier, as van der Kolk and van der Hart suggest in this volume, an important focus in the writing of Pierre Janet. He proposed that traumatic recall remains insistent and unchanged to the precise extent that it has never, from the beginning, been fully integrated into understanding. The trauma is the confrontation with an event that, in its unexpectedness or horror, cannot be placed within the schemes of prior knowledge—that cannot, as George Bataille says, become a matter of "intelligence"—and thus continually returns, in its exactness, at a later time. Not having been fully integrated as it occurred, the event cannot become, as Janet says, a "narrative memory" that is integrated into a completed story of the past. The history that a flashback tells—as psychiatry, psychoanalysis, and neurobiology equally suggest—is, therefore, a history that literally *has no place*, neither in the past, in which it was not fully experienced, nor in the present, in which its precise images and enactments are not fully understood. In its repeated imposition as both image and amnesia, the trauma thus seems to evoke the difficult truth of a history that is constituted by the very incomprehensibility of its occurrence.

For the survivor of trauma, then, the truth of the event may reside not only in its brutal facts, but also in the way that their occurrence defies simple comprehension. The flashback or traumatic reenactment conveys, that is, both *the truth of an event,* and *the truth of its incomprehensibility.* But this creates a dilemma for historical understanding. For on the one hand, as van der Kolk and van der Hart suggest, the amnesiac reenactment is a story that is difficult to tell and to hear: "it is not addressed to anybody, the patient does not respond to anybody: it is a solitary activity." The trauma thus requires integration, both for the sake of testimony and for the sake of cure. But on the other hand, the transformation of the trauma into a narrative memory that allows the story to be verbalized and communicated, to be integrated into one's own, and others', knowledge of the past, may lose both the precision and the force that characterizes traumatic recall. Thus in the story of Janet's patient Irène, her cure is characterized by the fact that she can tell a "slightly different story" to different people: the capacity to remember is also the capacity to elide or distort, and in other cases, as van der Kolk and van der Hart show, may mean the capacity simply to forget. Yet beyond the loss of precision there is another, more profound, disappearance: the loss, precisely, of the event's essential incomprehensibility, the force of its *affront to understanding*. It is this dilemma that underlies many survivors' reluctance to translate their experience into speech:

> People have said that only survivors themselves understand what happened. I'll go a step further. We don't. . . . I know I don't. . . .
> So there is a dilemma. What do we do? Do we not talk about it? Elie Wiesel has said many times that silence is the only proper response but then most of us, including him, feel that not to speak is impossible.
> To speak is impossible, and not to speak is impossible. (Schreiber Weitz, 1990)

The danger of speech, of integration into the narration of memory, may lie not in what it cannot understand, but in that it understands too much. Speech seems to offer only, as Kevin Newmark says, the attempt "to move away from the experience of shock by reintegrating it into a stable understanding of it." The possibility of integration into memory and the consciousness of history thus raises the question, van der Kolk and van der Hart ultimately observe, "whether it is not a sacrilege of the traumatic experience to play with the reality of the past?"

The impossibility of a comprehensible story, however, does not necessarily mean the denial of a transmissible truth. "I have precisely begun with the impossibility of telling this story," Claude Lanzmann writes of his film of Holocaust testimonies, *Shoah*. "I have made this very impossibility my point of departure" (Lanzmann, 1990b, 295). How does one precisely *begin* with impossibility? Challenging our usual expectations of what it means to tell, to listen, and to gain access to the past, Lanzmann suggests that historical truth may be transmitted in some cases through the refusal of a certain framework of understanding, a refusal that is also a creative act of listening. In her introduction to Lanzmann's address before the Western New England Institute for Psychoanalysis that appears in this issue, Shoshana Felman quotes his own eloquent statement of this refusal:

> It is enough to formulate the question in simplistic terms—Why have the Jews been killed?—for the question to reveal right away its obscenity. There is an absolute obscenity in the very project of understanding. Not

to understand was my iron law during all the eleven years of the production of *Shoah*. I had clung to this refusal of understanding as the only
possible ethical and at the same time the only possible operative attitude.
(Lanzmann, 1990a, 279)

The making of *Shoah*, Lanzmann suggests, proceeds, precisely, from what it
does not understand. The act of refusal, here, is therefore not a denial of a
knowledge of the past, but rather a way of gaining access to a knowledge that
has not yet attained the form of "narrative memory." In its active resistance to
the platitudes of knowledge, this refusal opens up the space for a testimony
that can speak beyond what is already understood. Indeed, *Shoah*, Lanzmann
suggests, was created not simply through the positive and straightforward
acquisition of facts—although the details of each person's story do indeed
form its very core—but also through the process of discovering the ways in
which understanding breaks down:

> I was like someone who is not very gifted in dancing, who takes lessons as
> I did 20 years ago, and then tries and doesn't succeed. There was an
> absolute discrepancy between the book-knowledge that I had acquired
> and what these people told me. I didn't understand anything anymore.
> (Lanzmann, 1990b, 294)

The refusal of understanding, then, is also a fundamentally creative act:
"this blindness was for me," Lanzmann writes, "the vital condition of creation" (Lanzmann 1990a, 279). What is created does not grow out of a
knowledge already accumulated but, as Lanzmann suggests, is intricately
bound up with the act of listening itself. In his appearance before the Western New England Institute for Psychoanalysis, Lanzmann enacts a kind of
refusal and creation by turning what was intended to have been the discussion of a film on a Nazi's inner development into the event of his own refusal
to watch the film and his explanation of why such a refusal took place. It is
precisely in the struggle to make sense of this refusal that the possibility of a
truly pedagogical encounter emerges, an encounter that, by breaking with
traditional modes of understanding, creates new ways of gaining access to a
historical catastrophe for those who attempt to witness it from afar.

Lanzmann thus provides, in *Shoah* and somewhat differently in his own
appearance before the psychoanalysts, the possibility of a speech that is not
simply the vehicle of understanding, but also the locus of what cannot yet be
understood. It is, as Shoshana Felman says of Celan's poetry in her essay in
Part I, "the event of creating an address for the specificity of a historical

experience that annihilated any possibility of address." It is thus also, in itself, a project that discovers the paradoxical foundation of address as the transmission of a gap:

> Between all these conditions [unemployment in Germany, the Nazi soul, and so on] and the gassing of three-thousand persons, men, women, children, in a gas chamber, all together, there is an unbreachable discrepancy. It is simply not possible to engender one out of the other. There is no solution of continuity between the two; there is rather a gap, an *abyss*, and this abyss will never be bridged. ("The Obscenity of Understanding")

It is ultimately in the ways in which it exceeds simple understanding that the eventful speech of this address—an address that takes place in all the struggles to communicate traumatic experience—opens up the possibility of what could be called a truly historical transmission.

The attempt to gain access to a traumatic history, then, is also the project of listening beyond the pathology of individual suffering, to the reality of a history that in its crises can only be perceived in unassimilable forms. This history may speak through the individual or through the community, which in its own suffering, as Kai Erikson makes clear, may not only be the site of its disruption but the locus of a "wisdom all its own." Each of the essays in this volume engages, from different perspectives, in the difficult task of this historical listening. And they help us to recognize that this task may take place not only in relation to a traumatic past not yet acknowledged, but, as Gregg Bordowitz, Douglas Crimp and Laura Pinsky forcefully remind us, in relation to an address that attempts to speak out from a crisis that is not yet over.

## References

Freud, Sigmund. 1920 (1955). *The Standard Edition of the Complete Psychological Works of Sigmund Freud.* Vol. 18. Translated under the editorship of James Strachey in collaboration with Anna Freud, assisted by Alix Strachey and Alan Tyson. 24 vols. (1953–74). London: Hogarth.

Greenberg, Mark S., and Bessel A. van der Kolk. 1987. "Retrieval and Integration of Traumatic Memories with the 'Painting Cure.'" In *Psychological Trauma*, ed. Bessel A. van der Kolk. Washington, D.C.: American Psychiatric Press.

Krystal, John. 1990. "Animal Models for Post-Traumatic Stress Disorder." In *Biological Assessment and Treatment of Post-Traumatic Stress Disorder*, ed. Earl L. Giller Jr. Washington, D.C.: American Psychiatric Press.

Lanzmann, Claude. 1990a. "Hier ist kein Warum." In *Au sujet de Shoah—Le Film de Claude Lanzmann*, ed. Bernard Cuau et al. Paris: Berlin.

———. 1990b. "Le lieu et la parole." In *Au sujet de Shoah*, ed. Bernard Cuau et al.

Schreiber Weitz, Sonia. 1990. Videotaped interview. In *Understanding Psychological Trauma* (video), produced by David G. Doepel and Mark Braverman. CVA Media.

# The Intrusive Past:
# The Flexibility of Memory and
# the Engraving of Trauma

BESSEL A. VAN DER KOLK and
ONNO VAN DER HART

Who can find a proper grave for the damaged mosaics
of the mind, where they may rest in pieces?
—L. L. LANGER, *Holocaust Testimonies*

The current revival of interest in the role of overwhelming experiences on the development of psychopathology has stimulated a fresh look at how memories are stored in the mind and continue to affect day-to-day perceptions and interpretations of reality. Over a century ago, the very foundation of modern psychiatry was laid with the study of consciousness and the disruptive impact of traumatic experiences. Struck by the observation that some memories could become the nucleus of later psychopathology, Jean-Martin Charcot and Pierre Janet at the Salpêtrière and William James in the United States devoted much of their attention to studying how the mind processes memories. They recognized, on the one hand, the flexibility of the mind and, on the other, how certain memories became obstacles that kept people from going on with their lives. William James wrote in 1880: "the new conceptions, emotions . . . which evolve [in the mind] are originally produced in the shape of random images, fancies, accidental outbirths of spontaneous variations . . . which the outer environment simply confirms or refutes, preserves or destroys." At the same time the psychologists and psychiatrists around the turn of the century were fully aware that some memories are not evanescent and that "certain happenings would leave indelible and distressing memories— memories to which the sufferer was continually returning, and by which he was tormented by day and by night" (Janet, 1919–25, 2:205).

## Janet's Contributions

Using only careful clinical observations, these early psychologists, particularly Janet, developed a comprehensive formulation about the effects of traumatic memories on consciousness. Even though Janet's views were well known during the early part of this century (for example, he participated in the opening of the buildings of Harvard Medical School in 1908 and received an honorary doctorate during Harvard's tricentennial celebrations in 1936), and though he accurately anticipated the developments in the neurosciences in the 1970s and 1980s, his monumental legacy was crowded out by psychoanalysis, and largely forgotten, until Henri Ellenberger (1970) rescued him from total obscurity in *The Discovery of the Unconscious.* For the past seventy-five years, psychoanalysis, the study of repressed wishes and instincts, and descriptive psychiatry virtually ignored the fact that actual memories may form the nucleus of psychopathology and continue to exert their influence on current experience by means of the process of dissociation.

Janet noticed that there were marked temperamental differences between people in such areas as "psychological force" (overall energy level) and psychological tension (the capacity to focus on relevant information and utilize available data for appropriate action). Besides temperament, he viewed the memory system as the central organizing apparatus of the mind, which categorizes and integrates all aspects of experience and automatically integrates them into ever-enlarging and flexible meaning schemes (Janet, 1889; Perry and Laurence, 1984). Janet coined the word "subconscious" for the collection of automatically stored memories that form the map that guides subsequent interaction with the environment. According to Janet, the automatic transformations involved in synthesizing and adapting new perceptions into existing schemes make it extremely difficult to later decode the precise nature of any particular memory and its role in subsequent behavior (1904, 1898). Janet claimed that when people respond to new challenges with appropriate action they automatically integrate new information without paying much conscious attention to what is happening. Healthy psychological functioning depends on the proper operation of the memory system, which consists of a unified memory of all psychological facets related to particular experiences: sensations, emotions, thoughts, and actions (Janet, 1889). He quoted his former classmate, the philosopher Henri Bergson: "What characterizes the man of action is the promptness with which he can call up relevant memories, and the insuperable barrier at the threshold of consciousness produced by unrelated memories" (Bergson, 1896, 166). Janet claimed that the interplay of this memory system and temperament make each person unique and complex: "The personality is a human work of art: a construction made by human beings with the means at their disposal . . . good, bad, incomplete, and imperfect" (1929, 282).

Janet distinguished narrative memory from the automatic integration of new information without much conscious attention to what is happening. This automatic synthesis, or habit memory (which contemporary writers like Schacter (1987) call implicit memory), is a capacity humans have in common with animals. Ordinary or narrative memory, however, is a uniquely human capacity. In order to memorize well, one must pay special attention to what is going on. Narrative memory consists of mental constructs, which people use to make sense out of experience (e.g., Janet, 1928). Janet thought that the ease with which current experience is integrated into existing mental structures depends on the subjective assessment of what is happening; familiar and expectable experiences are automatically assimilated without much conscious awareness of details of the particulars, while frightening or novel experiences may not easily fit into existing cognitive schemes and either may be remembered with particular vividness or may totally resist integration. Under extreme conditions, existing meaning schemes may be entirely unable to accommodate frightening experiences, which causes the memory of these experiences to be stored differently and not be available for retrieval under ordinary conditions: it becomes dissociated from conscious awareness and voluntary control (Janet, 1889, 1919–25). When that occurs, fragments of these unintegrated experiences may later manifest recollections or behavioral reenactments:

> It is only for convenience that we speak of it as a "traumatic memory."
> The subject is often incapable of making the necessary narrative which we call memory regarding the event; and yet he remains confronted by a difficult situation in which he has not been able to play a satisfactory part, one to which his adaptation had been imperfect, so that he continues to make efforts at adaptation. (Janet, 1919–25, 2:274)

## The Case of Irène: A Paradigm for Traumatic Memory

In his frequent attempts to describe the differences between narrative memory and traumatic memory, Janet often used a clinical example that manifested both: his patient Irène, a young woman of twenty-three years of age who was traumatized by the tragic death of her mother of tuberculosis

(Janet, 1904, 1919–25, 1928, 1929, 1935). In the months preceding her mother's demise, Irène cared for her conscientiously. At the same time, Irène continued to work to provide for the family (her earnings were spent on her father's alcoholism and on food for her mother). She had hardly slept for sixty consecutive nights. Thus she was utterly exhausted when her mother finally died one night. Irène was unable to grasp the reality of this event; all through the night she tried to revive the corpse, trying to force it to speak, continuing to give it medications and cleaning its mouth. While this was going on, the corpse fell from the bed. Calling her father for help was of no use: he was completely drunk. She finally succeeded in putting the body straight and continued to talk to it. In the morning Irène left her house trying to get help from her aunt. However, she did not tell her that her mother was dead. Sensing something was amiss, the aunt went to the apartment, took charge of the situation, and made preparations for the funeral. Irène did not understand what was going on. Initially, she did not want to go to the funeral; during the funeral she laughed inappropriately. After a couple of weeks, her aunt brought her to Salpêtrière. The most absurd symptom, the aunt said, was that Irène, an otherwise intelligent young woman, had absolutely no memory of the death of her mother and did not want to believe that her mother had died.

During the admission, Irène could speak intelligently and was not confused. When Janet spoke with her about her mother, she said,

> If you insist on it, I will tell you: "My mother is dead." They tell me that it is so all day long, and I simply agree with them to get them off my back. But if you want my opinion, I don't believe it. And I have excellent reasons for it. If my mother was really dead, she would have been dead in her room, on a specific date, and I, who never left her and took very good care of her, would have seen it. If she was dead, they would have buried her and taken me to the funeral. Well, there has been no funeral. Why do you want her to be dead? (Janet, 1928, 207–8)

Irène gave another "excellent" reason why her mother had not died: "I love my mother, I adore her, I have never left her. If she were dead, I would despair, I would feel very sad, I would feel abandoned and alone. Well, I don't feel anything; I am not sad at all, I don't cry; thus, she is not dead." Irène returned to this point over and again. Janet could not get her to recount any memory of her mother's death. After six months of inpatient treatment and hypnotic therapy, Irène slowly started to tell the story of her mother's death. Whenever Janet returned to this subject, Irène started to cry and said:

Don't remind me of those terrible things. It was a horrible thing that happened in our apartment that night in July. My mother was dead, my father completely drunk, doing only horrible things to me. I had to take care of the deceased and all night long I did a lot of silly things in order to try to revive her. I talked to her, I wanted her to answer me, I tried to get her to drink, I tried to clean her mouth, to close her mouth and to stretch her legs. I managed to drop the corpse on the floor. I did everything to get her back on the bed and, in fact, in the morning I had more or less lost my mind. (Ibid., 208)

She also had found the emotional part of the memory: "I feel very sad. I feel abandoned." According to Janet, as her memory was now accompanied by feelings, it had become complete.

Janet concluded that the most striking problem of this patient was that she didn't have any memories of her mother's dying. However, Irène suffered from a second set of symptoms. Several times a week, the following scene took place: whenever Irène looked from a certain direction to an empty bed, she took on a bizarre posture. She stared at the bed, without moving her eyes, did not hear anybody anymore, did not have contact with anybody, and she began to engage in stereotyped activities. She brought a glass to the lips of an imaginary person, she cleaned her mouth, she talked with this person: "But open your mouth, drink something, answer me." She climbed on the bed in order to arrange the body, then she cried: "The corpse has fallen on the ground and my father who is drunk, who vomits on the bed, cannot even help me." She became busy in putting the corpse on the bed. This reproduction of the tragic scene lasted three or four hours. It ended usually by the patient looking desperate, by a convulsion, and, finally, by sleep. Irène had meticulously reproduced all the details of her mother's death.

Thus, Irène had two sets of symptoms: on the one hand she was amnestic for the death of her mother—she could not tell the story—and on the other hand she seemed to remember too much. Or did she? The reexperiencing of the tragic night was, in fact, an exact and automatic repetition of the acts Irène had performed during that night. It was automatic behavior, comparable to what all of us do while eating, walking, and so on. However, while people usually introduce slight variations in these habits, Irène repeated actions in these "traumatic memories" that had been performed only once, on that night only. It was the reproduction of a unique sequence of acts.

## Narrative Memory versus Traumatic Memory

Janet observed the following differences between "traumatic memory" and ordinary or narrative memory. First of all, traumatic memory takes too long: in Irène's case, it took her three to four hours to tell this story. When she was finally able to tell her tale, it took her only half a minute. And this is how ordinary memory should function; it should be an aspect of life and be integrated with other experiences. Irène's "traumatic memory" clearly was not adaptive at all. After retrieving the narrative memory, she was able to give the correct answer to the question asked by her doctor: adapted to present circumstances. For instance, Irène told a slightly different story to Janet than she did to other people: with strangers, she left out her father's abominable behavior. Thus, in contrast to narrative memory, which is a social act, traumatic memory is inflexible and invariable. Traumatic memory has no social component; it is not addressed to anybody, the patient does not respond to anybody; it is a solitary activity. In contrast, ordinary memory fundamentally serves a social function, illustrated by Irène's telling people about the death of her mother as an appeal for help and reconnection.

Another distinction Janet observed is that traumatic memory is evoked under particular conditions. It occurs automatically in situations which are reminiscent of the original traumatic situation. These circumstances trigger the traumatic memory. In Irène's case, it was her position near a bed that triggered reenactment of the death scene. Traumatic memory is produced by the mechanism that Janet called *restitutio ad integrum* (Janet, 1928). When one element of a traumatic experience is evoked, all other elements follow automatically. Ordinary memory is not characterized by *restitutio ad integrum*. When Irène tells her story, she does not need to sit in front of a bed. She does not repeat the affective and motoric elements of the death scene. She just responds to a question, a question which in her case stimulated a special reaction, that is, the act of remembering.

## Dissociation and Subconscious Fixed Ideas

Lack of proper integration of intensely emotionally arousing experiences into the memory system results in dissociation and the formation of traumatic memories. Janet called these new cores of consciousness "subconscious fixed ideas." Though subconscious, they continue to influence current perceptions, affect states, and behavior; they are usually accessible under hypnosis (Janet, 1894). Much of Janet's treatment of Irène consisted of memory work under hypnosis. As her case illustrates, traumatic memories of the arousing events may return as physical sensations, horrific images or nightmares, behavioral reenactments, or a combination of these. Since fixed ideas have their origin in a failure to make sense of a past experience, they fulfill no further useful function and lack continued adaptive value. People who have learned to cope with stress by dissociation often continue to do so in response to the smallest strain. Subconscious memories thus come to control ongoing behavior. People who react to stress by thus allowing the event to bypass consciousness become emotionally constricted and cannot experience a full range of affects within what we would call today the same ego state (Janet, 1909a, 1909b). The most extreme example is multiple personality disorder, where fixed ideas develop into entirely separate identities.

Like contemporary studies which have shown that between 20 and 50 percent of psychiatric inpatients suffer from dissociative disorders (e.g., Chu and Dill, 1990; Saxe et al., 1993), Janet, Prince (1910), and other nonpsychoanalytic psychiatrists noted that many patients responded to stress by dissociating. They reacted inappropriately to stress and behaved "automatically," with irrelevant stereotypic images, ideas, emotions, and movements that represented fragmented reexperiences of frightening past events: "These patients have a disturbance of action as well as a disorder of memory, and that hides the most serious trouble: that of will" (Janet, 1898, 532). Janet proposed that traumatized individuals become "attached" (Freud would use the term "fixated") to the trauma: unable to make sense out of the source of their terror, they develop difficulties in assimilating subsequent experiences as well. It is "as if their personality development has stopped at a certain point and cannot expand any more by the addition or assimilation of new elements" (Janet, 1893, 138).

### Freud's Evolution Concerning the Relevance of Traumatic Memories

Psychoanalysis was born on the wards of the Salpêtrière; when Freud visited Charcot at the end of 1885, he adopted many of the ideas then current in that hospital, which he expressed and acknowledged in his early papers on hysteria (James, 1894; Freud and Breuer, 1893; Freud, 1896; Macmillan, 1990, 1991). In his later writings, he forgot these early teachings and came to view himself as the conquistador of entirely unexplored territories. In much of what he wrote between the second half of 1892 and 1896, Freud followed Janet's notion that the "subconsciousness" contains affectively charged events encoded in an altered state of consciousness. In "On the Psychical Mechanism of Hysterical Phenomena: Preliminary Communication" Freud and Breuer (1893) wrote on the nature of hysterical attacks: "We must point out that we consider it essential for the explanation of hysterical phenomena to assume the presence of a dissociation—a splitting of the content of consciousness . . . the regular and essential content of a (recurrent) hysterical attack is the recurrence of a psychical state which the patient has experienced earlier" (30). When they expanded this work in 1895, in *Studies on Hysteria*, Breuer and Freud acknowledged their debt to Janet and stated that "hysterics suffer mainly from reminiscences." Breuer's theoretical chapter in *Studies on Hysteria* shows practically no shift from the lessons from the Salpêtrière: Breuer insists that the tendency to split was basic to hysteria and that a rudimentary dual consciousness was present in every hysteria (Macmillan, 1990, 1991). An idea becomes pathogenic because it has been received during a special psychical state (a dissociated state of consciousness) and has from the first remained outside the ego. With the French, he regarded trauma-induced hysteria as state-dependent (dissociated) learning. He called this state "hypnoid" and hysteria thus was regarded as "hypnoid hysteria." Breuer thus invoked no active psychological force to keep traumatic memories apart from the ego. Like Janet, he indicated that hysterical phenomena had a traumatic origin and stated that these memories "originated during the prevalence of severely paralyzing affects, such as fright." Starting in 1895 Freud developed the new concept of defense hysteria, which he postulated as not having its origin in dissociated states of consciousness: "I have never in my own experience met with a genuine hypnoid hysteria." With this declaration, Freud took his first steps away from the theories of trauma-induced dissociation and hysteria of Charcot, Janet, and Breuer. "He denied that dissociation was fundamental and had come to view all so-called hypnoid symptoms as really caused by repression" (Macmillan, 1991, 101).

As late as 1896, in "The Aetiology of Hysteria," Freud quite categorically proposed the extreme view that: "the ultimate cause of hysteria is always the seduction of a child by an adult. The actual event always occurs before the age of puberty, though the outbreak of the neurosis occurs after puberty. The symptoms of hysteria can only be understood if they are traced back to experiences which have a traumatic effect." In the dramatic *volte face* on this "seduction theory," Freud renounced his previously very passionately held belief that childhood sexual trauma was at the origins of hysterical neuroses, and with that, he lost interest in exploring dissociated states of consciousness. During the latter part of the 1890s, Freud changed his position to one in which he held that patients actively repressed memories of conflictual instinctual wishes. Rather than ascribing hysteria to trauma, he proposed that the capacity for conversion is the basic predisposition to hysteria (Macmillan, 1990, 1991). He henceforth argued that the memory disturbances and reenactments seen in hysteria were not the result of a failure to integrate new data into existing meaning schemes but of the active repression of conflict-laden sexual and aggressive ideas and impulses, centering on the oedipal crisis at about age five. In, for example, *The Interpretation of Dreams* (Freud, 1900), he clearly (and erroneously) claimed that infantile memories are stored in memory, but remain unavailable for retrieval because of actively repressed, forbidden impulses and wishes. While psychoanalysis thereby came to emphasize the force of forbidden wishes, it ignored the continued power of overwhelming terror. Psychoanalysis came to dismiss the terrifying reality of many patients' experiences and the profession disregarded such profoundly shocking experiences as incest with statements such as "she is upset, because her oedipal wishes came true."

It seems that Freud revisited the conception of dissociation only once more, in 1936: "Depersonalization leads us to the extraordinary condition of double consciousness, which is more correctly described as split personality. But all of this is so obscure and had been so little mastered scientifically that I must refrain from talking about it anymore." However, the reality of actual trauma in the genesis of psychopathology could not be entirely swept under the rug: after the First World War, psychoanalysis was faced with the dual challenge of explaining men's infinite capacity for self-destruction, and the reality of combat neuroses. In the foreword to the Ferenczi et al. monograph on war neuroses (1919), Freud stated that "the symptomatic picture presented by traumatic neurosis approaches that of hysteria . . . but surpasses it as a rule in its strongly marked signs of subjective ailment in which it resembles hypochondria or melancholia as well as the evidence it gives of a far more comprehensive general enfeeblement and disturbance of mental capacities." Ferenczi et al. traced many of the motor symptoms of paralysis in the war neuroses to a fixation on the moment that the trauma occurred. Freud was struck by the fact that patients suffering from traumatic neuroses experienced a lack of conscious preoccupation with the memories of their accident. He postulated that "perhaps they are more concerned with *not* thinking of it."

In *Inhibitions, Symptoms, and Anxiety* (1926), Freud returned to Janet's notion of attachment to the trauma. He proposed that the compulsion to repeat the trauma is a function of repression itself: "We found that the perceptual content of the exciting experiences and the ideational content of pathogenic structures of thought were forgotten and debarred from being reproduced in memory, and we therefore concluded that the keeping away from consciousness was the main characteristic of hysterical repression" (163). And, he noted a few years earlier that because the memory is repressed, the patient "is obliged to repeat the repressed material as a contemporary experience, instead of . . . remembering it as something belonging to the past" (1920, 18).

Psychodynamic psychiatry has always attached crucial importance to the capacity to reproduce memories in words and to integrate them in the totality of experience, i.e., to narrative memory. In *L'Etat mental des Hystériques*, Janet said "it is not enough to be aware of a memory that occurs automatically in response to particular current events: it is also necessary that the personal perception 'knows' this image and attaches it to other memories" (1911, 538). In *Inhibitions, Symptoms, and Anxiety*, Freud claimed that, if a person does not remember, he is likely to act out: "he reproduces it not as a memory but as an action; he repeats it, without knowing, of course, that he is repeating it, and in the end, we understand that this is his way of remembering" (1926, 150). Thus, both Freud and Janet claimed that the crucial factor that determines the repetition of trauma is the presence of mute, unsymbolized, and unintegrated experiences: "a sudden and passively endured trauma is relived repeatedly, until a person learns to remember simultaneously the affect and cognition associated with the trauma through access to language" (van der Kolk and Ducey, 1989, 271).

In his last published writing during his lifetime, Freud revisited the power of unverbalized memories, maybe unconsciously returning to his own "repressed" early lessons from the Salpêtrière. In *Moses and Monotheism* (Freud, 1939) he claimed that:

> what children have experienced at the age of two and have not understood, need never be remembered by them, except in dreams. . . . But at some later time it will break into their life with obsessional impulses, it will govern their actions. The precipitating cause, with its attendant perceptions and ideas, is forgotten. This, however, is not the end of the process: the instinct has either retained its forces, or collects them again, or it is reawakened by some new precipitating cause . . . at a weak spot . . . [it] comes to light as a symptom, without the acquiescence of the ego, but also without its understanding. All the phenomena of the formation of symptoms may be justly described as the "return of the repressed." (124)

## Repression and Dissociation

Freud's ambivalent position vis-à-vis trauma and dissociation is reflected in his concept of repression. As illustrated above, sometimes he used this term in the sense of actively repressed conflictual instinctual wishes: a defense against primitive, forbidden, Id-impulses, especially of a sexual nature. At other times, he used the term "repression" more or less in the sense of dissociated traumatic memories. The same confusion is seen in the psychoanalytic literature at large. With regard to trauma, the use of the term "repression" evokes the image of a subject actively pushing the unwanted traumatic memory away. Personal consciousness stays in its place, as it were; it is the traumatic memory that is removed. It is highly questionable whether this is actually the case. Contemporary research has shown that dissociation of a traumatic experience occurs as the trauma is occurring (Putnam, 1989). There is little evidence for an active process of pushing away of the overwhelming experience; the uncoupling seems to have other mechanisms. Many trauma survivors report that they automatically are removed from the scene; they look at it from a distance or disappear altogether, leaving other parts of their personality to suffer and store the overwhelming experience. "I moved up to the ceiling from where I saw this little girl being molested and I felt very sorry for her" is a common description by incest survivors. When survivors later on suffer from flashbacks and related phenomena and subsequently become amnestic again for the trauma, they keep dissociating the traumatic memory. As illustrated by Janet's patient, Irène, the re-experience of the trauma itself reevokes a dissociative reaction. It seems reasonable to reserve the use of the concept of repression for the defense against primitive, forbidden, Id-impulses. Apart from its meanings in hypnosis and related phenomena, we believe the concept of dissociation is best suited for application with regard to traumatic memories.

Although the concepts of repression and dissociation have been used interchangeably by Freud and others with regard to traumatic memories, there is a fundamental difference between them. Repression reflects a vertically layered model of mind: what is repressed is pushed downward, into the unconscious. The subject no longer has access to it. Only symbolic, indirect indications would point to its assumed existence. Dissociation reflects a horizontally layered model of mind: when a subject does not remember a trauma, its "memory" is contained in an alternate stream of consciousness, which may be subconscious or dominate consciousness, e.g., during traumatic reenactments (Janet, 1894). Attempts to relate both models to each other have, so far, been rather unsuccessful (cf. Hart, 1926; Hilgard, 1977; McDougall, 1926; Singer, 1990). One failure is that in these combined models, traumatic memories cannot not be both dissociated and repressed.

## Contemporary Concepts of Memory Processing

Over the past half century extensive research has been conducted to elucidate the nature of human memory processes. These studies have been done without psychoanalytic, or even clinical psychiatric input, and, in fact, rarely have addressed the so-called "functional disorders of memory," which so intensely intrigued our psychiatric forefathers. While it is not possible in this space to review fully the recent advances in understanding memory processing, traumatic or otherwise, we will briefly review some of the relevant findings and compare them with what the early psychiatrists espoused. Janet had said that the basic function of the memory system is the storage and categorization of incoming sensations into a matrix for proper integration of subsequent internal and external stimuli (1889). The neurobiologist G. M. Edelman (1987) has suggested that the basic function of the central nervous system (CNS) is to "carry on adaptive perceptual categorization in an unlabeled world . . . that cannot be prefigured for an organism" (7). Edelman goes on to say that, after birth, when the basic neural structures are in place, the focus of development turns to modifications in the strengths of the synapses between neuronal groups. Modern neurobiology asserts that categorization is the most fundamental of mental activities: "With sufficient experience, the brain comes to contain a model of the world" (Calvin, 1990, 261). Contemporary researchers have found that the fundamental feature of memory consists of the creation of particular connections between the neuronal groups that enable people to get around in the world, and thus agree with Janet that what memory processes best is not specific events, but the quality of experience and the feelings associated with it (Edelman, 1987). The mind thus engages in two paradoxical activities: on the one hand, it creates schemes, and tries to fit all new experiences to fit its preconceptions. At the same time, it also is constantly looking for new ways of putting things together, for new categories to create (Calvin, 1990).

## Schemes and Categories

In order to remember new information it helps to have prior knowledge about the subject: while one-trial learning exists, most skills and knowledge are acquired by repetition (Bransford and Johnson, 1972; Schacter, 1987). People who possess a prior store of information about a particular area of knowledge tend to integrate new data related to that subject more easily than do people who have little or no prior knowledge. It is now widely accepted that memory is an active and constructive process and that remembering depends on existing mental schemas, "an active organization of past reactions or of past experiences which must always be operating in any well-adapted organic response" (Bartlett, 1932, 201; Schacter, 1987; Neisser, 1967). J. M. Mandler (1979, 263) said that "a schema is formed on the basis of past experience with objects, scenes, or events and consists of a set of (usually unconscious) expectations about what things look like and/or the order in which they occur. The parts or units of a schema consist of a set of variables, or slots, which can be filled or instantiated in any given instance by values that have greater or lesser degrees of probability of occurrence attached to them." In other words, preexisting schemes determine to what extent new information is absorbed and integrated.

New experiences can only be understood in the light of prior schemas. The particular internal and external conditions prevailing at the time an event takes place will affect what prior meaning schemes are activated (Janet already observed that events are much more likely to be experienced as traumatic when a person is tired, ill, or under stress [Janet, 1889, 1898]). Early in this century, gestalt psychology emphasized that all experiences consist of integrated structures or patterns that must be apprehended as wholes rather than as their disconnected parts. Subsequent research has shown that only after an experience is placed in a meaningful context can inferences and suppositions about the meaning of an event be made (Schacter, 1987). As M. Minsky (1980) puts it: "so we shall view memories as entities that predispose the mind to deal with new situations in old, remembered ways— specifically, as entities that reset the states of parts of the nervous system. Then they can cause that nervous system to be 'disposed' to behave as though it remembers."

The mind organizes new sensory information into preexisting patterns: "the pattern is the message" (Young, 1987). Janet anticipated this when he said:

> The person must not only know how to do it, but must also know how to associate the happening with the other events of his life, how to put it in its place in that life-history which each one of us is perpetually building up and which for each of us is an essential element of his personality. A situa-

tion has not been satisfactorily liquidated, has not been fully assimilated, until we have achieved, not merely through our movements, but also an inward reaction through the words we address to ourselves, through the organization of the recital of the event to others and to ourselves, and through the putting of this recital in its place as one of the chapters in our personal history. (1919–25, 2:273)

This principle of organization of experience in patterns and schemas has been called many things, including population codes, parallel processing, and distributed functions. The understanding of this principle has given rise to the new science of neural networks, which works on the basis of the notion that, while neurons are the anatomical units of the nervous system, they are not the structural elements of its functioning. Populations of neurons work together to discriminate patterns. These cannot be further subdivided into separate neurons for the details of a particular sensory impression. These unconscious memory processes function in domain-specific divisions, such as musical, athletic, mathematical, knowledge of the self, and so on (Gardner, 1987). Only some modules seem to have access to others, and only a few come under voluntary control. Parallel processing allows information to be processed very rapidly within one module. Only after a bit of information is unconsciously analyzed does it, when suitable, become accessible to consciousness. On the other hand, when there are problems with categorization because of difficulties in interpreting the nature of the incoming stimulus, consciousness also gets activated. On the whole, however, most processing of incoming information remains outside of conscious awareness. None of this has anything to do with internal conflicts and unacceptable wishes.

Memories easily become inaccurate when new ideas and pieces of information are constantly combined with old knowledge to form flexible mental schemas. As Janet pointed out a century ago, once a particular event or bit of information becomes integrated in a larger scheme it will no longer be accessible as an individual entity, and hence, the memory will be distorted (1889). Edward O. Wilson (1978) put it most poetically when he said that "the brain is an enchanted loom where millions of flashing shuttles weave a dissolving pattern. Since the mind recreates reality from the abstractions of sense impressions, it can equally well simulate reality by recall and fantasy. The brain invents stories and runs imagined and remembered events back and forth through time."

## How the Mind Comes to Freeze Some Memories

As we have seen, almost all memories are malleable by constant rework-ing and recategorization. Yet some memories are fixed in the mind and are not altered by the passage of time, or the intervention of subsequent experi-ence. In our studies on post-traumatic nightmares, traumatic scenes were reexperienced at night over and over again without modification (van der Kolk et al., 1984). In our Rorschach tests of trauma victims, we saw an unmodified reliving of traumatic episodes of ten, twenty, or thirty years ago (van der Kolk and Ducey, 1989). So how does memory occasionally escape integration and, instead, get "fixed" to resist further change?

One way in which this occurs is by myelinization: developmentally, the brain is extremely plastic until myelinization, which occurs in different parts of the brain at different ages but which is complete by the end of puberty, assigns specific functions to particular parts of the CNS. Binocular vision, speech, and even attachment patterns depend on myelinization during criti-cal periods (van der Kolk, 1987). Modern research (Jacobs and Nadel, 1985; Schacter and Moscovitch, 1984) indicates that infantile amnesia is the result of lack of myelinization of the hippocampus. Even after the hippocampus is myelinized, the hippocampal localizaton system, which allows memories to be placed in their proper context in time and place, remains vulnerable to disruption. Severe or prolonged stress can suppress hippocampal function-ing, creating context-free fearful associations, which are hard to locate in space and time. This results in amnesia for the specifics of traumatic experi-ences but not the feelings associated with them (Nadel and Zola Morgan, 1984; Sapolsky et al., 1984). Cognitive psychologists have identified three modes of information encoding in the CNS: inactive, iconic, and sym-bolic/linguistic (Bruner and Postman, 1949). These different modes reflect stages of CNS development (Piaget, 1973). As they mature, children shift from primarily sensorimotor (motoric action), to perceptual representations (iconic), to symbolic and linguistic modes of organizing mental experience. When people are exposed to trauma, that is, a frightening event outside of ordinary human experience, they experience "speechless terror" (van der Kolk, 1987). The experience cannot be organized on a linguistic level, and this failure to arrange the memory in words and symbols leaves it to be organized on a somatosensory or iconic level: as somatic sensations, be-havioral reenactments, nightmares, and flashbacks (Brett and Ostroff, 1985). As Piaget (1962) pointed out: "It is precisely because there is no immediate accommodation that there is complete dissociation of the inner activity from the external world. As the external world is solely represented by images, it is assimilated without resistance (i.e., unattached to other memories) to the unconscious ego." They therefore cannot be easily translated into the symbolic language necessary for linguistic retrieval.

## Hyperarousal, Triggering, and State-Dependent Learning

Another way in which memories can be "fixed" is by the occurrence of intense autonomic activation at the time that an event occurs. Janet (1889, 1894) noted that intense arousal ("vehement emotions") interferes with proper information processing and appropriate action, and that trauma could lead to both hypermnesias and amnesias. Current research has shown (DSM IV Field trials, 1991) that hypermnesias are more common after one time traumatic events, particularly in adults, while chronic amnesias tend to occur after repeated traumatization in childhood. One of the hallmarks of Post-Traumatic Stress Disorder is the intrusive reexperiencing of elements of the trauma in nightmares, flashbacks, or somatic reactions. These traumatic memories are triggered by autonomic arousal (Rainey et al., 1987; Southwick et al., 1993) and are thought to be mediated via hyperpotentiated noradrenergic pathways originating in the locus coeruleus of the brain (van der Kolk et al., 1985). The locus coeruleus is the "alarm bell" of the CNS, which properly goes off only under situations of threat, but which, in traumatized people, is liable to respond to any number of triggering conditions akin to the saliva in Pavlov's dogs. When the locus coeruleus alarm gets activated, it secretes noradrenaline, and, if rung repeatedly, endogenous opioids. These, in turn, dampen perception of pain, physical as well as psychological (van der Kolk et al., 1989). These neurotransmitters, which are activated by alarm, affect the hippocampus, the amygdala, and the frontal lobes, where stress-induced neurochemical alterations affect the interpretation of incoming stimuli further in the direction of "emergency" and fight-or-flight responses.

Animal research has shown that, once the memory tracts have been activated under conditions of severe stress, subsequent high-intensity stimuli will preferentially travel along the same pathways, activating the memories that were laid down under similar conditions (long-term potentiation; see ibid.). High degrees of stress cause state-dependent returns to earlier behavior patterns in animals as well. D. Mitchell and his colleagues (1984, 1985) found that arousal state determines how animals will react to stimuli. In a state of low arousal, animals tend to be curious and seek novelty. During high arousal they are frightened, avoid novelty, and perseverate in familiar behavior regardless of the outcome. Under ordinary circumstances, an animal will choose the most pleasant of two alternatives. When hyperaroused, it will seek the familiar, regardless of the intrinsic rewards (Mitchell et al., 1985). Thus, shocked animals returned to the box in which they were originally shocked in preference to less familiar locations not associated with punishment. Punished animals actually increased their exposure to shock as the trials continued (Mitchell et al., 1984).

It is likely that in people, just as in animals, long-term potentiation of neuronal connections made during intense autonomic hyperarousal is at the core of the repetitive, fixed, intrusive reliving of traumatic memories when people later find themselves in a state that resembles the original one (van der Kolk et al., 1985; Putnam, 1989). Cognitive psychologists have found that "perceptual processing automatically activates preexisting semantic memory structures corresponding to the features of the stimulus event, as well as related nodes by virtue of spreading activation. If some of these nodes correspond to the goals and conditions of various production systems, certain procedures will (automatically) be executed" (Kihlstrom, 1984, 447) without conscious awareness of the processes involved. Previously traumatized people are vulnerable to experience current stress as a return of the trauma.

In traumatized people, visual and motoric reliving experiences, nightmares, flashbacks, and reenactments seem to be preceded by physiological arousal. Yale researchers Southwick and his colleagues (1993) have recently convincingly shown that autonomic stimulation (by injection of yohimbine) causes people with PTSD to immediately access sights, sounds and smells related to earlier traumatic events. The general state of physiologic arousal, activation of particular neurotransmitter systems, and access to particular memory tracks all seem to be intertwined.

Thus, in the latter part of this century, we are rediscovering that the retrieval of memories and trauma-related states is to a large degree state dependent (Bower, 1981; Putnam, 1989). E. Tulving (1983, 242) has been able to demonstrate that remembering events always depends on the interaction between encoding and retrieval conditions, or compatibility between the engram and the cue. The more the contextual stimuli resemble conditions prevailing at the time of the original storage, the more retrieval is likely. Thus, memories are reactivated when a person is exposed to a situation, or is in a somatic state, reminiscent of the one when the original memory was stored. Janet described the fact that traumatized people lose track of current exigencies, and respond instead, as if faced with past threat: (they have) "lost the mental synthesis that constitutes reflective will and belief; [they] simply

transform into automatic wills and beliefs the impulses which are momentarily the strongest" (1907, xxi, xxii).

The fact that traumatized people experienced, and continue to experience, extremes of hyperarousal and numbing is compatible with the notion
that they are amnestic for certain aspects of their experience at any particular
time. In line with this, M. Bower (1981) has suggested that multiple personality amnesia is an extreme manifestation of state-dependent retrieval, whereby information acquired in one emotional state is inaccessible in another.
Since traumatic memories are state dependent, Janet drew the conclusion
that patients needed to be brought back to the state in which the memory was
first laid down in order to create a condition in which the dissociated memory of the past could be integrated into current meaning schemes (1895, 1889,
1904, 1894, 1989a, 1898b).

## Action Is Necessary for Integration

Janet made one other observation which is relevant to the fixing and
dissociation of traumatic memories. He thought that successful action of the
organism upon the environment is essential for the successful integration of
memories: "the healthy response to stress is mobilization of adaptive action"
(1909b, 1575). He even viewed active memory itself as an action: "memory is
an action: essentially, it is the action of telling a story" (1919–25, 2:272). This
notion keeps coming back in the works of modern neurobiologists. For example, Edelman states that "action is fundamental to perception: both sensory and motor ensembles must operate together to produce perceptual categorization" (1987, 238). Many writers about the human response to trauma
have observed that a feeling of helplessness, of physical or emotional paralysis, is fundamental to making an experience traumatic (e.g., Maier and
Seligman, 1976; van der Kolk, 1987): the person was unable to take any
action that could affect the outcome of events. It is likely that psychological
and physical immobilization indeed is a central feature of the impairment of
appropriate categorization of experience, and may be fundamental to the
development of hypermnesia and dissociation. Oliver Sacks, in *Awakenings*
(1990), provides rich clinical material that illustrates how experience, unless
acted upon, cannot be integrated into existing meaning schemes.

## Conclusions

After a long hiatus, the memories that plague people have once again
become a focus of investigation in psychology and psychiatry. While losing

track of the rich knowledge base about the role of memory in psychopathology which evolved around the turn of this century, psychoanalysis has, by highlighting the unavoidable conflicts between individual desires and the demands of a civilized society, held the torch for listening carefully to people's internal transformations of external experience. Contemporary neuroscience, also unaware of the earlier observations, has slowly started to focus on issues that preoccupied the founders of modern psychiatry and, with contemporary research methodology, is arriving at similar conclusions as they did. At the same time, psychiatry is beginning to rediscover the reality of trauma in people's lives, and the fact that actual experiences can be so overwhelming that they cannot be integrated into existing mental frameworks and, instead, are dissociated, later to return intrusively as fragmented sensory or motoric experiences. We are rediscovering that some experiences are encoded in memory, but not in such a way that people can acknowledge and accept what happened to them and go on with their lives (Schacter et al., 1982).

Traumatic memories are the unassimilated scraps of overwhelming experiences, which need to be integrated with existing mental schemes, and be transformed into narrative language. It appears that, in order for this to occur successfully, the traumatized person has to return to the memory often in order to complete it. Janet's case of Irène illustrates a situation in which this integration initially was totally absent: Irène had complete amnesia for the death of her mother and only experienced traumatic reenactments. This case also illustrates the fear and repugnance with which traumatized persons respond when confronted with their hitherto dissociated traumatic memories. They suffer, as Janet (1904) said, from a *phobia for the traumatic memory*. In Irène's case, overcoming this phobia was extremely difficult. When she could already accept the memory of her mother's death in the hypnotic state, she initially responded in the waking state with syncopal attacks and crises in which she again reenacted the tragedy. Other traumatized persons may initially respond with suicide attempts or other self-destructive behavior.

In the case of complete recovery, the person does not suffer anymore from the reappearance of traumatic memories in the form of flashbacks, behavioral reenactments, and so on. Instead the story can be told, the person can look back at what happened; he has given it a place in his life history, his autobiography, and thereby in the whole of his personality. Many traumatized persons, however, experience long periods of time in which they live, as it were, in two different worlds: the realm of the trauma and the realm of their current, ordinary life. Very often, it is impossible to bridge these worlds. This is most eloquently described by L. L. Langer (1991) in his study on oral testimonies by Holocaust survivors who never succeeded in bridging their existence in the death camps and their lives before and after. "It can . . . never be joined to the world he inhabits now. This suggests a permanent duality, not exactly a split or a doubling but a parallel existence. He switches from one to the other without synchronization because he is reporting not a *sequence* but a *simultaneity*" (95). This simultaneity is related to the fact that the traumatic experience/memory is, in a sense, timeless. It is not transformed into a story, placed in time, with a beginning, a middle and an end (which is characteristic for narrative memory). If it can be told at all, it is still a (re)experience.

> Witnesses are both willing and reluctant to proceed with the chronology; they frequently hesitate because they know that their most complicated recollections are unrelated to time. . . . [Trauma] stops the chronological clock and fixes the moment permanently in memory and imagination, immune to the vicissitudes of time. The unfolding story brings relief, while the unfolding plot induces pain. (ibid., 174–75)

Switching from one's present-day world to the world of traumatic memory does not only imply the simultaneity of two utterly incompatible worlds, of an ordinary and a traumatic state of mind. As the trauma is fixed at a certain moment in a person's life, people live out their existences in two different stages of the life cycle, the traumatic past, and the bleached present. The traumatized, fixated, inflexible part of the personality has stopped developing (Janet, 1898b, 1904). This is a major complication in the attempt to bridge the two realms of experience. Langer (1991) hints at this in his comments on one Holocaust survivor's report:

> The bizarre spectacle of an adult speaking of a seven-year-old child meeting his parents [during a traumatic meeting directly after liberation] remembering his five-year-old self [as a member of street gangs of orphaned or vagrant children] as an unrecapturable identity reminds us of the complex obstacles that frustrate a coherent narrative view of the former victim's ordeal from the vantage point of the present. (112)

In even more extreme cases, in people with multiple personality disorder, the adult self may be entirely unaware of his childhood trauma, which then can only be related when the traumatized seven-year-old dominates consciousness ("has executive power"). She either reexperiences the trauma in its totality (as did Irène) or fluctuatingly and opaquely "senses" autobiographical episodes.

Thus, one extreme post-traumatic state consists of living in the unremembered past, reenacting in contemporary reality past traumatic experiences, as did Irène. A different state consists of a continuous switching from one internal world to another, as described by a survivor of Auschwitz (quoted in ibid., 6): "I live in a double existence. The double of Auschwitz doesn't disturb me or mingle with my life. As if it weren't 'me' at all. Without this split, I wouldn't have been able to come back to live." But when the person is (partially) aware of his traumatic memories, for example, of the Holocaust, then the meaning schemes with which current experiences are integrated correspond to traumatic experiences. They often can tell the story of their traumatization with a mixture of past and present, but their current life is characterized by doubt and humiliation, by feelings of guilt and shame: past meaning schemes determine the interpretation of the present. This is not only the case in Langer's witnesses of the Holocaust but also in many otherwise traumatized persons, such as incest victims and combat veterans suffering from PTSD.

Being unable to reconcile oneself to the past is at least in part dependent upon the objective nature of the trauma. Can the Auschwitz experience and the loss of innumerable family members during the Holocaust really be integrated, be made part of one's autobiography? Every therapist working with traumatized people is familiar with the patient's deep despair and anguish when faced with their horrendous life histories. How can one bring the traumatic experience to an end, when one feels completely unable and unwilling to resign oneself to the fact that one has been subjected to this horrendous event or series of events? How can one resign oneself to the unacceptable? Both Janet and many contemporary psychotherapists have tried to assist their patients in realizing this act of termination, by suggesting to them an alternative, less negative or even positive scenario. Janet suggested to his patient Justine, who was traumatized at age seventeen by the sight of horrendous nude corpses of victims of a cholera epidemic, to visualize these corpses with clothes on. He even suggested that one, dressed in the uniform of a Chinese general, got up and walked away. One contemporary therapist of a Holocaust survivor had the patient imagine a flower growing in the assignment place in Auschwitz—an image that gave him tremendous comfort. Many patients who are victimized by rape and other forms of violence are helped by imagining having all the power they want and applying it to the perpetrator. Memory is everything. Once flexibility is introduced, the traumatic memory starts losing its power over current experience. By imagining these alternative scenarios, many patients are able to soften the intrusive power of the original, unmitigated horror.

The question arises whether it is not a sacrilege of the traumatic experience to play with the reality of the past? Janet (1919–25) provided one example that illustrates the usefulness of such a therapeutic approach in some cases (cf. van der Hart et al., 1990). His case example concerns a thirty-one-year-old woman who had lost her two infants in close succession. She was in constant despair and suffered gastrointestinal cramps and vomiting. She was admitted to the Salpêtrière, emaciated, preoccupied with reminders of her children, and regularly hallucinating realistic scenes of their deaths. Janet began treatment by having her give him the reminders for safekeeping. Using hypnotic suggestion, he substituted her traumatic death images with those of flowers. He then made them fade away altogether. Subsequently, Janet focused her attention on the future and on her being trained in midwifery. At one-year follow-up, she was working again and was considered to be cured.

Recently, the psychoanalyst A. Modell (1990), deeply conversant with psychoanalysis, and knowledgeable about Edelman's work, has started to integrate some of the new knowledge of neuroscience with the clinical practice of psychoanalysis, focusing particularly on the nature and meaning of the transference. He considers that traumatic or unassimilated memories are activated in the transference, where "units of experience of the past [are] brought into present time. When the archaic affect category predominates over current perceptions, it may contribute to the psychopathology of everyday life" (1990, 66). He considers that at the core of healing in the therapeutic relationship is the fact that "Affects are communicative and contagious, so that the other person is involved in the affective repetition and will collude, either consciously, or unconsciously, in confirming or disconfirming the subject's category of perception" (68). "The process of disconfirmation of the painful past interactions (in the therapy situation) is essentially a process of retranscription [of meaning schemes]." His work illustrates the reality that the trauma, almost inevitably, will be revived in the therapeutic relationship and that the meaning schemes built around the traumatic experiences will be activated in the form of irrational perceptions and fears. The taming and utilization of these transference expressions of the trauma to integrate past horror with current experience is one of the great challenges in the therapy of traumatized patients.

## References

Bartlett, F. C. 1932. *Remembering*. London: Cambridge University Press.
Bergson, H. 1896. *Matière et mémoire*. Paris: Alcan.

Bower, M. 1981. "Mood and Memory." *American Psychologist* 36:129–48.

Bransford, J. D., and M. K. Johnson. 1972. "Considerations of Some Problems of Comprehension." In *Visual Information Processing*, ed. W. G. Chase. New York: Academic.

Brett, E. A., and R. Ostroff. 1985. "Imagery and Post-Traumatic Stress Disorder: An Overview." *American Journal of Psychiatry* 142:417–24.

Bruner, J. S., and L. Postman. 1949. "Perception, Cognition, and Personality." *Journal of Psychiatry* 8:14–31.

Calvin, W. H. 1990. *The Cerebral Symphony*. New York: Bantam.

Chu, J. A., and D. L. Dill. 1990. "Dissociative Symptoms in Relation to Childhood Physical and Sexual Abuse." *American Journal of Psychiatry* 147:887–92.

Edelman, G. M. 1987. *Neural Darwinism: The Theory of Neuronal Group Selection*. New York: Basic Books.

Ellenburger, H. F. 1970. *The Discovery of the Unconscious: The History and Evolution of Dynamic Psychiatry*. New York: Basic Books.

Ferenczi, S., K. Abraham, E. Simmel, and E. Jones. 1919. *Zur Psychoanalyse der Kriegsneurosen*. Leipzig: Internationaler Psychoanalytischer Verlag.

Freud, Sigmund. 1896 (1962). *The Standard Edition of the Complete Psychological Works of Sigmund Freud*. Vol. 3. Translated under the editorship of James Strachey in collaboration with Anna Freud, assisted by Alix Strachey and Alan Tyson. 24 vols. (1953–74). London: Hogarth.

———. 1900 (1953–58). *SE* 4–5.

———. 1920 (1955). *SE* 18.

———. 1926 (1959). *SE* 20.

———. 1936 (1964). "A Disturbance of Memory on the Acropolis." *SE* 22.

———. 1939. *Moses and Monotheism*. Trans. Katherine Jones. New York: Vintage.

———. 1950. "Beyond the Pleasure Principle." *International Psycho-Analytic Library*.

Freud, Sigmund, and J. Breuer. 1893 (1955). *SE* 2.

Gardner, H. 1987. *The Mind's New Science*. New York: Basic Books.

Hart, B. 1926. "The Conception of Dissociation." *British Journal of Medical Psychology* 6:241–63.

Hilgard, E. R. 1977. *Divided Consciousness: Multiple Controls in Human Thought and Action*. New York: Wiley.

Jacobs, W. J., and L. Nadel. 1985. "Stress-Induced Recovery of Fears and Phobias." *Psychological Review* 92:512–13.

James, William. 1880. "Great Men, Great Thoughts, and the Environment." *Atlantic Monthly* 46:441–59.

———. 1894. "Book Review of Janet's 'État mental des hystériques' and Breuer and Freud's 'Über den Psychischen Mechanismus Hysterischer Phänomene.'" *Psychological Review* 1:195–99.

Janet, Pierre. 1889 (1973). *L'automatisme psychologique*. Paris: Société Pierre Janet.

———. 1893 (1990). "L'amnésie continue." In *L'état mental des hystériques*, 2d ed. Paris: Alcan.

——. 1894 (1990). "Histoire d'une idée fixe." In *Névroses et idées fixes*. Vol. 1. Paris: Alcan.

——. 1895. "Les idées fixes de forme hystérique." *Presse Medicale* 3:201–3.

——. 1898a (1911). "Le traitement psychologique de l'hystérie." In *L'état mental des Hystériques*. 2d ed. Paris: Alcan.

——. 1898b (1990). *Névroses et idées fixes*. Vol. 1. Paris: Alcan.

——. 1904 (1983). *L'amnésie et la dissociation des souvenirs par l'émotion*. Marseille: Lafitte Reprints.

——. 1907 (1965). *The Major Symptoms of Hysteria*. New York: Hafner.

——. 1909a. *Les névroses*. Paris: Flammarion.

——. 1909b. "Problèmes psychologiques de l'émotion." *Revue de Neurologie* 17:1551–1687.

——. 1911. *L'état mental des hystériques*. 2d ed. Paris: Alcan.

——. 1919–25 (1984). *Les médications psychologiques*. 3 vols. Paris: Société Pierre Janet.

——. 1928. *L'évolution de la mémoire et la notion du temps*. Paris: Cahine.

——. 1929 (1984). *L'évolution de la personnalité*. Paris: Société Pierre Janet.

——. 1935. "Réalisation et interprétation." *Annales Medico-Psychologiques* 93:329–66.

Kihlstrom, J. 1984. "Conscious, Subconscious, Unconscious: A Cognitive Perspective." In *The Unconscious Reconsidered*, ed. K. Bowers and D. Meichenbaum. New York: Wiley.

Langer, L. L. 1991. *Holocaust Testimonies: The Ruins of Memory*. New Haven: Yale University Press.

McDougall, W. 1926. *An Outline of Abnormal Psychology*. London: Methuen.

Macmillan, M. 1990. "Freud and Janet on Organic and Hysterical Paralysis: A Mystery Solved?" *International Review of Psycho-Analysis* 17:189–203.

——. 1991. *Freud Evaluated: The Completed Arc*. Amsterdam: North-Holland.

Maier, S. F., and M. E. P. Seligman. 1976. "Learned Helplessness: Theory and Evidence." *Journal of Experimental Psychology: General* 105:3–46.

Mandler, J. M. 1979. "Categorical and Schematic Organization of Memory." In *Memory Organization and Structure*, ed. C. R. Puff. New York: Academic.

Minsky, M. 1980. "K-Lines: A Theory of Memory." *Cognitive Science* 4:117–33.

Mitchell, D., A. S. Koleszar, and R. A. Scopatz. 1984. "Arousal and T-Maze Behavior in Mice: Convergent Paradigm for Neophobia Constructs and Optimal Arousal Theory." *Learning and Motivation* 15:287–301.

Mitchell, D., E. W. Osborne, and M. W. O'Boyle. 1985. "Habituation under Stress: Shocked Mice Show Non-Associative Learning in a T-Maze." *Behav. Neural Biol.* 43:212–17.

Modell, A. 1990. *Other Times, Other Realities: Toward a Theory of Psychoanalytic Treatment*. Cambridge, Mass.: Harvard University Press.

Nadel, L., and S. Zola Morgan. 1984. "Infantile Amnesia: A Neurobiological Perspective." In *Infant Memory*, ed. M. Moskovitz. New York: Plenum.

Neisser, U. 1967. *Cognitive Psychology*. Englewood Cliffs, N.J.: Prentice-Hall.

Perry, C., and J. R. Laurence. 1984. "Mental Processes outside Awareness: The Contributions of Freud and Janet." In *The Unconscious Reconsidered*, ed. K. S. Bowers and D. Meichenbaum. New York: Wiley.

Piaget, J. 1962. *Play, Dreams, and Imitation in Childhood*. New York: Norton.

———. 1973. *Structuralism*. New York: Basic Books.

Prince, M. 1910. *The Dissociation of the Personality*. New York: Longmans, Green.

Putnam, F. W. 1989. *Diagnosis and Treatment of Multiple Personality Disorder*. New York: Guilford.

Rainey, J. M., A. Aleem, A. Ortiz, et al. 1987. "Laboratory Procedure for the Inducement of Flashbacks." *American Journal of Psychiatry* 144:1317–19.

Sacks, Oliver. 1990. *Awakenings*. New York: Harper Perennial.

Sapolsky, R., L. Krey, and B. S. McEwen. 1984. "Stress Down-Regulates Corticosterone Receptors in a Site-Specific Manner in the Brain." *Endocrinology* 114:287–92.

Saxe, G., Bessel A. van der Kolk, R. Berkowitz, K. Hall, G. Lieberg, and J. Schartz. 1993. "Dissociative Disorders in Psychiatric Inpatients." *American Journal of Psychiatry* 150:1037–42.

Schacter, D. 1987. "Implicit Memory: History and Current Status." *Journal of Experimental Psychology: Learning Memory, and Cognition* 13:501–18.

Schacter, D. L., and M. Moscovitch. 1984. "Infants, Amnestic, and Dissociable Memory Systems." In *Infant Memory*, ed. M. Moskovitz. New York: Plenum.

Schacter, D., P. Wang, E. Tulving, and M. Friedman. 1982. "Functional Retrograde Amnesia: A Quantitative Case Study." *Neuropsychologia* 20:523–32.

Singer, J. L., ed. 1990. *Repression and Dissociation*. Chicago: University of Chicago Press.

Southwick, S., J. Krystal, A. Morgan, D. Johnson, L. Nagy, A. Nicolaou, et al. 1993. "Abnormal Noradrenergic Function in Post-Traumatic Stress Disorder." *Archives of General Psychology* 50:266–74.

Tulving, E. 1983. *Elements of Episodic Memory*. Oxford: Oxford University Press.

van der Hart, O., P. Brown, and R. N. Turco. 1990. "Hypnotherapy for Traumatic Grief: Janetian and Modern Approaches Integrated." *American Journal of Hypnotherapy* 32, no. 4: 263–71.

van der Kolk, Bessel A. 1987. *Psychological Trauma*. Washington, D.C.: American Psychiatric Press.

van der Kolk, Bessel A., R. Blitz, W. A. Burr, and E. Hartmann. 1984. "Nightmares and Trauma: Life-long and Traumatic Nightmares in Veterans." *American Journal of Psychiatry* 141:187–90.

van der Kolk, Bessel A., and C. R. Ducey. 1989. "The Psychological Processing of Traumatic Experience: Rorschach Patterns in PTSD." *Journal of Traumatic Stress* 2:259–74.

van der Kolk, Bessel A., M. S. Greenberg, H. Boyd, and John Krystal. 1985. "Inescapable Shock, Neurotransmitters, and Addition to Trauma: Toward a Psychobiology of Post-Traumatic Stress." *Biological Psychiatry* 20:314–25.

Wilson, E. O. 1978. *On Human Nature*. Cambridge: Harvard University Press.

Young, J. Z. 1987. *Philosophy and the Brain*. Oxford: Oxford University Press.

# Notes on Trauma and
# Community

### KAI ERIKSON

In the past several years, research errands of one kind or another have taken me to the scene of a number of different human catastrophes—a mountain hollow in West Virginia called Buffalo Creek visited by a devastating flood; a town in southern Florida called Immokalee, where 200 migrant farmworkers from Haiti were defrauded of their meager savings; the ring of neighborhoods surrounding Three Mile Island; an Ojibway Indian reserve in northwest Ontario called Grassy Narrows that experienced not only the contamination of its local waterways but a disastrous relocation; and a housing development in Colorado called East Swallow plagued by an underground gasoline leak. It has seemed to me throughout that some form of the term "trauma" is the most accurate way to describe not only the condition of the people one encounters in those scenes but the texture of the scenes themselves. The term itself, however, is used in so many different ways and has found a place in so many different vocabularies that it is hard to know how to make of it a useful sociological concept. So I begin with matters of definition.

Trauma is generally taken to mean a blow to the tissues of the body—or more frequently now, to the tissues of the mind—that results in injury or some other disturbance. Something alien breaks in on you, smashing through whatever barriers your mind has set up as a line of defense. It invades you, takes you over, becomes a dominating feature of your interior landscape—"possesses" you, Cathy Caruth says in the introduction to Part I of this volume—and in the process threatens to drain you and leave you empty. The classic symptoms of trauma range from feelings of restlessness and agitation at one end of the emotional scale to feelings of numbness and bleakness at the other. Traumatized people often scan the surrounding world anxiously for signs of danger, breaking into explosive rages and reacting with a start to ordinary sights and sounds, but at the same time, all that nervous activity takes place against a numbed gray background of depression, feelings of helplessness, and a general closing off of the spirit, as the mind tries to insulate itself from further harm. Above all, trauma involves a continual reliving of some wounding experience in daydreams and nightmares, flashbacks and hallucinations, and in a compulsive seeking out of similar circumstances. Paul Valéry wrote (Felman, 1990): "Our memory repeats to us what we haven't understood" (76). That's almost it. Say instead: "Our memory repeats to us what we haven't yet come to terms with, what still haunts us."

"Trauma," however, is used in so many different ways and has found a place in so many different vocabularies that we need to resolve two terminological matters before proceeding.

First, in classic medical usage "trauma" refers not to the *injury* inflicted but to the *blow* that inflicted it, not to the *state of mind* that ensues but to the *event* that provoked it. The term "post-traumatic stress disorder" (a peculiar gathering of syllables, if you listen carefully) is an accommodation to that medical convention. The disorder, that is, is named for the stimulus that brought it into being—a logic very like the one that would be at work if mumps were known as "post-exposure glandular disorder."

In both clinical and common usage, however, that distinction is becoming blurred. The dictionary on my desk (to return to that excellent source) defines trauma both as "a stress or blow that may produce disordered feelings or behavior" and as "the state or condition produced by such a stress or blow." In a sense, then, the location of the term, its center of gravity, has been shifting from the first meaning to the second, and I am not only taking advantage of that shift here but encouraging it for general use.

There are good reasons for doing so. The historian who wants to know where a story starts, like the therapist who needs to identify a precipitating cause in order to deal with the injury it does, will naturally be interested in beginnings. But those are no more than details to everyone else (and not even very important ones at that), because it is *how people react to them* rather than *what they are* that give events whatever traumatic quality they can be said to have. The most violent wrenchings in the world, that is to say, have no clinical standing unless they harm the workings of a mind or body, so it is the *damage done* that defines and gives shape to the initial event, the *damage done* that gives it its name. It scarcely makes sense to locate the term anywhere else.

Second, in order to serve as a generally useful concept, "trauma" has to be understood as resulting from a *constellation of life experiences* as well as from a discrete happening, from a *persisting condition* as well as from an acute event. Now I know that in dragging across this already well-traveled and well-charted conceptual ground, I am scuffing up a widely observed line differentiating "trauma" from "stress." "Trauma," in this familiar distinction, refers to a violent event that injures in one sharp stab, while "stress" refers to a series of events or even to a chronic condition that erodes the spirit more gradually. But that line, I submit, was drawn in the wrong place to begin with, at least for such purposes as these. A difficult marriage is stressful, yes. So is a draining job. But Auschwitz? A prolonged period of terror or brutality? No, it only makes sense to insist that trauma can issue from a sustained exposure to battle as well as from a moment of numbing shock, from a continuing pattern of abuse as well as from a single searing assault, from a period of severe attenuation and erosion as well as from a sudden flash of fear. The effects are the same, and that, after all, should be our focus.

Moreover, as I noted earlier, trauma has the quality of converting that one sharp stab of which I spoke a moment ago into an enduring state of mind. A chronicler of passing events may report that the episode itself lasted no more than an instant—a gunshot, say—but the traumatized mind holds on to that moment, preventing it from slipping back into its proper chronological place in the past, and relives it over and over again in the compulsive musings of the day and the seething dreams of night. The moment becomes a season, the event becomes a condition.

With these clarifications, "trauma" becomes a concept social scientists as well as clinicians can work with. I want to use my broadened vocabulary, in fact, to suggest that one can speak of traumatized communities as something distinct from assemblies of traumatized persons. Sometimes the tissues of community can be damaged in much the same way as the tissues of mind and body, as I shall suggest shortly, but even when that does not happen, traumatic wounds inflicted on individuals can combine to create a mood, an ethos—a group culture, almost—that is different from (and more than) the sum of the private wounds that make it up. Trauma, that is, has a social dimension.

Let me begin by suggesting that trauma can create community. In some ways, that is a very odd thing to claim. To describe people as traumatized is to say that they have withdrawn into a kind of protective envelope, a place of mute, aching loneliness, in which the traumatic experience is treated as a solitary burden that needs to be expunged by acts of denial and resistance. What could be less "social" than that?

But traumatic conditions are not like the other troubles to which flesh is heir. They move to the center of one's being and, in doing so, give victims the feeling that they have been set apart and made special. One Buffalo Creek survivor said: "The black water came down the bottom we lived in. I couldn't stand it any more. It was like something was wiped over me and made me different" (Erikson, 1976, 163). That woman was talking of a feeling shared by millions of others. She viewed herself as having an altered relationship to the rest of humankind, to history, to the processes of nature. She viewed herself as marked, maybe cursed, maybe even dead. "I feel dead now," one of her neighbors said. "I have no energy. I feel numb, like I died long ago."

For some survivors, at least, this sense of difference can become a kind of calling, a status, where people are drawn to others similarly marked. The wariness and numbness and slowness of feeling shared by traumatized people everywhere may mean that relating to others comes hard and at a heavy price, so I am not speaking here of the easy comradeship one often finds among those who live through telling experiences together. Still, trauma shared can serve as a source of communality in the same way that common languages and common backgrounds can. There is a spiritual kinship there, a sense of identity, even when feelings of affection are deadened and the ability to care numbed. A compelling example is provided by the young married couple, described by Shoshana Felman in this volume, who survived the Holocaust miraculously and remained together afterward not because they got along (they did not) but because "he knew who I was—he was the only person who knew . . . and I knew who he was." At a recent reunion of Americans who had been held hostage in Iran, one explained to a reporter: "It is easy to be together. We don't have to explain things. We carry the same pain."

So trauma has both centripetal and centrifugal tendencies. It draws one away from the center of group space while at the same time drawing one back. The human chemistry at work here is an odd one, but it has been noted many times before: estrangement becomes the basis for communality, as if persons without homes or citizenship or any other niche in the larger order of things were invited to gather in a quarter set aside for the disfranchised, a ghetto for the unattached.

Indeed, it can happen that otherwise unconnected persons who share a traumatic experience seek one another out and develop a form of fellowship on the strength of that common tie. Veterans haunted by dark memories of Vietnam, for example, or adults who cannot come to terms with childhood abuse sometimes gather into groups for reasons not unlike the Holocaust couple cited earlier: they know one another in ways that the most intimate of friends never will, and for that reason they can supply a human context and a kind of emotional solvent in which the work of recovery can begin. It is a gathering of the wounded.

For the most part, though, trauma damages the texture of community. I want to suggest, in fact, that there are at least two senses in which one can say that a community—as distinct from the people who constitute it—has become traumatized.

When I first wrote about the Buffalo Creek catastrophe, I tried to make a distinction between what I then called "individual trauma" and "collective trauma." To quote myself:

> By *individual trauma* I mean a blow to the psyche that breaks through one's defenses so suddenly and with such brutal force that one cannot react to it effectively. . . . [The] Buffalo Creek survivors experienced precisely that. They suffered deep shock as a result of their exposure to death and devastation, and, as so often happens in catastrophes of this magnitude, they withdrew into themselves, feeling numbed, afraid, vulnerable, and very alone. (Erikson, 1976, 153–54)

> By *collective trauma*, on the other hand, I mean a blow to the basic tissues of social life that damages the bonds attaching people together and impairs the prevailing sense of communality. The collective trauma works its way slowly and even insidiously into the awareness of those who suffer from it, so it does not have the quality of suddenness normally associated with "trauma." But it is a form of shock all the same, a gradual realization that the community no longer exists as an effective source of support and that an important part of the self has disappeared. . . . "I" continue to exist, though damaged and maybe even permanently changed. "You" continue to exist, though distant and hard to relate to. But "we" no longer exist as a connected pair or as linked cells in a larger communal body. (ibid., 154)

To say that Buffalo Creek as a social organism was traumatized—at least when one reflects on the matter—is to run the risk of sounding obvious. Buffalo Creek is part of a cultural setting in which the sense of community is so palpable that it is easy to think of it as tissue capable of being injured.

Now one has to realize when talking like this that one is in danger of drifting into a realm of metaphor. Communities do not have hearts or sinews or ganglia; they do not suffer or rationalize or experience joy. But the analogy does help suggest that a cluster of people acting in concert and moving to the same collective rhythms can allocate their personal resources in such a way that the whole comes to have more humanity than its constituent parts. In effect, people put their own individual resources at the disposal of the group—placing them in the communal store, as it were—and then draw on that reserve supply for the demands of everyday life. And if the whole community more or less disappears, as happened on Buffalo Creek, people find that they cannot take advantage of the energies they once invested in the communal store. They find that they are almost empty of feeling, empty of affection, empty of confidence and assurance. It is as if the individual cells had supplied raw energy to the whole body but did not have the means to convert that energy back into a usable personal form once the body was no longer there to process it. (ibid., 194)

In places like Buffalo Creek, then, the community in general can almost be described as the locus for activities that are normally thought to be the property of individual persons. It is the *community* that offers a cushion for pain, the *community* that offers a context for intimacy, the *community* that serves as the repository for binding traditions. And when the community is profoundly affected, one can speak of a damaged social organism in almost the same way that one would speak of a damaged body. The Buffalo Creek incident provided a telling test case of that idea, by the way, since a number of residents who were clearly traumatized by what had happened proved to have been a long way from home when the disaster struck and thus never experienced the raging waters and all of the death and devastation at first-hand. They were injured by the loss of a sustaining community.

This does not mean that Buffalo Creek had become a desert, an empty space, as a consequence of the flood. The people of the hollow still had memory, kinship, contiguity in common, so there were materials to build with. But for the moment, at least, they were torn loose from their cultural moorings—alone, adrift, floating like particles in a dead electromagnetic field.

Now, tightly knit communities like Buffalo Creek are rare in this country and becoming more so. None of the other disaster scenes I have visited can be described in the same way. But trauma can work its way into the fabric of community life in other ways as well.

Among the most common findings of research on natural disasters, as I also noted in my report on Buffalo Creek, is that a sudden and logically inexplicable wave of good feeling washes over survivors not long after the event itself. For one dread moment they thought that the world had come to an end, that they had been "left naked and alone in a terrifying wilderness of ruins," as Anthony Wallace put it (1957, 127). But, according to Wallace, a "stage of euphoria" quickly follows in most natural disasters as people come to realize that the general community is not dead after all (1957, 127). The energy with which rescuers work and the warmth with which neighbors respond act to reassure victims that there is still life among the wreckage, and they react with an outpouring of communal feeling, an urgent need to make contact with and even touch others by way of renewing old pledges of fellowship. They are celebrating the recovery of the community they momentarily thought dead, and, in a way, they are celebrating their own rebirth. One well-known study spoke of a "city of comrades," another of a "democracy of distress," and a third of a "community of sufferers." Martha Wolfenstein, reviewing the literature on disasters in general, called the phenomenon a "post-disaster utopia," while Allen H. Barton, having surveyed much the same literature, talked about an "altruistic community." "Therapeutic communities," Charles E. Fritz called them in a classic essay on disasters. It is as if survivors, digging out from under the masses of debris, discover that the communal body is not only intact but mobilizing its remaining resources to dress the wound on its flank.

Nothing of the sort happened on Buffalo Creek. Nothing of the sort happened in *any* of the disaster situations I have visited, in fact, nor has it happened in many other incidents reported recently in the literature.

For one thing, these disasters (or near disasters) often seem to force open whatever fault lines once ran silently through the structure of the larger community, dividing it into divisive fragments. In a number of places where such emergencies have taken place, the people of the community have split into factions to such an extent that one wise student of such matters calls them "corrosive communities" to contrast them with the "therapeutic communities" so often noted in an earlier literature (Freudenberg and Jones, 1991). The fault lines usually open to divide the people affected by the event from the people spared, exactly the opposite of what happens in a "city of comrades." Those not touched try to distance themselves from those touched, almost as if they are escaping something spoiled, something contaminated, something polluted. "Corrosive" is a good word, too, because the disasters that provoke this reaction tend for the most part to involve some form of toxicity. This is what happened at Three Mile Island, and it was a prominent feature of the social landscape of Love Canal and elsewhere. The net effect is to set the afflicted apart.

In such circumstances, traumatic experiences work their way so thoroughly into the grain of the affected community that they come to supply its prevailing mood and temper, dominate its imagery and its sense of self, govern the way its members relate to one another. The point to be made here is not that calamity serves to strengthen the bonds linking people together—it does not, most of the time—but that the shared experience becomes almost like a common culture, a source of kinship. Something of that sort happened in each of the places I have described here, and it is in that sense that they can be fairly described as traumatized. (I do not have time to go into it now, but I would add that something of the sort can also happen to whole regions, even whole countries. I lectured to students on trauma and related matters in Romania not long after the end of one of the most abusive and arbitrarily despotic regimes on human record, and the flashes of recognition that erupted from those warm and generous audiences when I spoke in terms not unlike the ones I am using here—outbursts might be a better term—spoke volumes about the damage that can be done to a whole people by sustained dread and dislocation.)

So communal trauma, let's say, can take two forms, either alone or in combination: damage to the tissues that hold human groups intact, and the creation of social climates, communal moods, that come to dominate a group's spirit.

I also tried to make a distinction in the original Buffalo Creek report—although I am not sure that I really appreciated its significance until later—between those traumatic events that are thought to have issued from the hand of God and those that are thought to have been the work of fellow human beings. The people of Buffalo Creek were horrified when the corporation they all perceived as responsible for the flood called it "an act of God," and then explained: "The dam was incapable of holding the water God poured into it." Whatever others may say about so peculiar a theology, the residents of the hollow knew it to be blasphemy; and they knew, too, that it reflected a degree of indifference that bordered on contempt. This added sharply to the traumatic effects of the flood, and indeed it has added sharply to the pain experienced in all of the disaster situations I know firsthand, for they share in common the circumstance of having been caused by other people. This may be worth a brief excursion:

The ancients feared pestilence, drought, famine, plague, and all the other scourges that darken the pages of the Revelations. These miseries trouble us yet, to be sure, but it is fair to say that we have learned ways to defend ourselves against many of the worst of them. Some (certain epidemics, say) can now be arrested or even prevented altogether. Others (hurricanes, tidal waves) can be seen far enough in advance for people to move out of their path, thus neutralizing a part of their lethal force.

The irony, though, is that the technological advances that have afforded us this degree of protection from *natural* disasters have created a whole new category of what specialists have come to call *technological* disasters—meaning everything that can go wrong when systems fail, humans err, engines misfire, designs prove faulty, and so on. Earthquakes, floods, hurricanes, and volcanic eruptions are "natural"; collisions, explosions, breakdowns, collapses, leaks, and of course, crises like the one at Three Mile Island, are "technological."

Now technological disasters have clearly grown in number as human beings press the outer limits of their competence. We are encouraged to think that we can control both the best in nature and the worst in ourselves, and we continue to think so until the momentum of some adventure carries us beyond the edge of our own intelligence. But, more to the point, they have also grown in size. This is true in the sense that events of local origins can have consequences that reach across huge distances—as was the case, say, at Chernobyl. And it is also true in the sense that news of it is broadcast so quickly and so widely that it becomes a moment in everyone's history, a datum in everyone's store of knowledge—as was the case at Three Mile Island.

The distinction between natural and technological disasters is sometimes hard to draw exactly. When a mine shaft collapses in Kentucky, it is often a collaboration of restless mountain and careless people. When an epidemic spreads across central Africa, it owes its virulence both to tough new strains of bacillus and to stubborn old human habits.

However hard it may be to draw in actuality, however, that line is generally quite distinct to victims. Natural disasters are experienced as acts of God or whims of nature. They occur *to* us. They *visit* us, as if from afar. Technological disasters, on the other hand, being of human manufacture, are at least in principle preventable, so there is always a story to be told about them, always a moral to be drawn from them, always a measure of blame to be assigned in respect to them. It is almost impossible to imagine a commission of inquiry, called to discover the causes of some dreadful accident, concluding, "well, it just happened." We look for responsible human agents and we find them.

Now there is a sense in which it *did* "just happen." This is not because the fates are full of mischief sometimes but because accidents are bound to happen over time as human systems get more and more elaborate. When geologists describe a floodplain as the kind that is likely to be inundated once in fifty years, they are not using a system of reckoning all that different from nuclear engineers who describe a core melt as the kind of occurrence that is likely to take place once in every 20,000 reactor years of operation. The flood is an act of God, the core melt a human mistake. But both have been written into a kind of script. Both are "natural" in the sense of being foreseeable, inevitable, expectable. The flood lies beyond our control, we say, because nature is simply like that. But core melts can be described as beyond our control because human systems, too, are simply like that. We know in advance that hands will slip and machinery fail some predictable fraction of the time. This makes of them what Charles Perrow (1984) calls "normal accidents."

Technological catastrophes, however, are never understood by those who suffer from them as the way the world of chance sorts itself out. They provoke outrage rather than resignation. They generate a feeling that the thing ought not to have happened, that someone is at fault, that victims deserve not only compassion and compensation but something similar to what lawyers call punitive damages. Most significant, they bring in their wake feelings of injury and of vulnerability from which it is difficult to recover easily.

The scene has become an ever more frequent one in our times: a scattering of people, unaware for the most part of the risks they were running, is damaged by the activities of some kind of corporate group. The corporation is sometimes huge, as was the case at Buffalo Creek and Three Mile Island, and it is sometimes no more than a family business, as was the case with the migrant worker camp in southern Florida. But most of the time—so often, in fact, that we can almost think of it as a natural reflex—the company draws into its own interior spaces and posts lawyers around its borders like a ring of pickets. Nothing unexpected in that, surely. Anyone who reads newspapers knows how that reflex works.

Yet it always seems to come as a surprise. Those who manage corporations (or more to the point, perhaps, those who are hired to defend them) generally speak of them as if they were *things*, bloodless and inorganic. But victims of accidents rarely forget, even when company officials manage to, that corporate decisions are made by human beings and that corporate policies reflect the views of human beings. And it can be profoundly painful when the people in charge of a company at the time of a severe mishap deny responsibility, offer no apology, express no regrets, and crouch out of sight behind that wall of lawyers and legalisms. A miner from Buffalo Creek, stripped of everything by the flood, said:

> I've often thought some of this stuff [the law suit] could have been avoided if somebody would have come around and said, "Here's a blanket and here's a dress for your wife," or "Here's a sandwich, could I get you a cup of coffee?" But they never showed up. Nobody showed up to give us a place to stay. . . . The Pittston Company never offered me a pair of pants to put on, no shirt.

And a woman from East Swallow, whose losses were of a very different kind and did not need a dress or a cup of coffee, thought:

> In all of these years that the spill has been going on, not once has anyone [from the gas company] said, "Hey, we spilled gasoline under your street and, gee, we're sorry and we'd like to help you clean it up." Nobody has ever said that. It's been a matter of seeing how much they can cover up and how much they can get away with. . . . I just don't think that's right.

What these people were asking for is so elementary a feature of social life that its absence becomes inhuman. This is not the way of neighbors, fellow townspeople, countrymen. It is the way of hostile strangers who treat one as if one belongs to a different order of humanity, even a different species, and that makes it all the more cruel.

To be treated thus bewilders people at first, but when time passes and nothing happens, it can infuriate them (often to the point, it may be worth noting, of creating new energy for exactly the kind of legal action the corporation feared to begin with). It is rarely a healing anger, however, because it leaves people feeling demeaned, diminished, devalued. It is hard for people to resist the sense of worthlessness that often accompanies trauma when other human beings whose power they once respected and whose good will they once counted on treat them with such icy contempt.

The mortar bonding human communities together is made up, at least in part, of trust and respect and decency—and, in moments of crisis, of charity and concern. It is profoundly disturbing to people when these expectations are not met, no matter how well protected they thought they were by that outer crust of cynicism our century seems to have developed in us all.

They have already been made vulnerable by a sharp trick of fate, and now they must face the future without those layers of emotional insulation that only a trusted communal surround can provide. And in the long run, the real problem is that the inhumanity people experience comes to be seen as a natural feature of human life rather than as the bad manners of a particular corporation.

Persons who survive severe disasters, as I noted a moment ago, often come to feel estranged from the rest of humanity and gather into groups with others of like mind. They are not drawn together by feelings of affection (in the usual meaning of the term, anyway) but by a shared set of perspectives and rhythms and moods that derive from the sense of being apart.

Among those shared perspectives, often, is an understanding that the laws by which the natural world has always been governed as well as the decencies by which the human world has always been governed are now suspended—or were never active to begin with. Traumatized people calculate life's chances differently. They look out at the world through a different lens. And in that sense they can be said to have experienced not only a *changed sense of self* and a *changed way of relating to others* but a changed *worldview.*

Traumatized people often come to feel that they have lost an important measure of control over the circumstances of their own lives and are thus very vulnerable. That is easy to understand. But they also come to feel that they have lost a natural immunity to misfortune and that something awful is almost *bound* to happen. One of the crucial tasks of culture, let's say, is to help people camouflage the actual risks of the world around them—to help them edit reality in such a way that it seems manageable, to help them edit it in such a way that the dangers pressing in on them from all sides are screened out of their line of vision as they go about their everyday rounds. Daniel Defoe has Robinson Crusoe muse:

> This furnish'd my thoughts with many very profitable reflections, and particularly this one, how infinitely good that providence is, which has provided in its government of mankind such narrow bounds to his sight and knowledge of things; and though he walks in the midst of so many thousand dangers, the sight of which, if discovered to him, would distract his mind and sink his spirits, he is kept serene and calm, by having the events of things hid from his eyes, and knowing nothing of the dangers which surround him.

People stripped of the ability to screen out signs of peril, naturally, are unusually vigilant and unusually anxious. (A man from Three Mile Island says: "My mind is like a little computer. It's always ticking. I figure it even ticks when I'm asleep.") They evaluate the data of everyday life differently, read signs differently, see omens that the rest of us are for the most part spared. Those people to whom a statistically unusual event has happened are almost sure to work out new probability theories for the world they now find themselves in—theories based less on the calculations of experts than on the experiences of those who have seen up close how chance really operates. After all, how do you estimate the odds of being damaged by a given hazard when it has already happened to you? To consult a chart and then declare that it is a one-in-a-million shot is too abstract a procedure by far. The times call for something else.

Once persons who have been visited by trauma begin to look around them, evidence that the world is a place of unremitting danger seems to appear everywhere. It is a rare morning paper or evening broadcast that does not tell us of exactly the species of mishap we fear most, and if that is the kind of data your mind is sensitive to—the kind of data your eye, made sharp and canny by events of the recent past, knows how to pick out from the flow of news—the darkest of outlooks can seem abundantly supported. People whose view of the world has been tempered by exposure to trauma can easily lose faith not only in the good *will* but in the good *sense* of those in charge of a dangerous universe. It is not just that those in charge lie or cover up when it suits their purpose, but that they, too, are out of control. The *New Yorker*, reporting several weeks after the catastrophe at Bhopal when the casualty estimates had reached 2,000 dead and 200,000 injured, put it very well (a telling example, incidentally, of the event that becomes a moment in everyone's history):

> What truly grips us in these accounts is not so much the numbers as the spectacle of suddenly vanished competence, of men utterly routed by technology, of fail-safe systems failing with a logic as inexorable as it was once—indeed, right up until that very moment—unforeseeable. And the spectacle haunts us because it seems to carry allegorical import, like the whispery omen of a hovering future. ("Talk of the Town," 1985, 17)

The most important point to be made, however, is that when the dread is lasting and pronounced—as often happens in trauma—the spectacle of failed technology can become the spectacle of a failed environment as well. This is a view of life borne of the sense that the universe is not regulated by order and continuity, as clerics and schoolteachers have been telling us for so many centuries, but by change and a kind of natural malice that lurks everywhere. That is the "broken connection" of which Robert Jay Lifton speaks (1979).

When one begins to doubt the findings of scientists and the calculations of engineers, one can begin to lose confidence in the use of logic and reason as ways to discern what is going on. And that is a truly frightening thought, for it has been understood for a long time that deeply felt upheavals, at their worst, can act to upset the established order of things, and, in doing so, create a cultural mood in which dark but familiar old exuberances flourish—millennial movements, witchcraft, the occult, and a thousand other systems of explanation that seem to make sense of bewildering events and offer a means for coping with them.

Let me close by quoting the comments of two women who have pondered these matters deeply. They are both respected elders in their own communities, though still young when they spoke the lines below, and I look up to them both as uncommonly mature and sensible persons.

The first is from Buffalo Creek:

No, this world's going to blow all to hell one of these days, and it's not going to be long away. I believe in the Bible, and I believe what it said in the Bible is happening now. There ain't going to be a world very much longer. When you see things happening right before your very eyes, you've got to believe it. That's all there is to it. . . . Mostly I read Revelations and things like that to tell me what's going to come. It didn't seem so much to apply to the world and the way it was before the flood. But this disaster that happened to us, I believe it opened up a lot of people's eyes. . . . I believe there will be wars, and there will be a bomblike thing that will just destroy this place to pieces. Somebody, some fool, is going to blow it all to pieces. Sure as I'm sitting here and you're sitting there, it'll happen. . . . So the flood has more or less opened up my imagination. It's got me thinking more and more about the way of life we're having to live, the way our kids is going to have to live, and things like that. I wasn't thinking about those things before the flood. It just seemed like it woke up a new vision, I guess you'd call it, of what is and what used to be. You know, you're almost halfway afraid to turn on the TV anymore. Afraid something's broke out in the United States, afraid some railroad car has broken open with poisonous gases running out right in your brother's face. . . . Sometimes I'll go to bed and think about it, you know—the end of time, destruction, what's going on in wars. It's like growing up, I guess. Before I wasn't thinking about nothing but making sure the house was kept clean, making sure my husband had things he needed for his dinner bucket, making sure the kids had the right clothes on, making sure they was clean, making sure I went to this place at the right time and that place at the right time.

The second is from East Swallow:

Will we ever be able to be the same people we were before? No, I won't actually ever be the same person. As soon as we learned about this [the gas spill] we make ourselves a list of things we must be sure and check before we ever buy another house. These were not things that we checked before we bought this house, like if there's a gas station within two miles, like if there was ever a dump on the site, like if there was a railroad track within *x* number of miles, like if there was any kind of industry with a smoke-stack within *x* number of miles. Those things didn't used to be of impor-tance because we were ignorant. Perhaps they should have been impor-tant, but, like most people in the world, they weren't. I just can't imagine most people going out and asking all those questions before they buy a house, before they buy land. And whereas it could be argued that it's not a bad thing to become more knowledgeable, it is, I think, certainly a bad thing to become knowledgeable in the way that we've become knowl-edgeable. It's like a person who's an agoraphobic. If you're terrified to go out of the house, you don't live a very good life. And whether you feel that you have great reason to be terrified—I mean you can be struck by lightning, you can get run over by a car, you can get hit by a train, you're being logical in being afraid to go out—that doesn't change the fact that your life is not real exciting. And if our fears—no matter how well founded, now—affect our lives so profoundly that we can't find anyplace to live without becoming hermits. Alaska's no good anymore. Where can we go? Antarctica? So it has destroyed our future life as well as our present life. I hope that after this is over we'll be able to accept the knowledge we have gained and live with it, and still have a happy, normalish life. But I don't know that that's going to happen. And that's frightening. I mean, it can be a real significant problem if you're so paranoid and focused—not paranoid, just so aware—that you can't ever go back to being uncon-cerned. That's what I don't know yet, whether we'll be able to be con-cerned and still function.

Voices like those deserve to be listened to carefully.

In summary, then, the hardest earned and most fragile accomplishment of childhood, basic trust, can be damaged beyond repair by trauma. Human beings are surrounded by layers of trust, radiating out in concentric circles like the ripples in a pond. The experience of trauma, at its worst, can mean not only a loss of confidence in the self, but a loss of confidence in the surrounding tissue of family and community, in the structures of human government, in the larger logics by which humankind lives, in the ways of nature itself, and often (if this is really the final step in such a succession) in God. As Henry Krystal notes in an earlier chapter:

> Desperate attempts are made by many survivors to restore and maintain their faith in God. However, the problem of aggression and the destruction of basic trust resulting from the events of the Holocaust make true faith and trust in the benevolence of an omnipotent God impossible.

I suspect that matters may be a good deal more complicated than that, but I can report from my own research experience that doubt in even this most elementary of securities is among the cruelties of trauma.

I know that I am bringing these comments to a close just as I am getting ready to deal with the issues they raise, but let me conclude by repeating what I take to be the most important points I have been making. Trauma is normally understood as a somewhat lonely and isolated business because the persons who experience it so often drift away from the everyday moods and understandings that govern social life. But, paradoxically, the drifting away is accompanied by revised views of the world that, in their turn, become the basis for communality. The questions remaining to be asked, then, certainly include these two: To what extent may one conclude that the communal dimension of trauma is one of its distinctive clinical signatures? And to what extent does it make sense to conclude that the traumatized view of the world conveys a wisdom that ought to be heard in its own terms? Trauma can surely be called pathological in the sense that it induces discomfort and pain, but the imageries that accompany the pain have a sense all their own.

## References

Barton, Allen H. 1969. *Communities in Disaster.* New York: Doubleday.

Erikson, Kai. 1976. *Everything in Its Path.* New York: Simon and Schuster.

Felman, Shoshana. 1990. "In an Era of Testimony: Claude Lanzmann's *Shoah.*" *Yale French Studies* 79:39–81.

Freudenburg, William, and Timothy Jones. 1991. "Attitudes and Stress in the Presence of Technological Risk." *Social Forces* 69:1143–68.

Fritz, Charles E. 1961. "Disaster." In *Contemporary Social Problems,* ed. Robert K. Merton and Robert A. Nisbel. New York: Harcourt Brace.

Lifton, Robert Jay. 1979. *The Broken Connection: On Death and the Continuity of Life.* New York: Basic Books.

Perrow, Charles. 1984. *Normal Accidents.* New York: Basic Books.

"Talk of the Town." 1985. *New Yorker,* Feb. 18.

Wallace, Anthony F. C. 1957. *Tornado in Worcester.* Disaster Study 3. Washington, D.C.: National Academy of Sciences–National Research Council, Committee on Disaster Studies.

Wolfenstein, Martha. 1957. *Disaster: A Psychological Essay.* Glencoe, Ill.: Free Press.

# THE OBSCENITY OF UNDERSTANDING:
# AN EVENING WITH CLAUDE LANZMANN

### CLAUDE LANZMANN

*What follows is the literal record of an event, the provocative and controversial evening of Claude Lanzmann's appearance before the Western New England Institute for Psychoanalysis (WNEIPA) in April of 1990. The specific circumstances of Mr. Lanzmann's appearance, as well as the discussion that unfolded on the occasion of his address, raise in a particularly acute way the complex issues surrounding the nature of understanding and of communication in relation to the Holocaust. Mr. Lanzmann's address and the exchange that took place demonstrate, in the singular encounter between the maker of* Shoah *and his analytic audience, the contradictory roles that understanding may play in gaining access to traumatic experience.*

*Mr. Lanzmann was invited to speak to the WNEIPA on the occasion of his second visit to Yale. He was originally invited to participate in the showing and discussion of a film on the Nazi doctor Eduard Wirths, which had been made available by Dr. Louis Micheels, a psychoanalyst who is a survivor of Auschwitz and author of* Dr. 117641: A Holocaust Memoir.[1] *Mr. Lanzmann accepted the invitation before he had seen the film. However, when he arrived in New Haven and viewed the film privately, he refused to participate in its showing. He did agree, nevertheless, to appear before the WNEIPA, and his remarks addressed, precisely, his refusal to discuss the film, as well as the difference between the project of the Wirths film and that of* Shoah.

*The film (not publicly available) was made in Holland, and traces the life of Dr. Wirths through interviews, in Dutch and German, with family, friends, and survivors. It attempts in part to explain Dr. Wirths' development into a Nazi doctor, and focuses at certain points on what some people believe to be Dr. Wirths' ambivalence toward his Nazi activities, thought by some to be demonstrated by his attempt to save some prisoners (including Dr. Micheels), as well as by his suicide after he was captured. The interviews thus focus not only on his activities but on his early and late character and on his inferred psychological state. It is this psychological dimension and the kind of insight it represents—as an attempt to gain understanding of the Holocaust—that is at the center of the evening's discussion, and is engaged by Mr. Lanzmann's initial refusal to have the film viewed and by the audience's response to this act of refusal.[2]*

*The following record of speeches and exchanges begins after Dr. Micheel's opening remarks on Auschwitz, on returning to Holland many years after the war, and on the need to make a breach in the wall of silence surrounding the Holocaust.*

—CATHY CARUTH

### Introduction to Claude Lanzmann's Speech (Shoshana Felman)[3]

Claude Lanzmann was born in Paris some sixty years ago to a Jewish family that had cut its ties with the Jewish world. During the Second World War he was a student resistance leader in France organizing, at the age of seventeen, his fellow high school students as a resistance group against the Nazis. After the war he was an investigative reporter; as such, he crossed over to East Berlin and sent back to France the first reports from East Germany on the cold war; later, he traveled to Israel to report on the situation in the Middle East.

In 1970 Claude Lanzmann turned his attention to filmmaking. Besides serving as the director of the very important periodical in Paris, *Les Temps Modernes*, founded by the French philosopher Jean-Paul Sartre, Claude Lanzmann has produced two films: *Pourquoi Israel?* (*Why Israel?*, released in France in 1973) and in 1985 the film *Shoah*, which was described by critics immediately upon its appearance as "the film event of the century." We know today that it is more than the film event of the century, because it is not simply a film, but a truly revolutionary artistic and cultural event. And this is what we are still trying to discuss in the years following the appearance of the film, and what so many people in the United States and in Europe are still trying to study and to understand.

In what ways has *Shoah* (both in its content and in its procedures) opened up new ways for an understanding of culture, politics, history, and the trauma of our century? One of the things that have been most frequently remarked upon, especially in Europe, about the film *Shoah* is the amazing psychoanalytic presence of Claude Lanzmann on the screen, and the way in which the film incorporates—in ways that go beyond a simple understanding—the most revolutionary and most radical psychoanalytic insights. I will try to point out the ways in which the film appears to be relevant—crucially relevant—to psychoanalysis, and the ways in which psychoanalysis, as another cultural revolution in our century, is crucially relevant to the film.

On the one hand, there are questions of content that are very obviously common to the film and to psychoanalysis: first of all, the fact that the central subjects that each indelibly researches are suffering, love, hatred, fear, sadism, and violence. But what is even more striking than the question of content is the question of procedure that seems to be common to the film and to psychoanalysis. Of course, we have to understand the radical differences between the two: they are not at all the same kind of enterprise. But it is still striking to take note of the following points. First and most obvious is the fact that the film is a quest, a search for truth, in much the same way that psychoanalysis consists in an investigation of truth; and both are a search for truth through an act of talking, through dialogue, through the act of interlocution. And the process of generating the truth, or bringing it forth, is contingent, both in psychoanalysis and in the film, on a presence, the presence of the listener on the screen and behind the couch. There is an extraordinary presence of Claude Lanzmann throughout the film, a presence tangible both in the depth of his silence, and in the efficacy of his speech—in the success of his interventions in bringing forth the truth. But the presence itself consists first and foremost in a bodily and a physical presence, and this material presence is an essential factor in the process of generating that truth. The second point is that both the film and psychoanalysis institute a quest of memory, a quest for the past that nevertheless chooses to take place through the present, through images and events of the present and of the present alone, through the contemporaneous eventfulness of speech. Something happens in the present in speech, and this is what brings about a revelation of the past in both psychoanalysis and in the film.

The third common denominator is related to the temporality of the film, which disrupts chronology, disrupts a certain kind of linear temporality, even though it deals with history. The film, very much like psychoanalysis, works through repetition and through ever-deepening circles: its progress is achieved only through the process of going around in circles. The temporality of the film is also reminiscent of the process of psychoanalysis with regard to the factor of the tempo, the necessity of prolonged time, the fact that the process of the revelation of truth takes time and cannot really take place without taking time: the film in effect lasts nine and a half hours. This may not compare to some nine and a half years of psychoanalytic therapy, but it is almost as long for the viewer with respect to the habits of cinematic viewing. And it took Claude Lanzmann eleven years to produce the film, so the necessity of the process is obvious on every level. The production of the film, like psychoanalysis, takes time and occurs slowly, and cannot really occur more quickly and without this process, which evolves in time.

The fourth factor that is common to the approach of the film and to psychoanalysis is the interest in details and the interest in specifics, in the very, very particular detail. There is a constant passage in the film from abstract questions to concrete, minutely detailed questions, and from historical events that are ungraspable in their generality to the physical presence of particular, concrete fragments of memory on the screen.

The fifth point—and perhaps this is the most interesting because it reveals what is common both to the approach of the film and to the approach of psychoanalysis, and also what specifically differentiates the two procedures in a radical way—is that they both work at the limit of understanding. The relation to understanding is something that is very profound both in the film, and in the discipline of psychoanalysis as a new and innovative discipline: in psychoanalysis as inherently a new relation to understanding and to consciousness. The film and psychoanalysis both work through gaps in understanding and at the limit of understanding, and even though the film incorporates, as I said, the most radical psychoanalytic insights, it is very important to recognize that it is not a psychological film, and that it incorporates a refusal of psychological understanding, and in a vaster sense a refusal of understanding as such. This is the most difficult thing to understand about the film. However, this attitude is present implicitly in psychoanalysis as well, and especially in certain trends of psychoanalysis. I think that one of the most difficult and most crucial things about the work of Claude Lanzmann is his refusals, and I would like to venture some remarks about the complex significance of these refusals. But first I would like to quote from a passage from the work of a psychoanalytic thinker, which in turn addresses the question of understanding. The citation is by a compatriot of Claude Lanzmann, Jacques Lacan, and I believe it is a reminder very relevant to the attitude of the film. Lacan writes:

> What counts, when one attempts to elaborate an experience, is less what one understands than what one doesn't understand. . . . How many times

have I pointed it out to those that I supervise when they say to me—*I thought I understood that what he meant to say was this, or that*—one of the things which we should be watching out for most, is not to understand too much, not to understand more than what there is in the discourse of the subject. Interpreting is an altogether different thing from having the fancy of understanding. One is the opposite of the other. I will even say that it is on the basis of a certain refusal of understanding that we open the door onto psychoanalytic understanding. (Lacan, 1975, 87–88)

And now I would like to quote from Claude Lanzmann on a completely different level another formulation, concerning his own refusal of understanding in *Shoah*. Paradoxically enough, this refusal has to do, in my opinion, with the fact that his work allows us to understand *so much more* than what we had understood before about the Holocaust. Claude Lanzmann writes:

> It is enough to formulate the question in simplistic terms—Why have the Jews been killed?—for the question to reveal right away its obscenity. There is an absolute obscenity in the very project of understanding. Not to understand was my iron law during all the eleven years of the production of *Shoah*. I clung to this refusal of understanding as the only possible ethical and at the same time the only possible operative attitude. This blindness was for me the vital condition of creation. Blindness has to be understood here as the purest mode of looking, of the gaze, the only way to not turn away from a reality which is literally blinding. . . .
>
> "Hier ist kein Warum": Primo Levi narrates how the word "Auschwitz" was taught to him by an SS guard: "Here there is no why," Primo Levi was abruptly told upon his arrival at the camp. This law is equally valid for whoever undertakes the responsibility of such a transmission [a transmission like that which is undertaken by *Shoah*]. Because the act of transmitting is the only thing that matters, and no intelligibility, that is to say no true knowledge, preexists the process of transmission. (Lanzmann, 1990, 279)

We should bear in mind this quintessentially difficult reminder, even as we listen now to Claude Lanzmann himself.

## Claude Lanzmann

I wish to thank you for what you have said tonight. But I am in some trouble, because I don't know exactly what the topic or focus of this evening is and since I am responsible for this trouble, I think I have to give you an explanation.

Originally, it was arranged that we would see a film on Dr. Eduard Wirths. Dr. Wirths was a camp doctor in Auschwitz who made the selections on the ramp and conducted some experiments. And we were supposed to discuss this film—Dr. Micheels, myself, everybody. Yet the evening took another direction. Why? Because when I gave my consent for this discussion I had not seen the film, and had never even heard of it. Fortunately enough, I was able to see the film the day before yesterday, with Dr. Micheels and with Dr. Dori Laub. At the beginning I thought that perhaps Dr. Micheels was the author of this film, and after awhile I thought that he was the protagonist of the film, but it was not the case, fortunately for him. He did not do the film, and he's not in the film.

Well I have seen this film, which lasted fifty minutes, and it was very difficult for me to watch in every respect. First of all, it's a very bad film, in my opinion; one doesn't even know *who* did it (I think two people from Holland),[4] but it is a film without any kind of *signature*. I wonder who in fact did it; there is no desire behind this film. And one wonders, it is impossible to know, what is the topic of the film. At the end, I had to tell myself that the purpose of the film was the rehabilitation of this Nazi doctor, to explore the "soul" of this man.

Well, first of all I did not understand why, having done *Shoah*, I was required to participate in a discussion of this bad film that complacently sets out to explore a Nazi soul. And I am not sure that all of you have seen *Shoah* and am even convinced that probably many of you have not seen the film. Of course, I realize it is much easier to see this fifty-minute film about a Nazi doctor than to see *Shoah*. However, I thought that the only fair thing to do, fair towards me, and fair towards the truth, would be, if this film had to be screened, to screen *Shoah* too. But maybe it would have been too difficult to have done that, to stay the whole night—but after all why not? There are already people who seem to be asleep [laughter]. It's a matter of concentration, of "free-floating attention."

Well, I was very, very violent against my friend Dori Laub, and against Dr. Micheels, whom I respect very much. But more than this misunderstanding of myself as the creator of *Shoah*, this film represented for me all of the things I have always fought against, with all my strength. And Shoshana Felman talked rightly about what I have called the obscenity of the very project of understanding. This quotation was excerpted from a short text that I wrote in a recent issue of a psychoanalytic magazine in France, which is called *La Nouvelle Revue de Psychanalyse*. It was a special issue devoted to the topic of evil, "Le Mal." I was asked to write for it and, since I have done a very long film, my writing every day becomes shorter. I wrote less than a page, and in this page I said what Shoshana Felman has quoted, but also some other things she didn't quote. I talked about academic frivolities and *canailleries* [low tricks, vulgarities].[5]

I wish to give you the reasons for my revolt when I saw the film. The film that we were supposed to see, that I forbade, started with a picture of this Nazi doctor as a child, as a baby. He's a smiling child. Dr. Wirths was a smiling, good-looking adolescent. The so-called inquirer or interviewer goes to the hometown of the Wirths family, and speaks to the passersby, who were supposed to have known Wirths. He asks them "How was he?" and they say, "Oh, he was a very good man, a very nice man," and so on and so forth. There are some pictures of Hitler as a baby too, aren't there? I think that there is even a book written by a psychoanalyst about Hitler's childhood, an attempt at explanation—which is for me obscenity as such. Because what are we supposed to do with Hitler's childhood? Maybe we will discover that Hitler had some problems with his mother, or father, and this will permit us to *engender*—harmoniously, if I can say so—the killing, the mass murders, the destruction of six million people, and many others. Well this is what I call obscenity, because there is such a discrepancy, such a *gap* between the originary scene in Hitler's life, and the result. It is the same in the historical discipline, because usually when people want to understand—when they don't understand precisely the obscenity of the project of understanding—they start in 1933 or even earlier, talking about *volkisch* [folk] ideologies, the Jewish Spirit opposed to the German one, etcetera, or the image of the father in Hitler's mind. All these fields of explanation (referring to the unemployment in Germany, and so on) are all true and all false. They're all true together and all false in the same way. And it is a very flat truth, because you cannot proceed in that way—you cannot precisely engender the Holocaust. It is impossible. Between all these conditions—which were necessary conditions maybe, but they were not sufficient—between all these conditions and the gassing of three thousand persons, men, women, children, in a gas chamber, all together, there is an unbreachable discrepancy. It is simply not possible to engender one out of the other. There is no solution of continuity between the two; there is rather a gap, an *abyss*, and this abyss will never be bridged.

I remember when I was working on *Shoah* at the start, I read so many books by reputed academics, for instance George Mosse's book on the formation of the German spirit (1964; see also Mosse, 1975). It's a very good book. But after you have read it you have to say, "Well, is it because of all these conditions that the children have been gassed?" This is what I called the obscenity of the project of understanding—and more than this, it is not only obscenity, it is real cowardice, because this idea of our being able to engender harmoniously, if I may say so again, this violence, is just an absurd dream of nonviolence. It is a way of escaping; it is a way not to face the horror. And this escape has become now a fashion, more and more. It's what I call in French, *élever le neveau du debat*, to raise up the level of the debate.

I remember there was a discussion some months ago in Paris on television between the Cardinal Archbishop of Paris and Elie Wiesel. They were saying to each other in French, *tu*. Not *vous*, but *tu*. They were extremely friendly. Of course, I forgot to say that both are Jews. The Cardinal Archbishop is a Jew, but maybe he is a good representative of what I want to illustrate.[6] He wants to "raise up" the debate. And he said, when they were talking about Auschwitz, or Treblinka, "Well, my dear Elie, you know—*tu sais*—the true problem, the true question is the problem of evil. *This* is the real question." Well when you hear such things *les bras tombent*—you are flabbergasted. Wiesel was fighting, but he was fighting against another Jew, and because they were on tender terms with each other he could not fight very well. And the same cardinal said—and now it has become a saying everywhere—"the real question is not the question of the crimes against mankind, against humanity. The real question is that these crimes are crimes *of mankind*, crimes *of humanity*." Well, the Holocaust was a pure event, an unbreakable event, *infracassable*. And now with all these stupidities, all these *canailleries*, everything is allowed. One can say there are not only the revisionists, the people who deny that such an event took place, but that the revisionism is much larger: this discussion I am giving you between the archbishop and Elie Wiesel is in a way a much more perverse form of revisionism.

In this film, this Dutch film with no signature, Wirths surrenders to the British in September or October 1945, and it is said that the British officer to whom he surrendered told them, "Well, I am happy to shake the hand of a man who is responsible for the deaths of four million people. Think of it, and we'll talk again tomorrow morning." On the same night, Wirths committed suicide. Now everybody in this film conjectures on the meaning of the suicide, talks about the guilt Wirths supposedly expressed by this suicide—because the witnesses who are questioned are Wirths' wife, a good

German woman, Wirths' children, Wirths' friends, Wirths' father, and so on. And the viewer has to become complacent with these Nazi women with maternal dolorosa faces.

But what is the meaning of this suicide? Do you think that the suicide of this man is a way to plead guilty, to acknowledge his guilt? I don't think so at all, because, after all, Hitler too committed suicide, no? Goebbels committed suicide; he even killed his wife and all their children. Himmler committed suicide. Even Göring tried to kill himself when he was jailed by the Americans in Nuremberg before his execution. They all committed suicide for a very simple reason: they just wanted to escape, to *escape justice* and *escape execution*, and to *escape the truth*, and to *escape history*.

This is one of the reasons I was obliged, when I was making *Shoah*, to use devices, very special devices. I had to fool them, I had to deceive them. Why? They knew perfectly what was the magnitude of the event, they knew perfectly the horror of the crime.

And we are all victims of this conspiracy of silence. There are many ways of being silent. There are some good ways, and there are very bad ways as well. To talk too much about the Holocaust is a way of being silent, and a bad way of being silent. This happens in this country too often, to my taste.

So Wirths committed suicide. It is a military tradition, to commit suicide. Well, I don't mind very much that people take their own life. But not in such circumstances. Not this one. I happen to have a sister who killed herself at the age of thirty-six. For me what she accomplished was the utmost of human achievement. But not this. All these suicides cannot be on the same plane, on the same level.

And there is a man in the film too, Hermann Langbein, who was a secretary of Wirths and now is a specialist of Auschwitz, who writes books about Auschwitz, *Menschen in Auschwitz* (*Men in Auschwitz*). (I think that I am now giving you a strong desire to see this film [laughter], but now I am absolutely prepared that you see the film, because I have given "directions for use." And this was necessary because there are some virgin brains among you! [laughter]) This Langbein is a specialist writer about Auschwitz. I know him. I met him during the making of *Shoah*. I went to Austria to meet him. He had nothing to say. Really, not a thing. He is an empty memory. And I have built *Shoah* against such a man. And if you have seen *Shoah*, you will remember that in the second half of the film the Jewish survivors of Auschwitz arrive. And they are a very special kind of survivor. They talk about political prisoners in Auschwitz, about the German political prisoners who succeeded in taking over against the former prisoners—against the murderers, the criminals, and so on. They did this with the agreement and thanks to the complicity of the higher echelons of the SS hierarchy—and the conditions of life for these people improved very much. But maybe you remember the story of the massacre of the Jews of the Czech family camp, in *Shoah* (it is told by Rudolf Vrba and Filip Müller). Langbein was a member of the resistance movement in Auschwitz, he was one of the chiefs of the resistance movement. And they explain that every time an action of resistance was at stake, the chiefs of the resistance never did anything. And when the Jews of the Czech family camp asked for help from the heads of the resistance movement, the latter just did nothing. They gave them some bread and some onions, and that's all. And Rudolph Vrba who escaped Auschwitz on April 7, 1944, says very rightly (he talks explicitly about this in *Shoah*) that the resistance movement in Auschwitz was not geared for an uprising, but for surviving, for the survival of the members of the resistance.[7] Not for the survival of the Jews, for sure, because these political prisoners were all non-Jews. (This is just to explain to you my great violence the other day [in relation to the Dutch film, which treats Langbein as a real witness]. This is the only way to objectivity. The only objectivity is the *ésprit de parti*.)

Anyway, this Langbein is talking to me. He was a secretary of Wirths, and he is talking with a lying face, it is absolutely true. This is the reason why I said he has no memory at all of Auschwitz. Between his world, and the world of the people who worked at the gas chambers, not to say anything of the world—one cannot really use this word—the world of the people who were gassed, there is a complete gap. This man is not a witness. *He is not a witness.* He is a *false witness* for Auschwitz, this Hermann Langbein. And I will say it publicly. This is the reason why it was very difficult for me to watch him in this film, which seeks to rehabilitate the image of a Nazi.

Well, if you want to see the film now, I have nothing against it. But I understood that they have also prepared some excerpts of *Shoah*. Maybe you prefer to talk—whatever you want. I am a free man in a free country. I would feel more free if I could smoke. Now it's up to you. Do you want to talk?

## Responses

*Al Solnit:* I did not lose a word of what you said, Claude Lanzmann. You spoke to the heart and the head. I agree with Shoshana's introduction, that true knowledge is not the same as the idealization of complete knowledge, an illustration in all of Western society. I join you and Shoshana Felman in saying that true knowledge is when you know what the limits of that knowledge are. Your presentation was most dramatic. I don't agree with all of it, but then I think you would be disappointed if I did. There is the strength in your presentation of the artist, of a creative mind that describes how awesome man's inhumanity to man can be, whether it is as a national policy or in a more individual sense.

I think Shoshana Felman was right in saying there are places where psychoanalytic theory and the process of ongoing efforts to comprehend the Holocaust can meet, even if they are from different levels of human experience and even if they can only help each other to grasp from radically different points of view what is ultimately not encompassable. Despite seeing *Shoah* and hearing this extraordinary presentation, we need to think about it further in order to approach and engage what *Shoah* and you have shown and told us. I hope we will be thinking about it for *at least* the next twenty or thirty years. I am grateful that you came and spoke here as you did.

*Member of audience:* I wonder if the other speakers agree that seeing this film would be a danger to our health?

*Solnit:* I don't think it's dangerous to your health but I would much rather hear Claude Lanzmann speak.

*Member of audience:* I think that it's fair to say, in looking around at this audience, that seeing *Shoah* was in a sense part of the homework of this meeting. You can rest assured that everybody did their homework. I feel quite certain that everybody saw it and was deeply moved about seeing it and will never forget it and will continue to think about it for the rest of their lives. But I think that part of my reaction to having expected to see the Wirths movie and then having you tell us about it instead of having a chance to see it, I think maybe we're having a kind of transference experience here as our patients do in the clinic. Here the experience with you gives us a certain inkling of something of the whole process. I think one of the things I was very curious about—only a small thing, but it interests me—is when you say in part of your presentation that there were certain devices that were necessary to achieve the goals of *Shoah*. One way of looking at what happened tonight is that there was a device necessary here for your presentation, which was not to show us the film, or even part of it. It might have been fifty minutes, but then we would have been shortchanged on discussion. I wouldn't have had a chance to hear myself talk. And we would have been shortchanged on your discussion. I find all that very stimulating. And when you say that maybe we were made more interested in the film by your comments, I was one of those who said, "Yes, we were." And when the person commented before, that the film was dangerous to our health, I think maybe it felt like a device that wasn't necessary for us. We could have seen some of it, or maybe we'll have another meeting to see it; and then we'll have the advantage of your comments about it.

*Lanzmann:* All right. What do you wish?

*Member of audience:* I would prefer to hear your comments, but I would like you to address something that you talked about as perverse and as an obscenity, but it is truly a question in my mind: the question of evil, of man's inhumanity to man. As you said, we need to understand that the Holocaust is not explainable by certain conditions—perhaps they were necessary, but certainly not sufficient conditions, for this to have happened. I perceive your film as one way of trying to think about what does happen in the world and how this could have happened, while each of us also tries to confront this question. Because, after all, man did do this to man.

*Lanzmann:* Yes. But I cannot enter this realm of problems, of questions. I think that Shoshana said it, but I repeat, the real problem is to transmit; although I think that there is no real knowledge before the transmission. It is difficult to say, it is difficult to explain, it is difficult to understand. It is a way I see things and the way I feel them. Of course there are books of history. There are very good books. And in *Shoah* I did not try to add new things to the knowledge or to the documentations that we already have. It was not at all my problem, in spite of the fact that there are some things I have in turn taught to the historians, because they generally used to work only with written materials. I don't see the reason for this cult of written material, because we can as well lie in writing. But in spite of this what was really important to me, what was at stake, was precisely this transmission. I want to say that if my knowledge had existed before, I think I would have never made the film. I am often asked, "When did you know what happened to the Jews during the war?" The most honest answer that I can give is that I started to know really when I started to work on the film. Before, my knowledge had no strength, no force. It was an abstract knowledge, an empty one. The whole process of *Shoah* was to connect, to link up, to accomplish the whole work of rememoration. I think there is a word of Freud to describe this process: *Durcharbeitung* (working-through). What mankind can do to mankind, on the other hand, is for me as irrelevant as, for instance, the debate on the existence of God. I can do nothing with this.

*Member of audience:* I have appreciated your comments very much. You reminded me that there are many different ways of knowing and that knowing is different from understanding, not synonymous with it. Sometimes understanding is only one way of knowing and sometimes understanding gets in the way of other ways of knowing. And many of us spend most of our lives knowing things in only certain ways. In fact in some of our clinical work, one thought I had about the different ways of knowing in response to your comments was in thinking about the difference between primary process thinking and secondary process thinking. Primary process is a way of knowing and much of our work we spend trying to move things from primary process types of thinking into secondary process thinking and for some purposes that's appropriate and useful. And the question becomes the different ways of knowing for different issues or problems or events. Some ways of knowing may be more powerful, more enabling, or better than other ways of knowing.

*Lanzmann:* I want to add that I am not a psychoanalyst.

*Member of audience:* Is there anything about the experience of the perpetrators, the Nazis, that interests you?

*Lanzmann:* What is an experience of the perpetrators? What do you call the experience of the perpetrators?

*Member of audience:* In any way making sense of, obtaining knowledge, in the sense that you've come to an interface of some knowledge of the victims. Do you have any sense or any interest in exploring the perpetrator?

*Lanzmann:* No. No, absolutely not. It is clear in *Shoah* every time they want to tell me, "I did not know, I did not want," I said "No, we are not talking about you. I am not interested in this." It was the only way to get the truth out of them. You imagine a conversation between the SS of Treblinka, for instance, and me about their life, about how did they come to this point, how did they arrive there. This has been attempted already. They talk very much about their parents, about their childhood, about their schooltime. And there is a gap, and they know perfectly well that they cannot bridge it.

*Member of audience:* That becomes obscene.

*Lanzmann:* It would become obscene to try, precisely, to bridge the gap. It was a question of art and a question of ethics, too. A question of efficacy as well—of being *operative*; otherwise they would have never talked, and they never would have said what they say in *Shoah*. And what they say in *Shoah* is very important because these things have never been said. It's a description, minute by minute, of the machinery of murder, or the process of destruction. And even when they lie, it's clear that they are, it's obvious.

*Member of audience:* Mr. Lanzmann, I think, however, as I recall *Shoah*, which I saw on the occasion of your visit here three years ago, that in that film you also conveyed to us some understanding of the perpetrator. I remember very vividly the scene in front of the church with the peasants, and the comment of that woman whom you provoked a little bit through some devices. And the sense of the banality of evil. In some ways I have the feeling that your objection to the film about Dr. Wirths that I haven't seen was the banality of it. That it's showing this man as just an ordinary man with a childhood and an adolescence and adulthood. Well I think that that's the very point of it all. That evilness and brutality can in some ways emerge from almost anybody under certain circumstances. And that in fact evilness has a certain banality to it. I remember very vividly also looking at Eichmann's Rohrschach test. He was a petit bourgeois bookkeeper with some mild traces of sadism, but there was no madness.

*Lanzmann:* This is the reason why we have to dismiss psychology, isn't it? [laughter]—if the only result that we achieve, is to arrive again at the banality of evil. Because for me, first of all what you said is not true. You are talking about the church scene. In the church scene there are perpetrators. The perpetrators were the Germans. In the church scene, you have Poles. The Poles did not kill the Jews.

*Member of audience:* But I get the feeling that that woman could have become a perpetrator.

*Lanzmann:* This is far-fetched. It is difficult to say. I am not sure at all, and this story of the banality of evil—peace to Hannah Arendt, she wrote some things that were better, no?—I think that all these people knew perfectly that what they were doing was not banal at all. Maybe they were banal, but they

213

knew that what they were achieving was really not banal, surely not. [Lanzmann is referring to Arendt, 1963.]

*Member of audience:* What I have to say is very painful for me to say. It has to do with the difficulty of learning from history and history repeating itself in different guises. *Shoah* is the view that you present to us. I have no question about its being genuine, about its presenting an absolutely terrifying, awful, and incomprehensible aspect of human history. But the Nazis started with a kind of book burning. By saying that there are things that people should not see because they are bad for people. Because they are too upsetting to the ideas that they have. Because they misrepresent. Because people cannot be allowed to make their own minds up about it. I don't argue for the Wirths film at all. It may be a terrible film. But I'm very disappointed and very angry that I was not given the opportunity to make my own mind up about it and that you used as justification for that an ideological stance which is a repetition of exactly what it is that you're attempting to help us to understand. And that I find very upsetting. [Loud assent.]

*Member of audience* [to Mr. Lanzmann in explanation]: He feels that people should have been able to make up their own minds.

*Lanzmann:* I plead guilty. But I just want to say one thing. If the film is screened now, and it's very possible, I will just go into the corridor and I will smoke a cigarette. I don't want to see it twice, that's all. It is too much for me. I am not pressing on you really. If I did so, first of all I spoke very frankly. I take the responsibility for not showing this film.

*Member of audience:* I think it's absolutely fair for you to say it's too upsetting for you to see. That I can respect absolutely.

*Lanzmann:* It's just that it is absolutely boring. I don't know what this film wants to convey.

*Member of audience:* That I object to. Why should you have to know what it's going to convey before we can see it?

*Lanzmann:* I really wanted to protect you. But if there is a majority in this assembly for seeing the film, you have the film here.

*Member of audience:* I would be very interested if Dr. Micheels—he's a soft-spoken man, but it's a film that personally, Dr. Micheels, you're very involved in. You know the people. Could you make some comments on it? Almost none of us have seen the film. We've heard one person's view of the film. I'd be interested in yours.

*Lanzmann:* You are right. (I am soft, too!)

*Dr. Micheels:*[8] The reason I was interested in the film was that I happened to hear about it actually through the person, Nora, who was my fiancée at the time of the Third Reich's incorporation of Holland. When I visited with her maybe three, four years ago, she mentioned that she had participated in making that movie and that it had been quite well received. Not only, apparently, in Holland. And then she mentioned who else was in the movie, including Hermann Langbein, and I became very curious, like I think you must be by now, too. I made it my business the next time I came to Holland to make an appointment—it was not easy—with the maker of the movie. But I did finally get ahold of the man, Rolf Orthel. His helper showed me the movie. And I was rather impressed. First with seeing the people in the movie that I hadn't seen for a long time and some I had never seen. I was particularly impressed with seeing, after forty years—described in my book [1989] and Lifton's book [1986]—this SS doctor by the name of Münch, who had been extremely helpful to me and to many of us. In some ways I could say that I might not be alive now if it hadn't been for him bringing various medications to the hospital to treat me after I developed peritonitis following an appendix operation. So I have certain feelings of gratitude for this man. And besides, he tried to help us at other times. He was the only SS doctor who persisted in refusing to participate in "selections," and succeeded in being exempted from that murderous "duty." Perhaps you can say that when he gave us a gun he did so because that was his way of trying to get help for himself. That may be very true. It is difficult to imagine for anyone who was not under the yoke of the SS the powerful effect of the contrast, created by the very few exceptions. I am referring to those SS who showed a trace of humanity, such as addressing you by your name. I was also interested by the fact that this movie was about Wirths, who was the chief medical person in Auschwitz and all the camps around it. He was, being a medical man, responsible not only for only purely medical matters, but also, since the "Final Solution," for the killing of people in the gas chamber, and the crematorium. In the Nazi code, that was a medical matter, too. It was connected with the racial dogma of the Nazis that Jews and their blood were impure and could infect the German superrace and, as such, were considered a dreadful enemy. At least that was their rationalization. It is still extremely frightening that at least thirty percent of the German medical profession in those days enthusiastically supported Hitler, who depended heavily on them for his Nazi eugenics. So, Wirths was responsible for, I think, all the racial killing in Auschwitz.

I was, of course, seeing the film just for the first time. The mood I was in was such that I thought I wanted to know more about that movie. I wanted to see it again sometime and show it to some of my friends and see what they had to say about it. After about four years and very intricate attempts I finally got the maker of the movie to send it to me. I have shown it to a number of friends, and analysts too, and they were all very impressed with the movie. Nobody said they liked it or disliked it particularly, but everybody was puzzled and impressed. It does stir up all kinds of feelings.

One thing I must say about it, and that was one objection you [Claude] had to the movie, that it was an attempt to rehabilitate Wirths. I didn't see that in the movie. On the contrary, the participants certainly were not rehabilitating Wirths, except maybe Langbein, who had a certain influence over Wirths for the benefits of the inmates and at great risk to himself. Almost all of the participants were indicting Wirths.[9]

Now the question that you brought up about his suicide. Does that mean that he felt guilty? Who knows for what reason he committed suicide, but if you would ask what is a just punishment for these crimes, I believe we can't think of or imagine a suitable punishment for these crimes. The last time, recently, I was in Holland, two Nazis, Fischer and Aus der Funten, who were both in charge of all the deportations of the Jews of Holland, the destruction of the Jews of Holland, including my own parents, were let go after they had been in prison since the end of the war, and people asked me how I felt about that. I would say that it was very difficult to feel anything in particular. What they did is too incomprehensible for one really to respond to it emotionally in an adequate way. So what about their release? Yes, I think they should probably have stayed in prison, even though they were old and quite ill. It is so difficult if you want to take revenge on these people: how are you going to do it? Kill them? That's too easy. Not kill them? That's too easy, too. What are you going to do? There is nothing you can do in that sense.

When I was walking every day from Auschwitz to the laboratory where I worked for a year, with my Dutch cohorts, we would make up punishments for the various SS men that we were in contact with. The worst ones should have the worst kind of punishment. But we *never* could really think of an adequate one. However, there was one punishment we thought of for the Dutch traitor and Nazi-Führer, Mussert. There would be a big gathering, thousands of people, in a stadium in Amsterdam—big, huge, like a football stadium—there would be a pile of explosives in the middle, and he would sit on a chair on top of the dynamite. There would be a very long fuse starting in Rotterdam, and the radio would report where the fuse was burning, coming closer and ever closer. When it arrived in the stadium, a little boy would come close to the dynamite and would stamp out the fire only seconds before it would explode. Then it would be announced, "Now we will start all over again." Over and over again. As if that's the only way one could think of taking revenge. Of course, that is impossible. That's one of the big problems. This was really what *we* felt all the time—sitting on a powder keg, never knowing when it would blow up.

*Dori Laub:* I reserve the right to make a few closing comments. I do think that we are faced with questions that are horrendous and will continue and not with a resolution. To face the truth is very difficult. Shoshana alluded to it, Claude spoke about it. In that sense it is, for us, tempting to escape it. And I really disagree in this context with the term *device*, which implies trickery (as applied to Claude Lanzmann's procedures). If we are to hear the truth, there must be a certain force to make us face it. And if that requires something to bring it forth, so be it. Other arguments about freedom of decision dwarf before the need to face the truth.

Let me share with you my own experience of this film. I take a certain responsibility for inviting Claude to discuss it. I saw it for the first time three years ago without its English subtitles. I understood all the German in the film. I did not understand any of the Dutch narration of the witnesses. So, the Germans spoke. I came away with a certain feeling that there was an attempt at making sense by normalizing, by casting the characters into typologies that could be understood easily. Now I can understand that the Germans can go only so far in understanding history. This includes the father's remark, when Wirths complains that he can't take it any longer: "My son, this is the one place in the world in which you can do the most good. Hang in there." The father repeats this remark twice. I was for a moment touched. Because the father, who has been described as a virtuous man, is struggling to make sense of his son, who is a mass murderer. And this way of making sense is the only way in which he can live with that knowledge.

Perhaps this is the father's contribution to history, this struggle we see him enact before us.

About the beginning of March, I saw the film again, this time with a translation from the Dutch, and I heard the testimonies of the survivors. The woman who described the experiments that Wirths conducted, his posture, his sadism, the details she gave about Wirths' broken promise to protect pregnant women. And I realized that the film in that sense was a hoax. That there was no balance whatsoever between this feeble and fumbling attempt of German self-explanation and that of the survivors. The Germans' attempts were hardly substantive. They were not enough. There was a disproportion. And I thought it was right not to be exposed to this kind of information. If we wanted to dedicate an evening to the inadequate study of the Nazi character, this was simply not a right way of spending our time.

I would like to end here with an example that the president of the Psychoanalytic Institute in Frankfurt, Clemens de Boor, told me about his own analysis. He approached the famous Dutch analyst Hempl de Groot after the war and asked to become his analysand. Dr. de Groot responded to Dr. de Boor, "Were you a Nazi in the war? If yes, go to somebody else. I cannot analyze you." As this example shows, I think the analyst has the right to sometimes refuse to extend his understanding and his analytic empathy.

*—Edited by Cathy Caruth with*
*David Rodowick*

## Notes

1. Louis Micheels is a member of the WNEIPA and associate clinical professor at the Yale School of Medicine. The other organizers of the evening were Dr. Rosemarie Balsam, associate clinical professor of psychiatry at Yale and, at that time, program chairman of WNEIPA; Shoshana Felman, Thomas E. Donnelly Professor of French and Comparative Literature at Yale; Dori Laub, psychoanalyst and child survivor, and cofounder of the Fortunoff Holocaust Video Archive at Yale; and Albert Solnit, Sterling Professor Emeritus of Pediatrics and Psychiatry and senior research scientist, and director of the Gardiner Seminar for Psychoanalysis and the Humanities at Yale University.

2. The seminar on *Shoah* that Mr. Lanzmann held for David Rodowick's course and the Department of Comparative Literature, which raises issues that are related to those in the following address, has been published in Lanzmann (1991). Additional considerations of these issues can be found in Lanzmann (1990).

3. The introduction by Shoshana Felman and the address by Claude Lanzmann were spoken spontaneously (not from prepared texts).

4. The creators of the film are not named in the film itself; according to Dr. Micheels (who obtained the film from them) the two men responsible for the making of the film are Rolf Orthel and Hans Fels, who reside in Holland.

5. The sentence that Mr. Lanzmann refers to reads as follows: "To gaze directly at the horror demands that one renounce distractions and evasions, beginning with the chief among them, the most falsely central, the question of why, with the indefinite train of academic frivolities or vulgarities [*canailleries*] it never ceases to induce" (Lanzmann, 1990, 279).

6. The Archbishop of Paris, Jean-Marie Lustiger, converted to Catholicism from Judaism.

7. This testimony can be found in Lanzmann (1985, 165).

8. *The following note is an addition by Dr. Micheels, who reviewed this article as it was published in* American Imago *and said that he "felt a need and obligation as a person who 'lived' in Auschwitz for nearly two years to correct some errors of fact, highlight my different point of view and make the discussion a more balanced one." Dr. Micheels writes:* Shoshana Felman and Claude Lanzmann use a quotation from an SS man given by Primo Levi: "Hier ist kein Warum." *Hier* is the important word for my argument. It refers to the world of Auschwitz, which has become synonymous with the Holocaust. I have described this world from my personal experience as so different and foreign that I called it another planet, light-years away. It was inhabited by creatures that had little in common with what we considered human beings. I mean not just the SS, the perpetrators, but also the inmates, such as Kapo's, muselmen and others—except for a few saints, if there were any. Saints are not quite human either. In that world, I agree, *ist kein Warum* (there is no *why*). However, in the civilized world, to which so few of us, including Primo Levi, returned there should be a *why*. Without an attempt, no matter how difficult and complex, at understanding, that very world, where truth is most important, could be lost again. [*End of note by Dr. Micheels.*]

9. *As in note 8, the following addition was provided by Dr. Micheels after his review of the original article:* Lanzmann called Hermann Langbein a man with "an empty memory." He met with him and "built *Shoah* against such a man." He mentioned the books by Langbein, but if he really read them as I did, it is impossible to see Langbein as a "lying face." These books give a very factual account of Auschwitz I, especially the camp hospital and its official—"legal"—and underground "illegal" organizations and Wirths' role in it (see Langbein, 1972). Under Langbein's influence, Wirths not only improved the camp hospital but the conditions in Auschwitz I as a whole. At least thousands were given a better chance of survival. This fact is confirmed by Rudolf Vrba in *Shoah*. He points out that the lower mortality rate left less room for new arrivals, which resulted in more gassing of arriving prisoners. It would be a terrible injustice to blame Langbein. Because of these improvements, the Political Department (the camp Gestapo) accused Wirths of conduct unbecoming an SS officer, and Langbein spent two months in the bunker (the prison in the prison camp). Langbein was one of the very few who emerged alive from this bunker. The fact that he was non-Jewish and

German was of little help there. Some of the other non-Jewish and Jewish associates of Langbein in the underground were betrayed while attempting to escape to establish contact with nearby partisans in the fall of 1944. They were all hanged during roll call, for everybody, including myself, to see. Langbein, who was very much part of the plan, escaped by sheer luck. A few weeks before, he was forcibly, against his will, transferred into northern Germany. To denounce Langbein as being a member of the Resistance for his own survival only is totally unjustified. Concerning the question about Wirths' suicide: the night after his surrender to the British, I have to correct an error made by Lanzmann in a quotation from the movie: the British officer did not say to Wirths, "Well, I am *happy* to shake the hand of the man who is responsible for the death of four million people." He said, rather, according to the movie, "Now I have *touched* the hand, etcetera." This quotation makes it less easy to call the movie a rehabilitation of Wirths, as Mr. Lanzmann suggested. [*End of note by Dr. Micheels.*]

# References

Arendt, Hannah. 1963. *Eichmann in Jerusalem: A Report on the Banality of Evil.* New York: Penguin.

Lacan, Jacques. 1975. *Le séminaire.* Vol. 1. *Les écrits techniques de Freud.* Paris: Seuil.

Langbein, Hermann. 1972. *Menschen in Auschwitz.* Vienna: Europaverlag.

Lanzmann, Claude. 1985. *Shoah, an Oral History of the Holocaust: The Complete Text of the Film by Claude Lanzmann.* New York: Pantheon.

———. 1990. "Hier ist kein Warum." In *Au sujet de Shoah: Le film de Claude Lanzmann,* ed. Bernard Cuau et al.

———. 1991. "Seminar on *Shoah.*" *Yale French Studies* 79.

Lifton, Robert Jay. 1986. *The Nazi Doctors: Medical Killing and the Psychology of Genocide.* New York: Basic Books.

Micheels, Louis J. 1989. *Doctor 117641: A Holocaust Memoir.* New Haven: Yale University Press.

Mosse, George L. 1964. *The Crisis of German Ideology: Intellectual Origins of the Third Reich.* New York: Grosset and Dunlap.

———. 1975. *The Nationalization of the Masses: Political Symbolism and Mass Movements from the Napoleonic Wars through the Third Reich.* New York: Howard Fertig.

# Concerning the Accounts Given by the Residents of Hiroshima

### Georges Bataille

Let's admit it; the population of hell increases annually by fifty million souls. A world war may accelerate the rhythm slightly, but it cannot significantly alter it. To the ten million killed in the war from 1914 to 1918 one must add the two hundred million who, during the same period, were fated to die natural deaths. People are quick to speak of the evil effects of science, but these remain outweighed by its benefits. The average life span in the seventeenth century was lower than it is today. Furthermore, all sorts of plagues used to decimate humans.

If such is the case, the relative apathy of the masses is not so surprising. When we encounter nothing but powerlessness, the desire to react exhausts us, and we forget that the margin of unhappiness at stake is not so great, that a core of darkness remains untouchable. Who doesn't want to free the world from fear? It is a task that takes precedence over all others. And yet the most ardent of would-be liberators are not so deeply troubled as they would like, while the masses can only shake their heads. The last wars have broken out in spite of the general will; their slaughter revolted the conscience. But the dread they provoked, however great, remained a stupid, inconsistent one . . . and laced with curiosity.

Following such experiences, whose horror should have, in principle— but in the end, what is this principle?—left the world quaking, the desire to put an end to them is more powerless than it ever was. We live in a darkness without fear and without hope. Even political parties no longer have the heart to use as an instrument of propaganda, with the blind passion of faith, their former "struggle against war." In fact, they have nothing arresting to say; they prefer to attract (isn't it really to distract?) our attention onto closer goals. According to the "wise men," we continue to cry needlessly, failing to see what really matters; we resemble the patient that Hersey mentions, who lay without hope in a Hiroshima hospital, fearing that he had syphilis (this was on August 6, 1945, a little before 8:15 A.M.). But this man, who died the moment after from an entirely different cause, could not possibly know what was in store for him. Our case is different. We know. And it is due to our lack of imagination, our foolish levity, that, whining, we busy ourselves with "blood tests." At least so the "wise men" keep telling us.

But the enlightened wisdom of these "wise men" is not always more correct than the blind wisdom of the people. The levity with which, on the whole, the atomic effect is generally faced—levity in a relative sense, when the importance of the effect is taken into consideration—is not this levity itself taken lightly? The double current of panic (in the realm of discourse) and indifference (practically total in the realm of decisionmaking, and quite substantial in the realm of feeling) is almost the same as it was ten years ago. Might we not have exaggerated the eventual consequences of the atom bomb? (People even fear proudly the destruction of the globe. We can no more exclude the possibility of such a denouement than we can that of a cosmic cataclysm; but for the moment, the chances of a global explosion, of either human or celestial origin, have remained very slight.) The blind wisdom [of the masses] is perhaps right to react as if losses of life and of useful accomplishments could never put an end to civilization. Civilization is no longer a matter of an aristocracy sheltering the order of an empire from the invasion of nomadic peoples. A world that would survive the torrents of bombs might not be the desert people have predicted. And we have been too quick to believe that the moral resources of man are not equal even to a truly insane experience. It seems to me that Albert Camus is wrong to affirm without reservation that "the coming war will leave humanity so mutilated and impoverished that the very idea of law and order would become decidedly anachronistic" ( *Combat*, 26:11–46, in the remarkable series of articles entitled *Neither Victims nor Executioners* [Camus, 1947 (1986)]). And yet . . .

The possibility of seeing the world delivered up to uranium obviously justifies some general reaction. And it is strange that, in the malaise in which it called men to holy war (to conquests, to crusades, to religious wars) or to revolution, the human voice, formerly so powerful, no longer has the slightest force, even given the most compelling reason ever. The leaders of the smallest and weakest parties evoke some echoes, but one does not even see *born* the uprising that would meet the grave concerns of the modern world with anything other than phrases.

It is fair to say that between the mind's habitual standards and the atomic effect there remains a disproportion that makes one's head spin, leaving the imagination before the void. On the other hand, the remoteness of where the bombs fell is not merely geographic; one cannot deny that the spiritual bonds between the Nipponese world and our own are weak. Thus the bombs that fell on Hiroshima and Nagasaki offer more for reflection than for feeling. One has to admit that had they fallen on Bordeaux or on Bremen (supposing these cities intact, and not yet evacuated), the bombs would not have had for us the sense of quasi-scientific experiments—whose magnitude overwhelms the imagination, but whose tragic effect is no less outside of sensory representation than it is undeniable. The Americans, geographically closer and linked to the Japanese by the sad ties created by years spent trying to destroy each other—besides being obsessed by the fact of having invented, manufactured and launched the bombs—are far more unhappy than the French: their nervous sensibility is affected.[1] (Similarly with the British, who were closely involved in the war against Japan and in the invention of the atomic weapon.) Thus the little book by John Hersey— the first to give a meticulously precise account (made up in large part of layer upon layer of details) of the experience of the bomb undergone by those who endured it—corresponds more to the problems of the Anglo-Saxons than to those of the French. Yet it therefore has greater interest for the French, who most lack what the book essentially provides: a sensory representation of the cataclysm.

We can recognize the life and character of those whom in Hersey's book we see suddenly engulfed in horror. They resemble those men, women and children whom we see every day and with whom we are familiar. The doctors Fujii and Sasaki, the German Jesuit Kleinsorge, Mr. Tanimoto, Miss Sasaki, Mrs. Nakamura and her children, all are not so different from the doctors, Jesuits, secretaries, widows of soldiers and children that we know. We see them, on the sunny day of the calamity, get up, and take the place assigned them at that moment by fate, where thanks to an unforeseen delay or a tiring chore, they somehow escape from the horror of death. The blow fell upon them from a serene sky, just after the all-clear siren had sounded (the still undestroyed city was in fact living in expectation of being bombed). But it is in isolation and in complete ignorance of what was suddenly upon them, that the revelation—the meager, shattering, unending revelation—began for each of them. It was even in a sense the opposite of a revelation, mocked, as they were, by their own laughably inaccurate hypotheses (throughout the day the disaster was attributed to "a Molotov flower basket," the Japanese name for the cluster of bombs that disperse themselves as they fall). The entire world learned before the inhabitants of Hiroshima did that the city had been the first to have a go at the invention that would shake up the earth and leave its inventors themselves shattered. The individual in the streets of Hiroshima, dazzled by an immense flash—which had the intensity of the sun and was followed by no detonation—learned nothing from the colossal explosion. He submitted to it like an animal, not even knowing its gigantic scope. On the ground, for the isolated man, a bomb had exploded right near by; there was no momentous event, no leap into the future like the one the President of the United States announced to a wonder-struck (but worried) world. For Truman's listeners, it was, from the very start, a question of a "historic event," projecting consequences into the future. The man of State announced that the "bomb had more power than twenty thousand tons of T.N.T. It had more than two thousand times the blast power of the British 'Grand Slam,' which is the largest bomb ever yet used in the history of warfare." At about three kilometers from the center of the city, Mr. Tanimoto, pastor of the Methodist church of Hiroshima, "a small man, quick to talk, laugh and cry," paused to catch his breath by the side of the road: the handcart containing a cabinet filled with clothes, which he was pulling with a friend, Mr. Matsuo, had tired him out:

> There was no sound of planes. The morning was still; the place was cool and pleasant. Then a tremendous flash of light cut across the sky. Mr. Tanimoto has a distinct recollection that it travelled from east to west, from the city toward the hills. It seemed a sheet of sun. Both he and Mr. Matsuo reacted in terror—and both had time to react (for they were 3,500 yards, or two miles, from the center of the explosion). . . . Mr. Tanimoto took four or five steps and threw himself between two big rocks in the garden. He bellied up hard against one of them. As his face was against the stone, he did not see what happened. He felt a sudden pressure, and then splinters and pieces of board and fragments of tile fell on him. He heard no roar. . . . When he dared, Mr. Tanimoto raised his head and saw that the rayon man's house had collapsed. He thought a bomb had fallen directly on it. Such clouds of dust had risen that there was a sort of twilight around. In panic . . . he dashed out into the street. . . . The first thing he saw was a squad of soldiers. . . . The soldiers were coming out of the hole, where they should have been safe, and blood was running from their heads, chests, and backs. They were silent and dazed. Under what seemed to be a local dust cloud, the day grew darker and darker. [Hersey, 1946 (1985), 6–7]

John Hersey's decision to reduce his reporting to a succession of scenes recorded in the memories of his various witnesses conforms to the methodical principles of modern news gathering (the American effort to give reporting a rigorous foundation is hardly known in France). The method leads to this notable result: the recollections that the author reports with the most praiseworthy care—since in them the immediate experience of the catastrophe is isolated—are reduced to the dimensions of *animal* experience. The *human* representation of the catastrophe is that given by President Truman; it immediately situates the bombing of Hiroshima within history and defines the new possibilities that it has introduced into the world. Mr. Tanimoto's representation, on the other hand, has only sensory value, since what there is of *intelligence* in it is mistaken. Error is the human aspect in the description, while what stands out in it as true is what the memory of an animal would have retained. The entire first chapter, in which the recollections of various witnesses follow one upon the other, all dealing with the fall of the bomb and the moments that followed (according to a mode of expression that Jean-Paul Sartre's *Le Sursis* introduced in France), is the view of the *animal*, walled in, deprived, by an error, of a passage into the future, deprived of an event whose essence is to alter the destiny of man. This difference that sets apart likewise opposes the account of the battle of Waterloo in *The Charterhouse of Parma* to the historical representation of the same event. But a concern *humanizes* the battle in Stendhal, who aims at another kind of *human* interest; his famous account inserts *historically* into human representations the formerly quasi-animal perspective of the individual. Relative to this, John Hersey's reporting is benign, and the view that it introduces is merely the unintended result of his precise method.

However interested we are in learning what the immediate reactions were to the explosion, it must be said that in itself, independent of any previous curiosity, this opening chapter is only of the slightest interest. What we learn from John Hersey about the arrival onto the scene of the atomic bomb is no different from, or differs little from, what has been reported of thousands of large bombs. The impression is not much stronger; it only requires multiplying by the large number—more than two hundred thousand—of those who, in varying degrees, experienced the bomb. But the necessity of multiplying, which gets one closer to the intelligible—human—reality of the event, only appears in Chapter Two. Mr. Tanimoto has had to help a woman who, while crying, was carrying a small child on her back:

By this solicitous behavior, Mr. Tanimoto at once got rid of his terror. At the school [previously designated for use as a temporary hospital and where he had just brought the woman], he was much surprised to see glass all over the floor and fifty or sixty injured people waiting to be treated. He reflected that . . . several bombs must have been dropped. He thought of a hillock . . . from which he could get a view . . . of the whole of Hiroshima. . . . From the mound, Mr. Tanimoto saw an astonishing panorama. Not just a patch of Koi, as he had expected, but as much of Hiroshima as he could see through the clouded air was giving off a thick, dreadful miasma. Clumps of smoke, near and far, had begun to push up through the general dust. He wondered how such extensive damage could have been dealt out of a silent sky; even a few planes, far up, would have been audible. (24–25)

The question that Mr. Tanimoto was not able to answer at least introduced, in his searching for it, the human meaning of the event. And the interest of John Hersey's remarkable book has to do with the slowness of a revelation that gradually changes a catastrophe, which strikes in an isolated, animal way, into an intelligible representation.

These distinctions will perhaps seem idle. But I can at this point explain myself. What struck me on first reading *Hiroshima* was that, if I had not had any other reason, the isolated view of horror would have left me, as it were, indifferent. If, however, I read in anguish, feeling in contact with the most oppressive reality, it was because I knew: right away I related all the banal reactions to the consciousness of the possibilities opened up by the manufacture of atomic bombs. I understood then that the annual death of fifty million human beings had no humane meaning. (We cannot, indeed, avoid it—and if we could, we should soon see that we should have done nothing, that the resulting misfortunes would be more serious than a thousand Hiroshimas, since numberless death is necessary for the uninterrupted renewal of life.) But the death of sixty thousand is charged with meaning, in that it depended on their fellow men to kill them or to let them live. The atom bomb draws its meaning from its human origin: it is the possibility that the *hands of man* deliberately hang suspended over the future. And it is a means of action: the fear produced by a tidal wave or a volcano has no meaning, since neither of them makes one afraid *in order* to compel surrender; whereas uranium fission is a project whose goal is to impose, by fear, the will of the one who provokes it. At the same time it puts an end to the projects of those whom it strikes. It is by representing possible projects, which in turn are intended to make other projects impossible, that an atom bomb takes on a *human* meaning. Otherwise, it would merely have the *animal* meaning of smoking out termites.

If we continue with John Hersey's narrative, the disproportion of the effect [of the bomb to the mind's habitual standards] soon brings us back into the *depths* of the termites' nest. Those who were its witnesses, enduring the effect without dying, no longer had the strength necessary to form an intelligible representation of their misfortune: they submitted to it as the termite submits to the unintelligible destruction of its nest. At first, they could not distinguish this effect from those of ordinary bombs; then, it seems, they perceived the immensity of the disaster, but without, for all that, escaping from their inhuman daze. This very human vertigo caused by the idea of catastrophe, which supposes at least the sort of proximity created by the sensory imagination, probably also supposes a minimum of distance. The horror reached the point where reflection—which requires sustaining not only concern, but beyond concern, that hope which is its foundation—could only exert itself weakly. Brief passages cannot replace reading the whole book, with the multiplication of details, monstrous and minute. [There are, for instance,] mixed in with the dead, the ten thousand wounded, bleeding, vomiting, and dying, overflowing the stairwells, the hallways and the court-yards of a hospital, and cared for by six doctors . . . but that is the simplest image of calamity. Mr. Tanimoto, running through the ruins in search of his wife and his church, is represented to us as the only one uninjured among the hundreds and hundreds of wounded that he meets along the way: "The eyebrows of some were burned off and skin hung from their faces and hands. Others, because of pain, held their arms up as if carrying something in both hands. Some were vomiting as they walked. Many were naked or in shreds of clothing. . . . Many, although injured themselves, supported relatives who were worse off. *Almost all had their heads bowed, looked straight ahead, were silent, and showed no expression whatever*" (my emphasis [38–39]). A little farther, Mr. Tanimoto discovered, lying on the bank of a river, some wounded who were too weak to move when the tide rose; he endeavored to save them: "He reached down and took a woman by the hands, but her skin slipped off in huge, glove-like pieces. He was so sickened by this that he had to sit down for a moment." With the help of a boat, he succeeded, with great difficulty, in lifting the bodies onto a higher part of the bank. Nevertheless, by the next day, the tide had washed them away. I do not cite this fact for the horror of such useless courage, but for a sentence that completes the account: "*He had to keep consciously repeating to himself,* 'These are human beings'" (my emphasis [59]). What emerges from the entirety of the account is that whatever humanity was maintained by these unfortunate people of Hiroshima, had to be painfully kept up against a background of animal stupor.

At first sight one imagines that the intelligible representations of the catastrophe whose return we must dread lack the emotive element provided by sensory representations, and in the absence of which reflection has no effect (since it is not followed by the necessary intense reactions). But one quickly realizes that the appeal to feeling is of negligible interest. Undoubtedly, it is even at the expense of effectiveness that feeling enriches the sentimentality of those who are depressed, since the result of reflection is either a virile attitude or none at all. If, besides, as is human, we reject sentimentality and go resolutely to the limits of the possibilities of feeling, we find only the infinite "absurd" of animal suffering. And in the meaningless world into which our reflection draws us, a cataclysm is limited to the instant it takes place—and its representation exceeds any concern for subsequent consequences. So much so that feeling cannot be the point of departure for action. And one can say with certainty that the most vivid imagination can place only a negligible force at the service of those who wish to ward off the return of misfortune. The sensibility that goes to the furthest limits moves away from politics and, as is the case for the suffering animal, the world has at a certain point nothing more to it than an immense absurdity, closed in on itself. But the sensibility that looks for a way out and enters along the path of politics is always of cheap quality. It cheats, and it is clear that *in serving* political ends it is no more than a *servile*, or at least subordinated sensibility. The cheating is quite apparent. If the misfortunes of Hiroshima are faced up to freely from the perspective of a sensibility that is not faked, they cannot be isolated from other misfortunes. The tens of thousands of victims of the atom bomb are on the same level as the tens of millions whom nature yearly hands over to death. One cannot deny the differences in age and in suffering, but origin and intensity change nothing: horror is everywhere the same. The point that, in principle, the one horror is preventable while the other is not is, in the last analysis, a matter of indifference. The standpoint of *sovereign sensibility*, which has nothing to do with sentimentality, or even with pity—which are equivocal—seems to me to have been represented perfectly by Malraux, when he asked the communists: "At this moment, what do you do about the man run over by a train?" Malraux was wrong to confront the communists with this difficulty, since they openly subordinate sensibility to reason. But the objection would be valid if addressed to those who think that they obey their sentiments.

In truth, if one singles out Hiroshima for lamentation, it is because one does not dare to look misfortune in the face—misfortune's profound non-sense, which is not only the result of the avoidable violence of war, but a basic component of human life. As a consequence, one takes refuge in the world of activity, dominated by the principles of a virile reason. But instead of responding to the concern about an impossible horror, one serves the ends of a narrow system. The man of equivocal sensibility is, at the same time, the man of civilization, which he normally supports without relying any more on reason than on feeling. In his faith, he neglects the fact that civilization is made up of autonomous systems, each opposing the others. He knows well that there is evil here, but he does not want to see that the "civilization" that he opposes to the savagery of wars is this same civilization—undistorted by any idealistic dream—that, since it is formed out of conflicting elements, is itself the cause of wars. More precisely, and more generally, he defends human systems that are based on concern for the future, on anxiety about difficulties that might arise unexpectedly, and therefore on regularly pruning back the world's possibilities. I do not mean that such systems should not be defended, nor that one can simply give up being concerned about the future. But anxiety and concern, which are the foundation of civilization, always necessitate certain patterns of activity, which the various States that are built on them can never agree to give up. Each civilized unit (thus, civilization) proclaims the primacy of its undertakings—by which it means to secure the future—over all considerations of feelings. This means that, [when forced to choose] between the horrors of war and giving up any of the activities through which it believes it must secure its future, society chooses war. The exceptions result either from the impossibility of struggle, from mistakes, or from the apparent insignificance of the concessions. Thus each nation responds without reservation to the demands of activity, and concedes only a minimum to those of sensibility. It is strange that concern for the future at the level of the State immediately diminishes the individual's security and chances of survival. But this is precisely the sign of human indifference toward the present instant—in which we suffer and in which we die—[an indifference] that leaves powerless the desire to live. The need to make life secure wins out over the need to live. On one point only does the sensibility of feeling coincide with the rational interest of the State. The destruction of life does not just affect the moment of the individual's death: it can bring disorder and depression to the collectivity as well. For the State, the constant ravage of death is without importance: it is made up for by the birthrate. But the victims of wars, not to mention the fear of defeat, represent a reduction of active strength. Napoleon's "one night of Paris," which would restore the losses of battle, expresses rather faithfully the Nation's point of view, but the blows struck by the enemy nevertheless threaten to sap the life from the social body. The Nation itself gives the man of equivocal sensibility his due. But it is striking that, at this point, the latter limits his sensibility rather closely to points that correspond to the rational preoccupations of States. It is true that on the surface his sensibility upsets preconceived notions: it considers the misfortunes of foreign countries, even enemies, on the same plane as those of the Nation. This is because sentimentality rationalizes (universalizes) and cannot *in principle* keep within the limits of State reason. But for the most part, in fact, it finds itself back within them: the majority of suffering souls are a lot more sensitive to national losses. They get from the state, in any event, the very rationalism that takes them beyond their own country: they only go (weakly) beyond geographical limits by maintaining moral ones; for these souls as for the State, the only truly shattering losses are those that affect, and profoundly disrupt activity. While some will say that this is a matter of guarding against losses that might be avoided, the equivocal sensibility is nonetheless placed *as a minor element* in the service of this "civilization," whose essence is limited to separate States. And one cannot say that the results of this servility justify it without question. If one serves the very cause of the misfortunes one wants to avoid, I'm not sure one has the right to call them avoidable. And the fact remains that in the end, nothing was avoided.

But if it is true that sensibility is caught in a dead end, if subordination to principles external to sensibility is at the origin of the miscalculation, it does not follow that a refusal of all subordination opens a way. On the contrary, it closes it, or at the very least gives up on any remaining illusion that there is a way out. In truth, the moment of sovereign sensibility differs in every respect from that of servile sentimentality. In one sense, it is quite close to pure animal sensibility, since it is similarly free from the limits of reason—that is, from all concern for the future. Like an animal, the man of sovereign sensibility does not see beyond the present moment. He is not interested if one offers him, as compensation for the misfortune that *is*, a happiness that *will be*. For him, the only valid response to misfortune is the one that counts that same instant, without delay. But he differs profoundly from the animal in that immediate sensibility is what, by definition, gets subordinated to reason—as soon as the being reaches the stage of reason— whereas sovereign sensibility is placed above reason, which it recognizes within the limits of goal-oriented activity, but which it transcends and subordinates. It is natural that it should at first appear in the form of sentimentality; in a sense, its first movement is the vain revolt of a sensibility that remains within the limits of reason. But this still empty sentimentality, which would have liked to have operated like reason but was, for its own ends, inoperative, frees itself when feeling cuts too deep. And one shouldn't be surprised that this liberation is confirmed at the moment when sensibility experiences this new proof of its own uselessness: when the military art of destruction gains unprecedented means. Indeed, the man of sovereign sensibility is not unrelated to the birth of the atomic bomb:[2] his excessive nature corresponds to that of the sciences, which is to say of reason.

To represent this attitude of sovereign sensibility, I will start from the "crucial" experience of sensibility found in the Christian meditation on the Cross and in the Buddhist meditation on the boneheap. Both these meditations, far from plunging the spirit into the depths of depression, create a passage and a rapid movement of "communicating vessels" from extreme anguish to "the joy that transcends joy." But the Christian and the Buddhist sensibilities presuppose, if not a stable subordination, at least a fundamental concession, to the sovereignty of reason. Both condemn the moment— which is to say, what exists, or the world; they condemn the sensible world, which they carry in one and the same movement to the farthest limits of the possible, and they can condemn it only in the name of the truths of an intelligible sphere. But such a trick is not so easy any more, at least to the extent that the crisis of sensibility reaches the point where it becomes unbearable. It is the instant, such as it is, without expression and without detour, that encloses being and, if one reaches an extreme state, can be neither balanced nor compensated for by anything that follows. Nietzsche was the first to experiment with this; or at least he was the first to express it with some degree of clarity. The state where extreme misery and ecstasy are blended, into which the idea of "eternal recurrence" would plunge him, is at first difficult to grasp. Apparently, the same idea, communicated to numerous readers, has not seriously affected their sensibilities. It is, however, no less possible or necessary to identify Nietzsche's experience with the moment of sovereign sensibility, in which the instant is lived without attempt at evasion. Now, this "mystical state" of Nietzsche's,[3] furthermore, differs from the Buddhist or Christian religious states only in the trickery that is suddenly exposed (only in a difficulty of access which is as a consequence made worse): the instant, the sensible moment, is sovereign here, no longer shifting the weight that crushes it onto a reality—or a nothingness—free from chance. And what in such a perfect gamble makes ecstasy inevitable, liberating it with a burst, transforming unimaginable exhaustion into radiance, is the suppression of hope. (Hope, conceived negatively here, is nothing more than postponement.) If the unrelieved instant that is before me, or rather within me, with each throw carries eternity in its fall, like a roll of the dice—if there is no salvation and if the rationalized future of the world cannot alter the world's being open to all that is possible—then nothing counts *more than* this cry, which fills the air like the wind or the light and, however powerless, leaves no room for fear, that is to say, for worrying about the future. But if this is the case, if there is affirmed within me a boundless suffering that is joy, or a joy that is infinite suffering, if I say, if I must say: "Nothing counts more than this joy that situates me," my affirmation immediately places me at the point where my sensibility meets its most difficult test. But this point cannot *now* be the suffering of Christ nailed to the Cross, extolled by a mythical narrative, nor the humble boneheap of the Buddhist, but rather, if one likes, the unequaled horror of Hiroshima. Not because any given horror should by itself grip me more than another that is less striking, but because the horror of Hiroshima holds, in fact, the attention of my fellowmen, like a lamp attracts a swarm of insects. It is not particularly surprising if Hersey's book takes on, in this sense, the meaning of a lamp: I imagine that for a while it will give an intolerable brilliance to the possibilities of human suffering, whose symbol and sign it has become even as those possibilities exceed it infinitely. And if it is necessary to place the cry of the instant on the level of the unbearable, the feeling evoked by *Hiroshima* may pass for an acceptable, if superficial, expression of it.

At this point the first aspect of a particular attitude stands out: the man of sovereign sensibility, face-to-face with misfortune, no longer immediately exclaims, "At all costs let us do away with it," but first, "Let us live it." Let us lift, in the instant, a form of life to the level of the worst.

But no one, for all that, gives up doing away with what one can.

I would not have written the preceding if I had only wanted to show that it is vain to want to avoid misfortune. I have described an effort, based on evasion, that can only *reduce* the portion of misfortune. I merely recalled that while following the route one has already taken might stir up a vague concern, one remains powerless. And certainly it is better to live up to Hiroshima than to lament it, unable to bear the idea of it. In truth, man is equal to all possibilities, or rather, the impossible is his only measure (would the human being be *fully* what he is prior to the instant when the possible—or the future—disappears in front of him?). But these thoughts mark a summit, and were one to live in its vicinity, one would not for all that have let go of this human life, which goes on and which, perceived in its totality, is beautiful, and admirable, and worthy of being loved. Thus at the very moment when the sovereignty of the instant appears to me to dominate utility, in no way do I abandon this enduring humanity: I will say that it is beautiful and admirable only to the extent that the instant possesses and intoxicates it, but this does not imply on my part any overestimation of the duration of the instant, doomed, from beginning to end, to a vanishing splendor. It even seems to me that a movement that carries me beyond limits is more helpful than an oppressive worry and a fear of the future, which lead to eloquence and the common overemphasis on action. The powerlessness of this world, established by the primacy of action, and by the atomic bomb, the latest expression of this powerlessness, is obviously detestable. And if I have spoken of a world of sovereign sensibility, it is not only because the sensible value of Hersey's book leads me to it. It's because—I cannot doubt it—this world of sovereign sensibility, that is, of the primacy of the instant, is the only one where the dead ends I have pointed out might be gotten around (though of itself, at least at first, this sensibility could not be the motor of action). And it is not completely utopian to evoke this possibility, *if it is already given in the nature of the present economy* (which does not mean that it is within quick reach nor even ever realizable).

Everyone knows that the industrial development of the United States has reached, from this point on, such a high level that the United States must no longer expect compensation for its overproduction, which it has to sell abroad. This difficulty in finding outlets must itself, on the other hand, speed up the growth of its productive power. One cannot forget in this light that the mobilization of atomic energy, in the form of the bomb, is likely to increase to an important extent the resources of productive energy (the production for military purposes of explosive uranium or of plutonium could even in a short time release as a by-product large quantities of heat available for electricity).

*Thus the normal and necessary progress of American activity should without particular effort lead to the outfitting of the entire globe without any corresponding compensation.* This is impossible within the customary conditions of activity submitted to the law of profit. But the impossibility cannot be final, since renouncing such a possibility would leave one before an equivalent impossibility. At this point, but slowly, a perfect reversal of the sphere of activity takes place. Worrying about the future is from now on the only foundation for worrying about the future: it is only to the extent that activity generally, by its origin, is based on this worry—and no longer due to a lack of resources—that we are still ruled by concern for the future. Supposing minds freed from such a concern, bodies would immediately be freed as well. This situation, from the point of view which we have taken up here, has, moreover, other consequences. Outfitting the USSR (bringing the USSR in a fairly short period of time up to the superabundant level of the United States) would be less costly to the latter than a military victory. Carrying out such an operation would even, in a sense, be easier than avoiding it. Now, this would radically alter the conditions of life throughout the world: beyond a certain point of general—and superabundant—development of productive forces, economic problems each day become more serious (and more strange). They cease to be susceptible to military solutions, which are ruled out by the certainty of wealth—which only the certainty of wealth can rule out: this would be the transition from the primacy of the future to that of the present. It would obviously be childish to deny the very basic difficulties. But it would be equally childish not to see that a dead end demands, despite the difficulties, this impossible leap: in any case the untenable nature of the present system is complete. The world, trapped in a corner, is doomed to abrupt metamorphosis.

In the end, the old sponge of anxiety that is the world of activity, whose movement leads to destruction, remains at the mercy of the chain reactions of a morality of the instant, of the morality that says: "I am. In this instant I am. And I do not want to subordinate this instant to anything"; or, "Riches will be squandered on earth as they are in heaven." It is true that a morality, even an expressly economic one, cannot overturn the foundations of economics. But these foundations are overturned all by themselves and morality is born of this overturning like a sudden escape of light.[4]

*— Translated by Alan Keenan*

## Notes

Bataille's essay originally appeared in *Critique* 8–9, January and February 1947, under the title, "A propos de récits d'habitants d'Hiroshima." A partial translation of the text by R. Raziel appeared in *Politics*, Vol. 4, No. 2 (July–August, 1947). This translation, which is the first complete translation into English, is based on the definitive French version published in Bataille (1947) and appears here with the permission of Editions Gallimard. The translator would like to thank Chantal Klein for her help. Bracketed passages are translator's notes; all others were written by Bataille.

John Hersey's reports were originally published in an issue of *The New Yorker* devoted entirely to him, on the 31st of August, 1946. It had, from the very first, an immense impact. The issue was sold out in a few hours. A number of newspapers reprinted the text, both in the United States and abroad. *France-Soir* published a complete translation from the 10th to the 28th of last September (1946). It appeared as a book simultaneously in the United States and England in November (1946).

1. The word translated here as "sensibility" is *sensibilité*. Quite frequently in the text it could equally well be translated as "sensitivity." Bataille uses this word and related ones throughout the essay to resonate with each other: *sensibilité* (sensibility, sensitivity), *sensible* (sensible, sensory), *sensiblerie* (sentimentality), and also *sentimentalité* and *sentiment*. A full understanding of the text would require close attention to the differing uses of these words and their resonance with each other.

2. It is interesting to note that the "man of sovereign sensibility," being the "man of the instant," may, by a play on words, also be called "the man of the atom," since the Greek word, "atom," served to designate the *instant*. (Aristotle and St. Paul used it in this sense.)

3. In this case, the meaning of the word "mystical" is uniquely connected with the sensible state. Nietzsche wrote (Posthumous Notes, 1884): "The new feeling of power: the mystical state; and the most lucid, the most daring rationalism providing the path by which to attain it."

4. The following footnote appears in the version of Bataille's article in *Critique*, but not in the *Oeuvres complètes*: "I cannot develop here a general theory of which I have given, in a completely provisional fashion, a very brief sketch in an article that appeared in *Constellation (La France Libre)*, no. 65, 1946, p. 57."

## References

Bataille, Georges. 1947 (1988). *Oeuvres complètes*. Vol. II. Paris: Gallimard.
Camus, Albert. 1947 (1986). *Neither Victims nor Executioners*. Trans. Dwight Macdonald. Philadelphia: New Society.
Hersey, John. 1985. *Hiroshima*. New York: Bantam.

# TRAUMATIC POETRY:
## CHARLES BAUDELAIRE AND THE
## SHOCK OF LAUGHTER

KEVIN NEWMARK

*for P.E.N.*

Faced with the difficulty of explaining what he considers to be the undeniable loss of contact suffered in modern times between lyric poetry and the experience of its readers, the literary critic and philosophical thinker Walter Benjamin wonders whether this is because the structure of their "experience" itself is no longer what it once was, or was believed to be (1969, 156). In conformity to a historical scheme that recurs in many of his writings, Benjamin identifies such a transformation in the structure of experience with the "decreasing likelihood" that the modern subject will be able to assimilate with any degree of success all the data with which he is confronted by the tumultuous world around him. Since "experience" (*Erfahrung*) in the strict sense, for Benjamin, always consists in the coordination of individual elements within a larger pattern or tradition, such experience would be possible only where "certain contents of the individual past combine with material of the collective past" (159). But in an age of information like ours, this associative structure of experience is threatened from the very start by an opposite tendency on the part of consciousness. Assaulted on all sides by unheard of numbers and kinds of impressions, consciousness learns to protect itself against the injurious effects of these invasive stimuli by preventing them from ever entering into real contact either with the subject's own past or with the unified tradition in which he would otherwise find himself.

What happens to the subject's experience in the modern world, then, at least in Benjamin's version of it, would be a kind of "atrophy" (*Verküm-merung*) in its ability to provide the necessary links or connections (*Zusam-menhänge*) between individual and collective patterns of memory. Instead of embedding any given occurrence within the total lived experience of the subject or the community, consciousness would adopt a defensive stance toward its own experience, merely sterilizing incidents by assigning them a precise point in time and space, and at the cost of the integrity of their contents (159, 163).

Should such an atrophy in the structure of experience indeed have taken place, Benjamin goes on to speculate, then it would be necessary at some point to turn to philosophy in order to find a model of thought capable of articulating and understanding this particular historical alteration within the very structure of experience. Starting out from a reference to Dilthey's philosophy of life, Benjamin then deflects the discussion toward Bergson's investigations into the durational structure of subjective "memory," and finally seeks a more substantial framework for the entire problem by invoking Freud's hypothesis, in *Beyond the Pleasure Principle*, about the relation and possible distinction within the subject's experience between the faculties of "consciousness" and "memory." "Freud's fundamental insight," Benjamin writes, "is formulated by the assumption that 'consciousness arises on the site of, or instead of, a memory trace' " (1920, 160). And what allowed Freud this great insight into the altered structure of contemporary experience was his suspicion, also quoted by Benjamin, that "becoming conscious and leaving behind a memory trace are processes incompatible with each other within one and the same system" (25). But how, precisely, can the hypothesis that consciousness and memory belong to two radically different systems of experience help to explain the general structure of experience in today's world, and how can any of these more or less philosophical speculations be of help to us in reading the poetic output of Charles Baudelaire, the ostensible subject of Benjamin's own essay?

The answer Benjamin himself begins to sketch out to this question, surprisingly enough, has to do with a dream characteristic of *accident* victims. In many accident victims, Freud reminds us, the dream reproduces the catastrophe in which they were originally implicated, and it does so in order, retrospectively, to allow the victim to gain some control over the unsettling occurrence and effects of this accident. But why should Benjamin base his considerations on poetry and the structure of contemporary experience on a peculiarity Freud himself associated with the special case of *trauma*? Although Benjamin himself nowhere says so explicitly, by pairing in this way the mnemonic capacity to reproduce or repeat an occurrence with the subjective experience of undergoing an accident, his essay begins to suggest that the structural distinction in Freud between consciousness and memory corresponds for him to the more fundamental question of the *historical* relationship between tradition and modernity. When the formal patterns of continuity that are presumed to have been grounded in traditional experience by the assimilation of consciousness to memory are disturbed by the truly alien experience of modernity, the coherence of subjective experience is itself displaced in an unexpected way. Consciousness and memory, whatever their relationship in some more or less mythic past, are no longer able to function as associative elements within the same system of individual and collective identity. According to this model, then, modernity would itself be structured like a historical "accident" that has at some prior moment befallen and disrupted the homogeneous structure of experience. And the traces of this accident manifest themselves whenever consciousness, as in Freud's text, can no longer be made fully compatible with memory. That is, modernity names the moment when the thinking subject can no longer be said to be completely in control or conscious of the actual events that necessarily comprise "his" own past.

For the very possibility of memory's coming into being, according to Freud in *Beyond the Pleasure Principle*, is predicated to some extent on a breach (*Durchbrechung*) in what otherwise would remain the unquestioned autonomy and coherence of consciousness's own system: "Consciousness is characterized by the peculiarity that in it . . . excitatory processes do not leave behind any permanent change in its elements but expire, as it were, in the phenomenon of becoming conscious" (Freud, 1920, 25). In other words, memory, as the site where change can be produced, where traces can be left, and where no one system or process of experience can ever sufficiently ensure that all foreign elements will merely "expire" (*verpuffen*) without effect on it, is also, at least for Benjamin, the historical site of modernity. As such, memory also would be the place where the wholly unexpected and accidental can now happen to the subject, making it into something different or other than it previously was, as was in fact the case when "modernity" occurred historically to interrupt once and for all the unified structure of what we continue to call "traditional" experience. Memory, that is, in its very capacity to repeat an event that lies outside or beyond the subject's own control, names the place where the subject of knowledge and experience is always susceptible to being overcome and transformed by the disruptive force of *shock*. Benjamin seems, ultimately, to generalize Freud's hypothesis—produced in response to the traumas of World War I—about the destabilizing and repetitive memory-traces left in accident victims into a global economy of modern life.[1] And in doing so, he gives himself the means of repeatedly bemoaning the traumatic loss of "experience" entailed for the subject when the mode of all possible experience is recognized as a recurrent strategy of defense against "the inhospitable, blinding age of large-scale industrialism" (157).

Now it is also at this point that it would be possible to describe with somewhat more precision the relationship that exists here between Benjamin's philosophical theory about the loss, or atrophy, of experience incurred in the age of industrialism and his understanding of Baudelaire's poetic output. Once subjective experience in the strict sense has been deprived of its capacity to assimilate events directly into a continuous tradition of consciousness and memory—and begins instead merely to ward off, or "parry" shocks—then it becomes obvious what role, both historical and philosophical, can and will be assigned to the aesthetic production of lyric poetry. Occupying an intermediate position between the punctual defensiveness of the consciousness that produces it and the retentive duration of the memory it serves to replace, Baudelaire's poetry—like the dream characteristic of accident victims, moreover, but on a far greater scale—affords its reader the opportunity to reproduce and develop the traumatic events that underlie it in order, retrospectively, to gain some control over them. In other words, Baudelaire's poetry would assume importance for any philosophical understanding of modernity to the precise extent that it provides a permanent memory-trace for the actual event, or shock, of the dissociation of memory from consciousness that occurs in and to the idea of a self-conscious tradition of experience. It is this special characteristic of Baudelaire's writing that sets him apart in the eyes of Benjamin. Baudelaire himself, Benjamin insists, paid dearly for coming to term (*das Einverständnis*) with the age of modernity in this way, but the disintegration of traditional experience (*Erfahrung*) brought on in it by the omnipresent shock experience (*Chockerlebnis*) remains nonetheless the "law of his poetry." And such poetry, Benjamin affirms, is ultimately capable of lending even this traumatic disintegration of experience, for those that can read it, "the weight of an actual experience (*das Gewicht einer Erfahrung*)." By thus making available for philosophical analysis the disruption of traditional modes of consciousness and understanding that occurs traumatically in the very experience of modernity, Baudelaire is finally able to appear at the end of Benjamin's essay, and in the words of Nietzsche, as a "rarefied star" in the otherwise dreary sky of the Second Empire (194).

The question that cannot fail to suggest itself here, of course, is how any properly philosophical understanding can have as its basis an aesthetic experience for which the event of shock has become the norm. For if shock in fact names the dissociation of memory from consciousness or, in slightly different terms, the dissociation of the actual event from its understanding within one and the same system, then how would it ever be possible to determine with certainty whether any philosophical model whatsoever had adequately understood and explained precisely this self-obliterating "experience"? In other words, how is it possible to test Benjamin's affirmation that a recuperation, or redemption, of unified experience ( *die Erfahrung der Aura*) is possible on the far side of Baudelaire's depiction of its very disruption and dissolution in modernity ( *die Zerstrümmerung der Aura im Chockerlebnis*)? One indication that Benjamin's own critical understanding of Baudelaire's writing, for instance, may not be wholly immune to such complications becomes apparent through a retracing of the vocabulary that is used in this essay to characterize Baudelaire's traumatic encounter with modernity.

Of particular relevance in this regard is Benjamin's citation of the following lines from the poem, "The Sun":

> When the cruel sun strikes with redoubled rays
> The city and the fields, the roofs and the grain,
> I go about alone practicing my fantastic art of fencing,
> On the lookout in every corner for chance encounters with rhyme
> Stumbling on words just like paving stones,
> Colliding now and then with long dreamed of verses.

> [Quand le soleil cruel frappe à traits redoublés
> Sur la ville et les champs, sur les toits et les blés,
> Je vais m'exercer seul à ma fantasque escrime,
> Flairant dans tous les coins les hasards de la rime,
> Trébuchant sur les mots comme sur les pavés,
> Heurtant parfois sur des vers longtemps rêvés.]

Benjamin offers these lines as a privileged example in Baudelaire's writing, as perhaps the one moment in *The Flowers of Evil*, in fact, where the poet actually portrays himself at work. It is, Benjamin will go on to claim, this struggle with "the ghostly crowd of words, of fragments, of verse incipits" that eventually produces what he calls "the subterranean *shocks* by which Baudelaire's poetry is shaken" (165, 164, emphasis added).[2] The German word Benjamin himself uses here to describe Baudelaire's writing is *Stösse*, a word that does indeed convey the sense of jolt, concussion, collision, or shock that is clearly involved in Baudelaire's portrayal of the accidental encounter with words befalling the poetic subject in modernity.

What is most surprising, however, and what constitutes a true challenge for any understanding of the essay on Baudelaire, is that this is precisely the term Benjamin uses to characterize what happens to our own thought when we turn to philosophy, as we eventually must, for an explanation of the "shock experience" underlying modernity. In other words, according to Benjamin's own writing, whenever we turn to philosophy to understand the subterranean shocks (*Stösse*) inscribed in Baudelaire's poetry, we always run the risk of receiving an unexpected bump, jolt, or shock in our turn:

> If conditions for a positive reception of lyric poetry have become less favorable, it is reasonable to assume that only in rare instances does lyric poetry maintain contact with the experience of its readers. This may be due to a change in the structure of their experience. Even though one might approve of this development, one would be all the more hard put to say precisely in what respect there may have been a change. Thus one turns to philosophy for an answer, though in doing so one encounters a peculiar state of affairs. [Dabei *stösst* man auf einen eigertümlichen Sachverhalt.] (156)

The peculiarity of the situation is, in part at least, constituted by the repeated encounter in our reading of the lexical variants of *Stösse* and *stossen*, which in Benjamin's text must carry the burden of characterizing both the trauma inscribed in Baudelaire's poetry and the turn to philosophy that is meant to recover from it. But how, we cannot now avoid asking, would it ever be possible to recover from a condition of trauma where the treatment necessarily entailed sustaining a new set of shocks? Benjamin's philosophical understanding of Baudelaire's poetry is thus itself shaken (*gestossen*) and threatened with dissolution at the very moment it names the shock experience as the law and principle of modernist writing. To the extent that it does so, however, it does manage to bring us as close to an actual encounter with this experience as would be possible without undergoing it directly.

Baudelaire himself, at any rate, was sensitive enough to these issues to have made them the basis for at least one of his most important and far-reaching critical texts. In the essay entitled, "On the Essence of Laughter," Baudelaire (1976) develops a theory of laughter that, like Benjamin's theory of modernist writing, takes as its model the production of *shock*:

> In fact, since laughter is essentially human, it is essentially contradictory, that is, it is at the same time a sign of infinite grandeur and infinite misery, infinitely miserable by comparison to the Supreme Being of which it possesses only the conception, and infinitely grand by com-

parison to the natural world. It is from out of the perpetual *shock* of these two infinities that laughter emanates. (532, emphasis added)

The Pascalian overtones of this passage, organized as it is around the polar opposition, *grandeur infinie* and *misère infinie*, are more than obvious. They should also go a long way toward alerting us to the fact that "laughter," at least the way Baudelaire understands it, is not necessarily a laughing matter. For Pascal, it was precisely the "abyss" produced within the self by the collision of such heterogeneous infinities that had as its existential correlate "fear," and that Freud later associated with the sudden start of fright (*Shreck*) that confirmed the failure of the shock defense. The structure of experience that interests us here, then, could not be easily subsumed under the reassuring rubrics of "humor" or the "comic" without reducing its complexity a great deal more than would be legitimate.

On the contrary, for Baudelaire it is of the essence of laughter to bring us face to face with a radical discrepancy or disjunction within the very composition of the human self, and such a recognition could be considered a source of mere merriment only from the point of view of the simplest naiveté or the bleakest cynicism. If it is true, on the other hand and as Friedrich Schlegel once remarked, ironically enough of course, that *irony* is the one philosophical category that is definitely not to be joked with—"Mit der Ironie is durchaus nicht zu scherzen"—then we could with some justification speak of Baudelaire's essay on laughter as constituting in its profoundest intention a special theory of irony. Baudelaire's own characterization of laughter as the sign of a *choc perpétuel* between two infinities, moreover, is not so far removed from offering us a helpful translation for Schlegel's more notorious, and therefore less accessible and intelligible, definition of irony as a "permanent parabasis"; that is, a permanent disruption or interruption of any state of equilibrium whatsoever. Again though, the question cannot help but arise: if the production and experience of shock were in this way to become truly infinite, or "perpetual" in Baudelaire's words, then just what sort of treatment would be appropriate to it, and what sort of recovery could ever be hoped for it?

At the beginning of the essay, "On the Essence of Laughter," which started out as a practical study of contemporary caricature, the subject who speaks—whom we call Baudelaire—addresses questions such as these when he refers to his own state of mind as being caught in the grip of a kind of "obsession." It is his repeated reflections on laughter, Baudelaire tells us—which, as we also soon learn, emanates from the perpetual shock of two incommensurable infinities—that have become obsessive to the point of requiring him to write them down in this text. And by introducing into these obsessive reflections on the "shock" of laughter a certain amount of rigor or order, the subject who speaks in the essay also hopes that he will finally be able to communicate them effectively. Communicate effectively in this context, of course, turns out to mean both in the sense that the speaker would be able to make these obsessive reflections intelligible to others, and in the sense that he would in the process find himself at last relieved of their obsessional character:

> I do not want to write a treatise on caricature; I simply want to share with the reader some of the reflections that have often come to me on the subject of this peculiar genre. These reflections had become a kind of obsession for me; I wanted to relieve myself. I have made every effort, moreover, to introduce a certain order into them and in this way to facilitate their digestion. This article, therefore, is exclusively that of the philosopher and artist. (525)

The key term here is undoubtedly, "digestion," a word that names, albeit metaphorically by the time Baudelaire was writing in the mid-nineteenth century, the intellectual operation of systematic organization and assimilation of foreign elements that is necessary to the healthy maintenance of any consciousness. The disruption that is produced within consciousness by the explosive collision of two irreducible infinities—which traumatic phenomenon, as we have seen, can also always become an obsessive distraction for the consciousness that tries perpetually to reflect on it from the outside—is therefore the true subject of Baudelaire's essay on laughter. And the test of whether and to what extent any consciousness will eventually be able to digest, that is to say, to order, assimilate, and ultimately understand, such a proliferation of disruptions can be undertaken only by compulsively reflecting on, in other words, by learning to read in the fullest sense of the term, all the texts in which they have been inscribed.

In Baudelaire's case, this would mean learning to become aware of and reflect on the various thematic and existential levels on which the model of shock is made to function in the essay on laughter. First of all, shock as it is articulated in this text exhibits the fundamental character of a "fall." Whether it is associated with the literal spectacle of somebody falling in the street (53), the poetic representation of an innocent young thing falling into vice (528–29), or the psychological symptom of a subject falling mentally ill (530), the shock disclosed by laughter is one that involves a loss of balance or equilibrium. In all cases, Baudelaire suggests, the loss of balance involved with laughter can be traced back to mankind's universal fallen condition with respect to a transcendental principle of unity and wholeness: "In the earthly paradise (whether it be conceived as having been or yet to come, recollection or prophecy, according to the theologians or the socialists) . . . joy was not expressed through laughter . . . man's face was simple and all of a piece; his features were undistorted by the laughter that now agitates all nations" (528). Baudelaire's reference here to teleological models of origins and ends as they are classically conceived, either theologically or politically, as closed and potentially totalizable systems of experience and cognition thus makes one thing perfectly clear. Such models, to the extent that they are based on an ideal concept of a prior or subsequent unity, are not capable of fully accounting for laughter—laughter is indeed the symptom that the teleological model is susceptible of being exceeded at every point. And so the very possibility of laughter, according to Baudelaire, also necessitates a different model of thought for dealing with the physiological, intellectual, and ethical modes of experience with which laughter is intimately tied in the essay, if only as an accident or aberration whose occurrence is nonetheless always possible.

As a consequence, moreover, it is laughter itself, rather than some transcendental principle of lost or promised unity, that is made here to provide the essential link between the individual and the larger structures of temporal and spatial experience named by the term "nations"; "man's features were undistorted by the laughter that now agitates all nations." If laughter is the sign that henceforth deforms the face of man, it also becomes by the same token the characteristic sign of commotion and even redirection (*agiter*: to agitate, to trouble, but also to propel or impel) for the course of nations. As such, laughter can no longer be circumscribed by any one or combination of the regions in which it functions—physiologically as grimace and explosive sound, epistemologically or psychically as the potential for error and madness, ethnically as a potential fault or depravity. Extended by Baudelaire to encompass the entirety of the individual subject as well as of the nations and their mobile links, laughter comes to name the fallen mode of all experience; it thus becomes another name for a radically secular, that is to say, nonteleological and indeterminate, mode of history. The shock of laughter in Baudelaire's text designates the loss of equilibrium that is always entailed by an actual fall into history, where history itself can be experienced only nonteleologically, as a constant falling.

Such a perpetual falling, however, whose ultimate impact or shock would

by definition also be forever suspended in the very same moment it is triggered, continues to recall the teleological dimension it nevertheless always
eludes. In Baudelaire's essay on laughter, for instance, significant traces of
these principles remain visible in the way the original intention to reflect
directly on laughter from a strictly philosophical and artistic point of view
becomes doubled in the second section by the need to analyze a slightly
different, at bottom *theological,* proposition. And this time, rather than supposing an unbridgeable distance between a lost or promised teleological
principle and the actual but seemingly aimless condition of individual and
collective laughter, Baudelaire focuses the discussion on a possible mediation
between them. For tradition has it that one man, at least, did not laugh, and
the hypothesis of this single exception may be enough to help bridge the
gap between the perpetual shock of laughter and a teleological principle of
unity and understanding that would otherwise remain forever impossible to
ground. Thanks to a kind of philosophical integral calculus, Baudelaire
seems, in the second section of the essay, to use man's irrefutable but fallen
condition of laughter to reconstruct in reverse order a transcendental principle of mediation capable of reconciling even the most irreconcilable of differences: between God and man would finally stand the mediator par excellence,
Christ.

Starting out from the French maxim, "Le Sage ne rit qu'en tremblant"
(The Sage does not laugh without trembling), Baudelaire is eventually able
to derive in a wholly consistent manner the following proposition: "The
ultimate Sage, the Verb incarnate, never laughed. In the eyes of Him who
knows all and can all, the comical ceases to be" (527). For once it has been
established, thanks to the maxim about the worldly Sage, that laughter is
susceptible to occurring by degree—a laughter that is qualified by "trembling" is not really the same thing as unqualified laughter—then it is an easy
matter to extend the incremental difference out to infinity: there should be a
point at which all laughing stops.[3] And if laughter, the very shock or concussion that "shakes" (*agite*) the entire world can in this way be made itself to
"tremble," then there is no reason why such a "wisdom" cannot be put to
work to redeem the original fallibility of laughter. Indeed, such a possibility
would ultimately be the result of a double logical inversion. By assuming the
standpoint of "wisdom" in the first place, any number of reversals become
possible, and it is even permitted to face up to the full negativity of laughter:
"Now," Baudelaire concedes at last, "by inverting the propositions [about
Christ and the Sage], it would follow that laughter is generally the privilege
of the insane" (527). But if this final reference to the laughter of insanity

seems bleak to us, we should remember that it is introduced here only by way of a logical "inversion" of wisdom's priority—both human and divine. And a merely inverted wisdom is a far different matter than a "perpetual" recurring shock of incomprehension, for it can always be inverted in its turn. Once the shock of laughter is touched by the self-conscious reflex of a tremble, as it seems to be in the maxim quoted and analyzed by Baudelaire in this section, it becomes possible to break the pattern of its incessant fall and to envisage again or for the first time a final state of genuine equilibrium.

Such a promise is in fact ultimately held out by Baudelaire's essay, both in the teleological schema of laughter that is reintroduced there immediately after it has been shown to be impossible, and in the more strictly philosophical and artistic sections that articulate the main argument and conclusion of the essay. Just after insisting on the radical separation between laughter and the divine, "laughter and tears can have no place in the paradise of delights," Baudelaire goes on to reverse this negative assurance into a progressively affirmative supposition: "And note how it is also with tears that man washes away the afflictions of man, and with laughter that he sometimes softens his heart and draws him near; for the phenomena engendered by the fall will become the means of its redemption" (528). The all-important turn is made in each case not when a deficiency, in this case laughter, is simply ignored or refuted, but rather when, thanks to placing it into a negative relation with precisely that which it is not and could never become, it is said to be known *as* a deficiency. The operation—which could be called dialectical, or hermeneutical, or analytical, depending on the context—is still very close to the one familiar to readers of Pascal's famous *pensée*, referred to earlier and entitled *Grandeur et Misère*: "In a word, man knows he is miserable. He is therefore miserable simply because he is, but he is indeed great because he knows this" (1963, 514). The change in perspective that produces the reversal between the misery of being and the greatness of knowledge can be repeated on any number of levels, and it is a further variation of the same pattern that is involved in Baudelaire's essay when he goes on to treat the specificity of artistic consciousness.

This becomes evident in the fourth section of the essay, where Baudelaire provides a "summary" for his theory of laughter and then makes fully explicit the crucial distinction that up to this point has been operating only implicitly:

> The comical, the power of laughter, that is, belongs to the one who laughs and has nothing to do with the object of laughter. It is by no

means the man who falls who laughs at his own fall, unless he is a philosopher, a man who has acquired through force of habit the capacity to split himself rapidly in two [*la force de se dédoubler rapidement*], and to look on the phenomena of his own self as a disinterested observer. (1976, 532)

It is, then, only because the collision, or shock, between the two infinities that produces the laughter can be subsequently *divided* and thus analyzed, that it becomes possible to envisage a standpoint that could ultimately exist beyond all of its disruptions. This division or analysis of the traumatic experience of laughter is performed, according to Baudelaire, by making a distinction, or split, between the experience itself and what he calls the "disinterested observation" of it. Now, it is precisely this potential for "disinterested observation" that characterizes the philosopher and that makes the pathological phenomenon of laughter subject to an act of self-reflexivity, or *dédoublement*, that would be capable of rising above and curing it.[4]

The vocabulary of pathology and cure is Baudelaire's own, moreover, and he uses it near the conclusion of the essay to refer to the self-reflexive component he associates with artistic production in general, and with certain authors, like the German writer E. T. A. Hoffmann, in particular: "it is likely that [in the case of Hoffmann] we are dealing with a most profound physiologist or physician of the insane, and that in his case he has chosen to put this profound science into poetical forms" (542). The artist, who in this regard is like the Sage as well as the philosopher, is also an analyst and a therapist because he knows about the madness of laughter without necessarily succumbing to it. The distance his disinterested knowledge provides him with also serves to shelter him from the traumatic collapse of knowledge that is the constant risk of an overt identification with laughter, which by the end of the essay Baudelaire has begun calling by the aesthetic name of the comical: "Artists create the comical; having studied and gathered together the elements of the comical, they know that such and such a character is comical, and that he is so only on condition of *ignoring* his own nature; in the same way and by an inverse law, the artist is only an artist on condition of being double and of *not ignoring* any phenomenon whatsoever of his double nature" (543, emphasis added). We seem to have come full circle from the beginning of the essay, and to have realigned the attributes of laughter's infinite duplicity in such a way that they no longer need function as a threat—in this case as a compulsion to repeat—to the consciousness that would reflect on them.

Indeed, by the end of the essay, the subject who speaks seems to have gained considerable control over his obsession with laughter by gradually distancing himself from it through his increasingly self-aware analysis and digestion, or understanding, of it. By describing with precision the momentary collapse of knowledge that occurs when two infinities of human nature come together in the shock of laughter, the author of the essay seems to become conscious of the infinite distance that can now separate his own knowledge of that traumatic occurrence from the repetitive experience of ignorance that lies forever inscribed within it. Self-reflexivity seems to be the key that allows the conscious subject to move away from the experience of shock by reintegrating it into a stable understanding of it.

The question remains, however, whether the very occurrence of trauma signals the breakdown of our ability to maintain the perspectival distinctions we ordinarily make between the inside of an empirical experience and the outside of an analytic cognition of it. Is there an outside standpoint ever stable enough to withstand an actual encounter with shock, no matter how mediated by self-reflexivity it might be? As we all know, there is something *contagious* about laughter, and Baudelaire himself does not fail to remark the difficulty of thus containing the explosive potential within laughter once it has been unleashed: "Once the vertigo has entered, it circulates through the air; one breathes it in the air; vertigo fills the lungs and flows through the blood . . . it was truly an intoxication of laughter, something terrible and irresistible" (540, 539). There is indeed a trace of tension left in the essay by this infectious element in laughter that ultimately *resists* a final cure by even the most advanced stage of consciousness. For, though the concluding section of the essay does in fact refer back to the beginning and claim to clarify it, it nonetheless makes no explicit statement with respect to relieving the motivation for Baudelaire's having written the essay in the first place. That is, the subject who speaks so assuredly at the end of the artist's self-reflexive knowledge makes no attempt whatsoever to reflect back on, and perhaps finally to exorcise, his own obsessive attempts to digest and thus rid himself once and for all of the recurrent reflections on laughter that originally prompted the essay.[5]

If it is true, as Baudelaire simply and emphatically affirms at the end of the essay, that no artist can be an artist and ignore any aspect, however small, of his double nature, then what are we to make of the status of this text we are now reading? Has it achieved the degree of self-conscious understanding that would entitle it to the appellation of genuine art, and if so does that mean that it now remains safely beyond the reach of laughter? Has this essay some-how become invulnerable to any further traumatic slips from the heights of its own wisdom and knowledge? The questions are far from being idle ones, since it should be obvious that only a firm decision about whether the text is artistic in Baudelaire's sense (and thus truly beyond laughter, or blindly compulsive, and in this case, a constant object of laughter in its own right) could allow us to support our own understanding of the shock, whose occurrence the text itself names as the essence of laughter.

That this situation represents a dilemma of significant proportions for any reading of the essay was quite clearly appreciated and remarked by one of the best recent commentators of Baudelaire, Paul de Man. After citing a pas-sage written by the Swiss literary critic and psychoanalyst, Jean Starobinski, on the mediating role played by the ironic consciousness within artistic pro-ductivity, de Man rather boldly reverses the terms of the argument to suggest that the effect of "irony," the term by which he consistently translates Baude-laire's "laughter," would be the exact opposite of the kind of therapy or cure for madness that is in fact proposed by Starobinski as well as by some of the main thematic statements in Baudelaire's own essay (1983, 216–17). "Irony," de Man says in flagrant opposition to both Starobinski and certain portions of Baudelaire, "is unrelieved *vertige*, dizziness to the point of madness . . . absolute irony is a consciousness of madness, itself the end of all conscious-ness; it is a consciousness of a non-consciousness, a reflection on madness from the inside of madness itself" (215, 216). The discrepancy here between de Man's text and the others has to do at bottom with his apparent insistence on characterizing irony solely as a principle of consciousness and self-reflexivity. On the one hand, he sees quite clearly that once the trauma of laughter occurs, it is exceedingly difficult to stop its proliferating effects on cognition, even on those who are best equipped to deal with and analyze it. On the other, by emphasizing the dimension of consciousness that persists in laughter at the expense of what he repeatedly calls "reality," de Man leaves open the pos-sibility that the ironic consciousness—however "mad"—could nonetheless somehow remain wholly enclosed within itself and therefore devoid of any substantial contact with material historical reality. This further possibility is one, moreover, that is not so clearly in evidence in Baudelaire's text.

Thus, whereas for Baudelaire the phenomenon of "laughter" must neces-sarily be studied from both a theoretical and a historical point of view, for de Man the turn back to history finally appears as though it constituted only a temptation to be withstood:

> Instead, the ironic subject at once has to ironize its own predicament and observe in turn, with the detachment and disinterestedness that Baudelaire demands of this kind of spectator, the temptation to which it is about to succumb. It does so precisely by avoiding the return to the world mentioned by Starobinski, by reasserting the purely fictional nature of its own universe, and by carefully maintaining the radical difference that separates fiction from the world of empirical reality. (217)

Whatever the hesitations in de Man's formulation, and they are real enough, the emphasis falls clearly on "avoiding" a return to the world, and on "maintaining" the radical separation between fiction and historical reality.[6] If, on the other hand, and as Baudelaire himself suggests, the occurrence of laughter is a historical phenomenon through and through, then no matter how self-reflexive it is allowed to become it will still have to leave a historical residue in its wake. The very possibility of maintaining the separation between pure fiction and reality may itself be something of a theoretical fiction in its own right, though one that is perhaps not so easily avoidable if we want to maintain our own distance from the contagious effects of Baudelaire's laughter. For—unless Baudelaire is referring here to the *shock* of laughter in a merely metaphorical way that would no longer be worthy of the claims he puts on it or the interest we pay to it—there must be some aspect of the trauma in this laughter that is as historically "real" as anything else that leaves its mark on the world. It becomes necessary therefore to ask about the actual historical traces that would be inevitably inscribed on the inside of Baudelaire's own theoretical project of understanding the shock of laughter.

To be historical in this sense, however, and as we have already seen, is also to be potentially disruptive with respect to the ways we usually think about the production and cognition of historical occurrences. According to Baudelaire's own definition, moreover, the occurrence of laughter, which eventually comes to stand in the essay for the fallen condition of all human experience, is peculiarly historical to the precise extent that it is neither divine nor natural, though it also seems to have something of both the divine and the natural about it. It is therefore located at an infinite distance from either the purity of divine knowledge or the simplicity of natural existence, yet it is only through the simultaneous reference to such knowledge and existence that we could ever gain any access to it. To this peculiar structure of laughter Baudelaire gives the name, "shock," and he makes it absolutely clear in what terms he understands the production, or occurrence, of such a traumatic event. The laughter that emanates from shock, Baudelaire tells us, possesses the linguistic structure of a *sign*: corresponding to neither pure knowledge nor simple existence, laughter can only occur on the site of their mutual impossibility to achieve the fullness of presence, as either simple being or thought. "*Sign* of superiority," Baudelaire writes, "in comparison to natural beings . . . laughter is a *sign* of inferiority in comparison to those with true wisdom" (532, emphasis added). Laughter occurs as shock because it occurs semiotically as language, and as language, laughter is traumatic because it always refers to its inability to occur as anything other than a compulsively repeated reference that is never allowed to come to rest in the fullness of a final meaning. The laughter of language can only refer, infinitely and compulsively, that is, traumatically, to its inability to reach the fullness of pure thought and being from which it is infinitely separated. Where is it in Baudelaire's text, we must now ask, that such a traumatic language is itself referred to and occurs historically?

*Le Sage ne rit qu'en tremblant*—The Sage does not laugh without trembling. These words, which open the second section of Baudelaire's essay on laughter, occur as an unattributed citation that disrupts as well as redirects the philosophical and artistic project announced and begun in the first section of the essay. Baudelaire says as much himself: "This peculiar maxim has been running through my head incessantly since I first conceived the project for this essay, and I wanted first of all to rid myself of it" (527).[7] Unlike the "reflections" on laughter mentioned in the first section, and that had become enough of an obsession with Baudelaire to have prompted the writing of the essay, the citation, *Le Sage ne rit qu'en tremblant*, seems to come from out of nowhere, since it is not in itself associated with any particular form of experience or knowledge, either philosophical or artistic. "I have a vague memory of having read it," Baudelaire admits, though he remains unable to identify with precision from just what pen or context this strangely gripping maxim ("étrange et saissisante maxime") has befallen him (526–27). And then he goes on to "analyze" it, step by step, eventually deriving from this one sentence the entire logic of the essay, in particular the fundamental opposition between the divine and human orders as well as the mediating point, occupied by Christ, that forms the bridge between them. But if the essay remains unable to explain how it has come to be in possession of, and to repeat compulsively, this bit of wisdom—*La Sage ne rit qu'en tremblant*—this also means that whatever bridge of mediation is eventually built thanks to it will itself be doubled by a gap in experience and knowledge even more difficult to account for and recover from.

For it is one thing to write an essay, philosophically and artistically, because one has intentionally reflected for a long time about the essence—empirical as well as cognitive—of laughter. It is quite another, on the other hand, to write an essay whose only essential motivation is to rid oneself of the purely mechanical repetition of an anonymous maxim: *Le Sage ne rit qu'en tremblant.* If it were true, and Baudelaire's text certainly does not permit us to rule out this possibility, that the elaboration of an entire theory of laughter—a theory of shock and its overcoming through a process of cognitive self-reflexivity—could be explained solely on the basis of the way this particular maxim, which associates laughter with the words for "wisdom" on the one hand and "tremor" on the other, just happens to be running constantly through one's head, then what could we ultimately say about the philosophical or artistic status of such a theory? In that case, would not all the following sentences of the essay be reducible to a monotonous variation on the inexplicably recurrent, and thus traumatic, refrain—*Le Sage ne rit qu'en tremblant*—that befalls the subject as soon as he conceives of the philosophical and artistic project of writing on laughter?

The unavoidability of these questions reveals that Baudelaire's text exists neither simply beyond laughter nor as a mere object of laughter, but is itself a text that laughs traumatically whenever it is read. That is, the text is not just a description and interpretation of the debilitating discrepancy between experience and meaning that we normally associate with traumatic experience. The text on the occurrence of shock occurs itself as a shock of laughter whenever the reading process necessary for its understanding discloses, as it always must, the two radically heterogeneous levels of which it is ultimately composed. This means that there can be no communication of the philosophical understanding of laughter that Baudelaire has achieved in writing his essay without communicating, and thus passing on to the reader, the shock that lies inscribed within that understanding.

Between the text as rigorous and controlled philosophical analysis of the essence of laughter and the text as compulsive unfolding of a blank citation randomly but irresistibly brought to mind, then, there lies only an unbridgeable fault. Or rather, whenever the text is read, this fault is produced anew when an understanding resulting from the philosophical and artistic reflection on laughter necessarily collides with the residue left in the text by the repetition, meaningless in itself, of a vaguely recollected, but nonetheless insistent, maxim. For the one element in the text on laughter—or in any text for that matter—to which the increasingly self-conscious subject who has written it can never have access by means of a purely philosophical or artistic logic is the actual production of this linguistic residue that always, and from the very beginning, confronts him as an inexplicable enigma. And it is precisely in the terms of this residue—*Le Sage ne rit qu'en tremblant*—that the end as well as the beginning of the textual process of his own understanding ultimately lies embedded. What we call trauma, then, in a technical as well as a clinical sense, is another, more pronounced, version of this radical dissociation within language that can always be experienced by the thinking subject as one between the registration of a given traumatic event and its eventual cognition. Textual trauma, however, like Baudelaire's laughter for instance, is all the more redoubtable to the extent that it, unlike many of the more clinical examples we are familiar with, eventually manages to conceal the fault of cognition inscribed within it behind a pretense of understanding, while remaining otherwise incapable of containing its effects.

It is now clear why Walter Benjamin singles Baudelaire out as the exemplary poet, or star, that lights up the sky of our modernity. The laughter that shakes his texts as well as our attempts to understand it emanates from the shock that in modernity dissociates once and for all the traditional cohesion of experience and cognition. For Benjamin, the writing of Baudelaire offers us a privileged access to the bumps and jolts the continuity of individual and collective consciousness sustains in the industrial age of the big city. As is evidenced by the shock that Benjamin's own philosophical vocabulary sustains when he tries to formulate this understanding in historical terms, however, the recourse to purely chronological models of progression and change may themselves be the superficial images of deeper lying tensions. Reading Baudelaire's own essay on the essence of laughter helps to disclose how even this picture of the more or less recently produced shock of modernity may have its roots in a traumatic experience that ultimately eludes temporal and spatial determinations altogether, even though these determinations remain inextricably bound up with it.

The resultant fall, or trauma, that lies hidden in reading the text is therefore one that now must befall the reader, whose sole task is to register and understand what actually does take place in all these texts. Because the trauma is hidden, it is accessible only by way of a necessary process of reading and interpretation. But because it is textual, its traumatic effects on the potential to understand it can always reproduce themselves on the one who erroneously believes it possible to remain forever sheltered from them. As Baudelaire himself reminds us in his poem, "The Sun,"

> *Trébuchant sur des vers comme sur des pavés,*
>
> Stumbling on words just like paving stones,

it is just as possible to be tripped up on our way to a given destination by words as by paving stones, though perhaps not so easy to recognize such a fall afterwards for the historical disruption to experience and comprehension it both describes and prolongs, or even initiates. Traumatic poetry, to the extent that it necessarily confronts the reader with these issues, also suggests how the language we speak in order to understand the experience of trauma is also irretrievably marked by it. What remains impossible to determine without further analysis is whether and to what extent such a suggestion could ever be put to use for understanding without leaving its own traumatic residue on it. The name for this impossibility that necessitates further understanding even as it risks proliferating incomprehension is language, though a language that could become accessible as such only once we have learned to listen to all the traumatic events through which, with trembling lips, it begins to speak.

## Notes

1. For the complications produced in Freud's own text by a confrontation with "trauma"—the one it would theorize as well as the one it must undergo—see Caruth, introduction to Part I of this volume, as well as Caruth, 1991.

2. Benjamin suggests that he is simply borrowing this characterization of poetic "shock" from the French critic Jacques Rivière, but Benjamin's reference to "die unterirdischen Stösse . . . von denen der Baudelairesche Vers erschüttert wird" is a good deal more inflected toward a traumatic connection than Rivière's conventionally aesthetic formulation: "Etrange train de paroles! Tantôt comme une fatigue de la voix, comme une modestie soudaine qui prend le coeur, comme une démarche pliante, un mot plein de faiblesse" (Rivière, 1911, 10).

3. The distinction introduced in Section 2 with respect to a "trembling" laughter will reoccur later in the essay in the more technical and developed distinctions made between "le comique ordinaire" and "le comique absolu."

4. The most straightforward formulation of this self-reflexive structure of knowledge can be found in Baudelaire's poem, "L'irrémédiable":

> Tête-à-tête sombre et limpide
> Qu'un coeur devenu son miroir!
> Puits de Vérité, clair et noir,
> Où tremble une étoile livide,
>
> Un phare ironique, infernal,
> Flambeau des grâces sataniques,
> Soulagement et gloire uniques
> —La conscience dans le Mal!

5. The last paragraph begins with the sentence, "And to return to my original definitions, though this time expressing them more clearly" (543). A note from the editor (1352) recalls that the essay as it was first written was altogether lacking in a speculative conclusion commensurate with the philosophical considerations of the beginning.

6. If the issue here were de Man's, rather than Baudelaire's, text, it would be necessary to develop more carefully the tension implicit in his supplementary stipulation that the ironic consciousness simply "observe" the temptation to which it is actually "about to succumb." The tension becomes explicit in de Man's own text a few pages later, when he goes on to insist that, "this consciousness is clearly an unhappy one that strives to move beyond and outside itself" (222). It is not clear from these passages just what "moving beyond" consciousness would entail for de Man, but it certainly could no longer be thought of simply in terms of an absolute separation between historical reality and pure fiction.

7. "Cette singulière maxime me revient sans cesse à l'esprit depuis que j'ai conçu le project de cet article, et j'ai voulu m'en débarasser tout d'abord." As the editors of the Pléiade edition point out, the citation is originally from Bossuet's *Maximes et réflexions sur la comédie*. What is of interest here, though, is that Baudelaire, even though he mentions the possibility of its having come from Bossuet, refuses to specify its origin and says only that he has "a vague memory of having read it," already as a citation, in a book.

## References

Baudelaire, Charles. 1976. *Oeuvres complètes*. Vol. 2. Paris: Gallimard, Bibliothèque de la Pléiade.

Benjamin, Walter. 1969. *Illuminations*. Trans. Harry Zohn. New York: Schocken. Translations are sometimes modified.

Caruth, Cathy. 1991. "Unclaimed Experience. Trauma and the Possibility of History." *Yale French Studies* 79 (Jan.).

de Man, Paul. 1983. *Blindness and Insight*. 2d ed. Minneapolis: University of Minnesota Press.

Freud, Sigmund. 1920 (1955). *The Standard Edition of the Complete Works of Sigmund Freud*. Vol. 18. Translated under the editorship of James Strachey in collaboration with Anna Freud, assisted by Alix Strachey and Alan Tyson. 24 vols. (1953–74). London: Hogarth.

Pascal, Blaise. 1963. *Oeuvres complètes*. Paris: Seuil.

Rivière, Jacques. 1911. *Etudes*. Paris: NRF.

# "The AIDS Crisis Is Not Over":
## A Conversation with
## Gregg Bordowitz, Douglas Crimp,
## and Laura Pinsky

CATHY CARUTH and THOMAS KEENAN

*The following conversation took place in New York City on Wednesday, September 25, 1991. Gregg Bordowitz is an activist, a videomaker, and a writer who has been involved in the movement to end government inaction on AIDS. Douglas Crimp is the author of* On the Museums' Ruins, *editor of* AIDS: Cultural Analysis/Cultural Activism *(1988), and co-author (with Adam Rolston) of* AIDS Demo Graphics. *Laura Pinsky is a psychotherapist in private practice and at the Columbia University Health Service, and director of the Columbia Health Service's Gay and Lesbian Health Advocacy Project, and has co-authored (with Paul Harding Douglas)* The Essential AIDS Fact Book.

*CC:* Trauma can be experienced in at least two ways: as a memory that one cannot integrate into one's own experience, and as a catastrophic knowledge that one cannot communicate to others. In what ways can the AIDS crisis be called traumatic?

*DC:* One of the unstated premises of my essay "Mourning and Militancy" [1989] was the incommensurability of experiences. What in this context would be something like trauma producing, I think, is that certain people are experiencing the AIDS crisis while the society as a whole doesn't appear to be experiencing it at all. Richard Goldstein [1987] said that it's as if we were living through the Blitz, except that nobody else knows it's happening. Here's a personal example of what I mean by incommensurability: I once was visiting a very, very sick friend in the hospital and, later that night, coming out of the hospital, experienced a minor form of fag bashing: somebody going by in a car, screaming "Fag, AIDS." Just when you feel most vulnerable and most deserving of sympathy, you get the opposite, an attack, for precisely what you are at the moment feeling the most vulnerable about.

*TK:* The complexity is that it's not simply that some people are living through the Blitz and other people don't know it, but that they *do* know it, in a different way. Because they knew something, you were addressed. After all, if there's one thing that everybody knows, or thinks they know, it's something about AIDS. Isn't one symptom of the crisis precisely the fact that there's not a clean boundary between the insider, what is experiencing it, and the outside, which isn't?

*GB:* People with AIDS, or people living with AIDS, and the people surrounding them are seen to have a kind of causal relation to AIDS, so that those who've heard about AIDS *are* living with AIDS, but are not directly affected by the experience of having it or knowing someone who has it. They know, and they do not want to know.

*LP:* People don't want to hear very much about the experiences of those who are living with AIDS, for all kinds of complicated reasons. People who are ill often want a chance to talk about it: about going to the hospital, sitting in the doctor's waiting room, about what their symptoms are, what their bodies feel like, what medications they are taking. It is often hard to find someone who is willing to listen to this.

*CC:* So part of the traumatic experience itself is the relation to other people, others who are actively aggressive or simply don't want to listen?

*DC:* Apart from the corporeal reality of the disease, we could say that, if there's trauma associated with it, it's a socially produced trauma. In that sense it's not like a catastrophe that just happens; it is of course itself catastrophic, a catastrophic illness, but at the same time the negative effects—the extremities—that most of us experience are social.

*CC:* Kai Erikson in this volume speaks of "community trauma," in the case of a town that was flooded through the negligence of a coal company (the kind of disaster he refers to as "technological disaster"). Part of the traumatic experience of the community as a whole was that sense that the catastrophe wasn't just an accident of nature, but that no one cared about what happened.

*TK:* There's a double trauma here. On the one hand, there's a cataclysmic event, which produces symptoms and calls for testimony. And then it happens again, when the value of the witness in the testimony is denied, and there's no one to hear the account, no one to attend or respond—not simply to the event, but to its witness as well.

*GB:* That's why Kimberly Bergalis is so important, because she does not speak as a person with AIDS identifying with the community of people with AIDS.[1] She never has a "Silence = Death" pin on, she is never seen in relation to or next to other people with AIDS, she has never been pictured talking about early intervention or what it's like living with AIDS. Kimberly Bergalis is the first member of the general public dying from AIDS. That's why she's significant, and that's why she's being pushed forward at us, over and over again: to make up for all the times that we've managed to get on TV as people with HIV or AIDS, to talk about what it's like living with AIDS.

*LP:* In contrast to Belinda Mason, who became completely identified with the community, and became part of the political struggle.[2]

*GB:* Kimberly Bergalis doesn't identify at all with the community affected by AIDS. In fact, this was "done to" her *by* that community—she identifies as its victim.

*TK:* There's a way in which the telling of the story, the testimony of the affected community, functions or can be received as an accusation, by those who thought they were uninvolved. The testimony is an address, which means that it's a provocation to a response. And that's what they don't want to give. They don't want to respond to the person who has called—for responsibility. When someone says, "I don't want to hear about it," or counters with a slur, they are telling the truth. They are creating themselves, as something insulated in its generality from the specificity of the address, by disavowing any involvement with the one who appeals.

*GB:* That's how the general public is constructed. Because if you look historically at the ways in which people with AIDS have been presented, on television for instance, we have been placed behind potted palms, given masked or scrambled faces, and pictured pretty much the same way as criminals, prostitutes, terrorists have been. Then eventually, somewhere in the late eighties, we were allowed to speak about our experiences, but only to some mediator. Finally, the last border, which has still to be transgressed, is the person with AIDS looking out into the audience and addressing another person with AIDS or HIV, forcing the realization that there are people with AIDS or HIV in the audience. Probably the closest we've come, as I recall, was a show that hybridized two different stories, a CNN news anchor who had AIDS together with the newscaster in San Francisco who did a weekly show on his illness. The trick was a kind of superimposition: showing the character with AIDS talking on his news show, but always *on television.* So it was television on television, but still it was the first time you ever saw a person with AIDS look out directly into the camera, into the audience, and address people with AIDS. And that is the only instance that I have actually seen.

Two years ago, at the international AIDS conference in Montreal, I was interviewed when [New York City Health Commissioner] Stephen Joseph announced his contact-tracing plan.[3] As an HIV-positive person who had gone through the anonymous testing procedures, I tried to talk about it on television. I kept trying to look into the camera, and to say that as an HIV-positive person, as a person who needed anonymous testing, I would never have gone had there been contact-tracing. I say I am HIV positive in public at great peril: there's an enormous amount of stigma attached to it, it's only because of a certain amount of privilege that I'm allowed to do it, I know I won't lose my job, etcetera. And I kept trying to look into the camera and say, "If you need HIV-antibody testing, you should go to an anonymous clinic, don't settle for confidential testing," etcetera. Because that was the content of most of what I said, none of that ended up on CNN. The only thing that ended up on CNN was a clip in which I said nothing: the camera just pointed to me, and the caption said "Person who went through anonymous testing." But they didn't picture me saying anything.

*DC:* The interviewer said, "Can't you put yourself in other people's shoes?" In other words, he wanted Gregg to identify with the HIV-*negative* "general public." They had no desire to hear from an HIV-positive person.

*GB:* The reporter said, essentially, "Answer the questions as though you were in my shoes"—as though I were HIV negative.

*CC:* We're back to the question of address: what Dori Laub [in this volume] calls the ability, or the inability, to say "thou." The problem of witnessing the Holocaust was that when you were inside the event, you could not address anyone outside: there was no "thou," as Laub puts it. Which meant that you could only be an object, without anything like a relation of address (which is what people are trying to establish now—during a time when, as people say, "the AIDS crisis is not over").[4] The attempt to address seems limited to two possibilities: either you can only address as someone completely different, or you can't address at all.

*DC:* Identifying oneself as HIV positive or as a person with AIDS has been the intent of a lot of people with AIDS and HIV in the arena of media—not merely to humanize or to give a face to the disease, but also to acknowledge that there could be people with AIDS or HIV in the audience. The primary function actually has been to engender an audience of people with AIDS and HIV, and not to sway people one way or the other who didn't identify with the community in some way.

*LP:* This problem comes up over and over again in terms of AIDS education. It's generally assumed that the reader is not HIV infected. That's the standard and has been for a long time, including most safe sex education. For a while it was very common to see as one of the safe sex guidelines: "Don't have sex with anybody who is HIV infected." It was crazy-making to think of what somebody was to do with that if they were HIV infected. In our educational work at Columbia, we've made a big effort to address our information to somebody who may be himself or herself infected. And sometimes this is seen as not addressing the general public. "You're being too specific, you're not talking to everybody."

*CC:* This raises the question of how you do address people, for example, when you address them as an activist. Do you address them as people who are like you, or who are different from you, that is, who have to recognize the specificity of people who are living with HIV or AIDS? What is the value or what are the problems of addressing a public by saying, "We all have to identify with each other?" When you're speaking into the camera directly, you say you are directly addressing people who are HIV positive. What relation are you trying to establish to those who are not?

*GB:* None.

*DC:* A relation could be established. . . . I would think that it could be very shocking, since it is not a habit of television—at least not for any group that is reported about, but never directly spoken to (this would be true of an address to queers)—to treat those people not as an ethnographic subject but as the very subject to whom you are speaking. I think that that would be shocking, there would be a kind of shock of recognition.

*GB:* When it first occurred to me that you could address people with AIDS or HIV in television interviews directly and try to engender them as an audience, the secondary effect was that people who were not HIV positive would realize that there were HIV-positive people in the audience.

*DC:* The biggest problem with even thinking about audiences is that one usually begins with some completely absurd fiction of generality, that is, with the notion that there could be a language that could reach everyone, or anything like a general public that could simply be addressed without exclusions. I don't think you could ever make any kind of cultural work that functioned as a general address. But the problem, of course, is that we live in a culture in which it is assumed that you can, always. And in fact almost every cultural work is made with that fiction of a general audience in mind.

*TK:* Which means that it is addressed to a particular audience, which masquerades as a general audience.

*DC:* Exactly.

*GB:* The general public is a market, a fictional market. Advertisements are posed to it, and the intention is to get people to identify as a group that would want to buy specific products for specific reasons. For activists, the point cannot be simply to address a general audience. That's why at GMHC we're trying to produce community-specific television, produced by members of the communities for themselves and in their own interests—because a mutually exclusive criterion has been established, either general or specific.[5] As Douglas has clearly articulated, that is a false dichotomy, an opposition which does not exist. *The general public does not exist.* Except for Kimberly Bergalis, the first example.

*DC:* There's a certain sense of trauma in the difference between one's own experience and a sense of something like "society's" experience which one gets in the daily assault of reading the *New York Times* (see Crimp with

Ralston, 1990, 108–14). I'm thinking of those occasional feature articles about the fears and anxieties of people who have in some way possible become infected—cops who get needle sticks making arrests or, for example, a story that appeared in the *Village Voice* about a woman who was raped and insisted that the rapist be tested. In this latter case (a curious one, since she had tested negative a number of times but nevertheless was taking AZT prophylactically), a significant portion of the article was devoted to her experience of her timer going off in public places in order to remind her that she had to take her AZT, and the embarrassment and the anxiety attached. Now, this was something that is the daily experience of a number of gay men who are my friends. And the people that I know who are taking AZT know that they are infected. I know of no stories in the media about the anxieties of gay people, or IV drug users, who have AIDS or are HIV infected. Nor have I seen a story in the mainstream media during the entire ten years of this epidemic that deals with the anxieties of gay men, generally, regarding for example what this epidemic has done to our experience of our sexuality. This is how one of the worst aspects of homophobia shows itself, in the suggestion that homosexuality is a simple choice, because it's assumed that we could all now make the choice not to be homosexual. It's as if the disruption of millions of gay men's lives could simply be wished away by the assumption that we could all become celibate or heterosexual or whatever. And that can be productive of a certain kind of traumatic experience.

*CC:* What do you think was happening there, in this substitution of people who are not identified with the AIDS community for those who are as witnesses of the crisis, as substitute witnesses? What does it do to the people who are not speaking but who could be, and who could be heard? Is it perhaps an active way of avoiding, not listening to others by listening to those people who have been constructed as the general public?

*GB:* I don't know if empathy is the right word, but the substitution intervenes in a kind of empathy that I think AIDS activists hoped they might be able to generate by being able constantly to bring our stories forward, to humanize the stories, to show that we are people in the communities, that we are people you know, and so on. It's very easy for Kimberly Bergalis to appear on television saying, "I am someone you know," because she is not gay and she is not other in ways that many of the people from the various communities hardest hit by AIDS are. And she refused to identify herself. So she reaffirms, and very quickly, what was a very stable notion that people with AIDS and HIV in the communities affected by it want to give it to "us," that they will not be happy until "we" are infected by it as well.

*DC:* The fact is that Kimberly Bergalis is a person with AIDS who has managed to achieve a kind of empathetic reaction in someone like Jesse Helms. It makes you wonder: if that's the way empathy gets constructed, is empathy anything we would even want to strive for? Because it seems that empathy only gets constructed in relation to sameness, it can't get constructed in relation to difference.

*TK:* In fact, you have to become Jesse Helms in order to receive the empathy: that's the structure of empathy. No one except these simulacra of the general public will receive the empathy. But that means that this phantom—the general public—is the most traumatized of all. It's having the nightmares, suffering from the flashbacks, uncertain about what has happened to it. It knows that it has undergone some change, that its world has been altered in a potentially life-threatening way, but it can't identify the event.

*DC:* So the general public as Kimberly Bergalis, as it gets constructed in all forms of representation—

*TK:* —in ways designated to marginalize the people who are actually undergoing it—

*DC:* —as a transfer of the experience of AIDS (whether or not *it's* a trauma)—there's a kind of a negation of that experience, through the construction and consolidation of a traumatized "general" subject.

*TK:* It's now allowed to happen to the people that it's happening to, and it's allowed to happen phantasmatically to the people that it's allegedly not happening to.

*GB:* I'll say it again: Kimberly Bergalis is the first member of the general public. There was a big effort to get Ryan White to play this role, but he resisted. Kimberly Bergalis does not resist: in fact, this is how she identifies herself.

*CC:* So empathy and a certain mode of understanding, or what you talked about, Doug, as the problematic structure of empathy, would be crucial in constructing this general public. Empathy is what the public is supposed to learn to feel, but it solidifies the structure of discrimination. In this case, empathy as a kind of understanding or of relation seems to reinforce the gesture of exclusion rather than the recognition—or what Douglas called a "shock"—that might come from some other mode of contact.

*GB:* It's always very complex, and the identities are constantly shifting. For example, on *Oprah* today the people who were HIV positive on the panel—other than Kimberly Bergalis, who was on a television next to the people on the panel—were gay white men. So immediately there was this opposition created, the dichotomy required for the formation of the general public: Kimberly Bergalis against the gay white men. And it's supposed to be the gay white men who want to conceal this, who want to hide this, who are dishonest. One member of the audience, speaking to a doctor on the panel, said "You are dishonest for not informing your patients you are HIV positive." Implicitly, it was the people on the panel who had infected Kimberly Bergalis, and they were dishonest about it: people in the audience actually stood up and said they were not courageous, they were cowards.

Now, the complexity resides in the fact that a huge portion of the audience were people of color, and they had legitimate questions and fears around infection—which clearly pointed to the fact that, more than anything else, there is still an enormous lack of education around how HIV is transmitted. What was interesting was that what was being constructed there, in fact what was being erased, was the fact that an enormous number of people with AIDS in this country are people of color.[6] It was simply a matter of white gay men threatening the general public. You know that on television today it's a rare instance where people of color are pictured as members of a viewing audience, and it seems to happen today particularly in the service of a certain kind of message. The fact that there was not one person of color with AIDS on the panel, and that only people of color in the audience (in the section I saw) were asking questions antagonistically to the doctors on the panel, structured a very divisive and very reactionary moment. It suggested that AIDS is primarily a disease of gay white men, who still threaten the rest of us.

*LP:* You know, I would raise one objection to the way our conversation is moving, which is that it keeps moving away from the experience of people who are HIV infected. I'm not criticizing what we're talking about, but it is easy to lose sight of the issue of the variety of actual experiences HIV-infected people have.

*GB:* If the distinction is between going into the realm of analysis and talking about specific needs, I would much rather do the former than the latter, because I'm really tired of identifying as HIV positive. I think that that's something to speak about, now, particularly historically. Now we're at a time when there are people who've been alive long enough, other than the very few people who are long-time survivors of AIDS, to have had the experience of having been consistently and constantly thrust into the public and defining themselves only as HIV positive. It's complex, and it's something to think about. It seems like it's no longer sufficient merely to put oneself forward as surviving and thriving and having a "chronic manageable disease"—there's actually a crisis of faith around these notions. Whereas three or four years ago a lot of us were disclosing our HIV status because we wanted to put out the message that you could live with this, that it was a chronic manageable disease, now that we've been experiencing more and more the deaths of our friends, and a lot of us have been getting increasingly ill, and there is actually nothing in the pipeline as far as treatments go, it is becoming a more and more desperate situation. It is becoming difficult to believe in the compelling notions that were once the reasons for disclosing one's status. It's like walking down the street, and seeing those posters with smiling faces that say in handwriting, "I'm living with HIV." And I just detest them.

*DC:* The difficulty is in the relation that existed between what you told yourself in relation to hopefulness and what you told the world in relation to hopefulness. In other words, by making it public, by adopting the rhetoric of "living with AIDS," you were actually, in a certain sense, persuading yourself. Now you have a crisis of faith around it, because you still recognize the necessity of the rhetoric, but it's no longer persuasive to you.

*GB:* At one time I thought it was an identity, and I realize now that it's not. I was on a panel yesterday at GMHC, and I knew I was on the panel as the HIV positive person. I realized, and I said, that it's important that in any group such as this someone who has HIV identify as HIV positive. But in fact, it's not an identity at all. I was of a generation of people who had to come out during the AIDS crisis, which meant pride around a sexuality that was stigmatized as a disease in a way that had never been done historically before in such a concrete sense, but nonetheless, my gay identity is not to be confused with my HIV status. Now more and more it seems to be important to talk, among ourselves anyway, about the sense of diminishment felt by a lot of us who have consistently and repeatedly identified ourselves as HIV-antibody positive, as though our identity is just reduced to the status of our health.

*LP:* There is no right place to be on this question. On the one hand, HIV-infected people sometimes need to feel that HIV disease is chronic and manageable—in some way you have to believe this. People have to keep up some kind of hope, since they have to go to the doctor, take AZT, and do other tedious and frightening things. On the other hand, it may feel embittering to have to talk in an optimistic way if you feel that you are going to die or if your good friend just died. One of the things you have to remember about HIV disease is that a lot of people are being diagnosed as having this disease when they're perfectly fine physically, with absolutely no clinical symptoms. There is a long period of time before people develop symptoms; the average time between infection and the development of symptoms serious enough to be called AIDS is eleven years. People are getting tested early on, and then living without symptoms but with a potentially fatal disease for more than a decade. And during that period of time there's a question for the individual about identifying with the person with AIDS. People can't always go around thinking of their identity as HIV positive, and yet they can't afford not to think about the disease.

*TK:* Is the problem that at a certain point the assertion of this identity constituted a political intervention—and was understood as making a certain kind of progress, even transforming the debate to a certain extent—and now the gesture doesn't have the same force? Or is it that having an identity itself is becoming a problem?

*GB:* No. It's that the gesture has to be rethought, because the terrain has shifted. There was a reason why. I identified as HIV positive for the same reason that most identities, particularly disenfranchised identities, are formed: through negation. The notion of the "AIDS carrier" was the precursor of the self-identified HIV-antibody-positive person, and that identity emerged in defiance and in resistance to the fantasy of the "carrier." Now it's no longer as compelling and as meaningful to me to say the same things over and over again—which might be just the effect of the repetition, but I do think that other things need to be said. It's not enough merely to say, "I'm living with this disease."

My discussions with Douglas, when he was writing "Mourning and Militancy," were useful to me because we were treading on ground I hadn't been on before, because I was speaking about death. It didn't seem to me that many HIV positive people felt as though they could speak about death, and I thought that was important. It seemed very difficult to talk about mortality, and it's still difficult to give voice to things that I think, and that other people who are HIV positive think, but that we don't necessarily think about. For example, sitting in a memorial service and fantasizing that it's yours. I don't know if everyone does that, but I certainly do that. And particularly since all the memorial services that I go to are for people with AIDS. I listen and hear what people say—and I usually think that nice things will be said about me. One of my closest friends died last year, and I've had three co-workers die over the past year at GMHC, in my department. And when I see somebody getting sick, I don't say, "That *could* be me," I say, "That *will* be me." So it's very painful and sometimes intolerable.

*LP:* And what people want to say is, "That *can't* be me." They want to find things that are different between themselves and that person. "They didn't take care of themselves, they had a bad attitude, they didn't think positively, etcetera." Blame can be a way of putting distance between yourself and someone else with whom you are afraid to identify.

*TK:* So the same inside-outside structure we saw in the case of the general public reproduces itself here, but within the "inside."

*GB:* Frankly, more than anything else, I think it's important to talk about the lack of real options, and the lack of secular thinking around death, the lack of philosophical options for people with AIDS and HIV. I think there's a paucity of different options for thinking about one's mortality. And that needs to be developed.

*LP:* There are two common pictures: either the image of people tortured by the world outside them yet feeling strong and fighting back (which is a partially useful propaganda picture) or the image of the victim alone, helpless, lying alone in bed. But neither of these pictures leaves room for understanding the complexity of the psychological issues of HIV disease, for example the way disease inevitably brings up preexisting conflicts. It's a difficult topic to discuss because, when you talk about intrapsychic issues, someone may feel blamed or that you do not understand that there is a real assault from the outside, that there are real political enemies, and that the medical care system is terrible.

*TK:* You both seem to be saying that now there's a therapeutic as well as a political necessity for the AIDS community to think about death. That in some way it hasn't been thought about, and that there are very few resources right now for thinking about it.

*GB:* I think that it has been thought about on the same kind of model we produced before—at once too little knowledge and too much knowledge. In the same way that the invention and exclusion of the person with AIDS has constructed the general public, we've experienced our deaths as spectacle for the general public. Until recently, the only thing you could see on national television would be images of the quilt. An aerial image of the quilt, "two football field sizes big," the shot of reading the names, and maybe someone famous like Michel Foucault—actually they always showed Rock Hudson— would have their name read. And so we experienced the representations of our deaths only as spectacle for the general public. There was a real resistance to allowing us to picture the deaths that we experienced, our experience of mortality. Things get worse because of the lack of philosophical options for thinking about death. Options are scarce, and people are desperate for ways of thinking about this. To the point where there's this notion, which I despise, this New Age philosophy, that AIDS is a gift and challenge and it's going to make me a better person. I don't think it's a gift and I don't think it's a challenge.

*DC:* It's actually a huge industry, especially on the West Coast. Louise Hay (1988) runs an enormous industry: she has meetings every week in Los Angeles, called "Hayrides," and thousands of people go to them and buy her books and tapes.

*GB:* Then there's religion. When my friend Ray died, he became extremely religious. He was not religious, was even somewhat antireligious, before he got sick. And when he got sick, he got religious, and I found myself in a predicament: I wanted to be supportive because I loved my friend Ray, but I don't believe in God. But I would be at his bedside often, and we talked about God a lot. I was instrumental in getting him a priest when he wanted it and negotiating these things, because we all had weird feelings around Ray's increasing religiosity. And it made me realize that there were no options. It has been my experience that the people who get sick and who are terminally ill have two choices: the New Age-ism of Louise Hay, and the religion of their childhood. And that's it. There's no specific writing about philosophical considerations around dying when you're a person with AIDS. That's changing—for instance, with the fiction of Allen Barnett (1990)—but slowly.

*TK:* And what about the political consequences for activism and other, say, public interventions?

*DC:* It certainly has political consequences in the sense, for instance, that divisions within ACT UP, or in the AIDS community, have entailed certain moralistic positions deriving from hierarchies of oppression. The splits in ACT UP chapters around the country have generally occurred because of a different sense of priority and urgency among members. On the one hand, those who are HIV positive tend to want to stress the short term and therefore emphasize development and testing of treatments. On the other hand, there are those in the movement—many of them HIV negative—who are more concerned with broader struggles and the long term, for example, the need to create national health care. This has often played itself out in very destructive ways.

*CC:* That makes me think again of what you, Douglas, said before about empathy, that its structure is something that somehow elides thinking about death. Something is not confronted there, when you think you're understanding or empathizing in a certain way. The construction of the general public, that we discussed before, also somehow doesn't allow that, to come into that kind of knowledge or empathy for anyone. And, as you point out in "Mourning and Militancy," the problem takes on an added urgency for those who *must* identify with the dead.

*DC:* I think there might be some kind of psychic prohibition about identifying with the dead, because then it's really about confronting your own mortality. I think that it's terribly difficult for anyone to do that in any full way.

# Notes

1. Two days after this interview took place, in a story datelined "Washington, Sept. 26," and illustrated with a front-page photograph of Kimberly Bergalis, *The New York Times* reported the following:

> Kimberly Bergalis, wearing pale flowers and the strands of short, sandy-colored hair she has remaining after her treatment for AIDS, was wheeled to the witness table in Congress to utter 15 seconds of testimony. In a weak, slurred voice, the 23-year-old woman said: "AIDS is a terrible disease that we must take seriously. I didn't do anything wrong, but I'm being made to suffer like this. My life has been taken away. Please enact legislation so other patients and health-care providers don't have to go through the hell that I have. Thank you." Though extremely frail, Ms. Bergalis traveled by train from her home in Florida to offer brief testimony in support of a bill that would require AIDS testing of health-care professionals who perform invasive procedures. [. . .] Ms. Bergalis and four other patients became infected after dental treatment [. . .] Ms. Bergalis has come to personify issues in AIDS as no one has since Ryan White, the Indiana boy who was infected through a transfusion and who died last year. She has attracted widespread news coverage, partly for the anger she has focused on the medical establishment. When Ms. Bergalis arrived here on the train from her home in Fort Pierce, Fla., on Wednesday, local television cameras covered the event live" (Hilts, 1991b).

2. Belinda Mason, a member of the National Committee on AIDS, died of AIDS on September 9, 1991 in Tennessee. The *New York Times* (Hilts, 1991a) reported in its obituary for her that in August she had pleaded with the President to oppose mandatory HIV testing of health care workers. She had become infected in 1987 through a blood transfusion during the birth of her second child.

3. On Stephen Joseph, and the lengthy campaign by ACT UP against Joseph's AIDS policies, including the Montreal contact-tracing proposal, see Crimp with Rolston, 1990, 72–76; and Crimp, 1989, 16–17.

4. For a reproduction of the 1988 activist sticker that bears this slogan, see Crimp with Rolston, 1990, 40–41.

5. Jean Carlomusto and Gregg Bordowitz have been producing the *Living with AIDS* cable television program, for over three years, at the Gay Men's Health Crisis (GMHC) in New York City. GMHC is the nation's oldest and largest AIDS service organization, providing services and advocacy to people with AIDS.

6. According to the Centers for Disease Control, 1991, of the 191,601 people currently diagnosed with AIDS, 54 percent were white, 28.8 percent were black, and 16.2 percent were Hispanic.

## References

Barnett, Allen. 1990. *The Body and Its Dangers.* New York: St. Martin's.

Centers for Disease Control. 1991. *HIV/AIDS Surveillance Report, September.* Atlanta: CDC.

Crimp, Douglas, ed. 1988. *AIDS: Cultural Analysis/Cultural Activism.* Cambridge: MIT Press.

Crimp, Douglas. 1989. "Mourning and Militancy." *October* 51:3–8.

Crimp, Douglas, with Adam Rolston. 1990. *AIDS Demo Graphics.* Seattle: Bay Press.

Goldstein, Richard. 1987. "A Plague on All Our Houses." *Village Voice*, Sept. 16.

Hay, Louise. 1988. *The AIDS Book: Creating a Positive Approach.* Santa Monica: Hay House.

Hilts, Philip. 1991a. "Belinda Mason, 33, U.S. Panelist and Bush Adviser on AIDS Policy." *New York Times*, Sept. 10.

———. 1991b. "AIDS Patient Urges Congress to Pass Testing Bill." *New York Times*, Sept. 27.

# CONTRIBUTORS

**Georges Bataille** was a French writer who lived from 1897 to 1962. He was director of the College de Sociologie with Roger Caillois and Michel Leiris from 1937 to 1939, and founder of the journal *Critique* (1946). Among his major writings are *L'experience interieure, La part maudite, La litterature et le mal,* and *L'Erotisme* (1957). He also wrote fiction.

**Harold Bloom** is Sterling Professor of Humanities at Yale University and Berg Professor of English at New York University. He is a MacArthur Fellow and a member of the Academy of Arts and Letters. He has written more than twenty books, among them, *The Anxiety of Influence, The Visionary Company, Poetry and Repression,* and *A Map of Misreading.* Other books that include essays on Freud are *Agon, The Breaking of the Vessels,* and *The Strong Light of the Canonical: Kafka, Freud and Scholem as Revisionists of Jewish Culture and Thought.* His most recent books are *The Book of J, The American Religion: The Emergence of the Post-Christian Nation,* and *The Western Canon: The Books and School of the Ages.* He is currently working on a book entitled *Angels, Dreams, and Not Dying: A Meditation for Millennium.*

**Gregg Bordowitz** is an activist, video-maker, and writer who for the past ten years has been involved in the movement to end government inaction on AIDS.

**Laura S. Brown**, Ph.D., is a clinical psychologist in the private practice of feminist therapy and feminist forensic psychology in Seattle, Washington, and Clinical Professor of Psychology at the University of Washington, who has written extensively in the area of feminist therapy theory and practice.

She is the author of *Subversive Dialogues: Theory in Feminist Therapy* (Basic Books). She is presently involved in research on the phenomenon of recovered memories of trauma.

**Cathy Caruth** is Associate Professor of Comparative Literature and English at Emory University. She is the author of *Empirical Truths and Critical Fictions: Locke, Wordsworth, Kant, Freud* (Johns Hopkins, 1990), and of *Unclaimed Experience: Trauma, Narrative and History* (forthcoming from Johns Hopkins). She is also the co-editor, with Deborah Esch, of *Critical Encounters: Reference and Responsibility in Deconstructive Writing* (Rutgers, 1994).

**Douglas Crimp** is visiting professor of visual and cultural studies at the University of Rochester. He is the author of *On the Museums' Ruins* (MIT Press, 1993) and *AIDS Demo Graphics* (with Adam Ralston) (Bay Press, 1990), and the editor of *AIDS: Cultural Analysis/Cultural Activism* (MIT Press, 1988).

**Kai Erikson** is Professor of Sociology and American Studies at Yale University. He is author of *Everything In Its Path: Destruction of Community in the Buffalo Creek Flood* (1976) and *A New Species of Trouble: Explorations in Disaster, Trauma, and Community* (1994) in which a version of the essay in these pages appears.

**Shoshana Felman** is Thomas E. Donnelley Professor of French and Comparative Literature at Yale University. She is the author of *Jacques Lacan and the Adventure of Insight: Psychoanalysis in Contemporary Culture* (1987), *Writing and Madness* (1985), and *The Literary Speech Act: Don Juan with J. L. Austin, or Seduction in Two Languages* (1983, English translation), and editor of *Literature and Psychoanalysis: The Question of Reading: Otherwise* (1982). She is also co-author, with Dori Laub, M.D., of *Testimony: Crises of Witnessing in Literature, Psychoanalysis, and History* (Routledge, 1991). Her most recent work is entitled *What Does a Woman Want?: Reading and Sexual Difference* (Johns Hopkins, 1993).

**Alan Keenan** teaches in the Rhetoric Department of the University of California at Berkeley. He is the author of "Promises, Promises: The Abyss of Freedom and the Loss of the Political in Hannah Arendt" (in *Political Theory*, May 1994) and is completing a dissertation on "Politics, Theory, and the

Impossible Law of Democracy" from the Humanities Center at the Johns Hopkins University.

**Thomas Keenan** teaches in the English Department at Princeton University. He is the author of *Fables of Responsibility* (forthcoming from Stanford University Press), and co-editor of *Paul de Man's Wartime Journalism 1939–43* (Nebraska, 1988) and *Responses* (Nebraska, 1989).

**Henry Krystal**, M.D. is Professor Emeritus of Psychiatry at Michigan State University and Lecturer at the Michigan Psychoanalytic Institute. A practitioner of psychiatry and psychoanalysis for thirty-five years, Dr. Krystal has long worked with Holocaust survivors in Michigan, Ohio, and Indiana, both in private practice and in connection with their claims under the Restitution Program for Victims of Nazi Persecution. He has also served as a consultant for survivors in Ontario, Canada. He is the author of *Integration and Self-Healing: Affect—Trauma—Alexithymia*, and the editor of the important collection *Massive Psychic Trauma*. He is most recently author of "Trauma Beyond DSM-III: Therapeutic Problems," in *The International Handbook of Traumatic Stress Syndromes* (edited by John P. Wilson and Berly Raphael), and with Andrew D. Krystal, "Psychoanalysis and Neuroscience in Relationship to Dream and Creativity" in *Creativity* (edited by P. Rankow).

**Claude Lanzmann** is director of the film *Pourquoi Israel* and of the pathbreaking testimonial film on the Holocaust, *Shoah*.

**Dori Laub**, M.D. is a psychoanalyst who has published analytic and psychotherapeutic essays about his work with Holocaust survivors and their children. He is the cofounder of the Fortunoff Video Archives for Holocaust Testimonies at Yale University and the co-author, with Shoshana Felman, of *Testimony: Crises of Witnessing in Literature, Psychoanalysis and History* (Routledge, 1992). He is Associate Clinical Professor of Psychiatry at Yale University.

**Robert Jay Lifton** is Distinguished Professor of Psychiatry and Psychology at the City University of New York, John Jay College of Criminal Justice. He is the author of numerous books, including *Death in Life: Survivors of Hiroshima, Home from the War: Learning from Vietnam Veterans, The Nazi Doctors: Medical Killing and the Psychology of Genocide, The Broken Connection:*

*On Death and the Continuity of Life*, and most recently *The Protean Self: Human Resilience in an Age of Fragmentation* (Basic Books).

**Louis J. Micheels**, M.D. is a practicing psychoanalyst and associate clinical professor in psychiatry at the Yale University School of Medicine. He is the author of *Doctor 117641, Memoirs of the Holocaust* (Yale, 1989), and has written an article entitled "The Bearer of the Secret" (*Psychoanalytic Inquiry*, 1985). He has also presented papers at various professional and public meetings, and was a discussant of *Shadows of the Holocaust* by Nathaniel Roth at the American Psychoanalytic Association winter meeting in December 1988.

**Kevin Newmark** teaches at Boston College and is the author of *Beyond Symbolism: Textual History and the Future of Reading* (Cornell, 1991).

**Laura Pinsky** is a psychotherapist in private practice and at the Columbia University Health Service, Gay Health Advocacy Project, and has co-authored with Paul Harding Douglas *The Essential HIV Treatment Fact Book* (Pocket Books, 1992).

**David Rodowick** is Professor of English and Visual/Cultural Studies, and the Director of the Film Studies Program at the University of Rochester. His most recent book is *The Difficulty of Difference: Psychoanalysis, Sexual Difference and Film Theory* (Routledge, 1991).

**Albert J. Solnit**, M.D. is a training and supervising analyst with the Western New England Institute for Psychoanalysis. He is also Sterling Professor Emeritus, Pediatrics and Psychiatry, and Senior Research Scientist, Yale University School of Medicine and Child Study Center; as well as Commissioner of Mental Health for the State of Connecticut. Dr. Solnit has been managing editor of *The Psychoanalytic Study of the Child* since 1971 and his extensive bibliography includes "From Play to Playfulness in Psychoanalysis," in *The Many Meanings of Play*, of which he is co-editor. He is also co-author of *Beyond the Best Interests of the Child, Before the Best Interests of the Child*, and *In the Best Interests of the Child*.

**Bessel A. van der Kolk** is Associate Professor of Psychiatry at Harvard Medical School and Director of the Trauma Clinic at the Massachusetts General Hospital. He is a past President of the International Society for Traumatic Stress Studies, and is author of *Post-Traumatic Stress Disorder* and *Psychologi-*

*cal Trauma.* The chapter in this volume, which deals with the psychology of traumatic memory, is the first part of a two-part series. The second part, entitled "The Body Keeps the Score" (*Harvard Review of Psychiatry*) is concerned with the biology of traumatic memory.

**Onno van der Hart**, Ph.D. is a Professor at the Department of Clinical and Health Psychology, Utrecht University, Utrecht, Netherlands, and Chief of the Dissociation Team, Regional Institute for Ambulatory Mental Health Care Amsterdam South/New West, Amsterdam, Netherlands. He is currently Vice-President of the International Society for the Study of Multiple Personality and Dissociation. He has written *Rituals in Psychotherapy* (New York, 1981), edited *Coping with Loss* (New York, 1987) and *Trauma, Dissociation and Hypnosis* [in Dutch] (Amsterdam, 1991).

Library of Congress Cataloging-in-Publication Data

Trauma : explorations in memory / edited, with introductions, by Cathy Caruth.
    p.    cm.
    Includes bibliographical references.
    ISBN 0-8018-5009-6. — ISBN 0-8018-5007-x (pbk. : alk. paper)
    1. Psychic trauma.    2. Post-traumatic stress disorder.    3. Recollection (Psychology)
4. False memory syndrome.    I. Caruth, Cathy, 1955–    .
BF175.5.P75T73   1995
155.9'35—dc20    94-46167